Mastering Finance and Accounting

Mastering Finance and Accounting

DAVID FARROW

McGRAW-HILL BOOK COMPANY

London · New York · St Louis · San Francisco · Auckland
Bogotá · Caracas · Lisbon · Madrid · Mexico · Milan
Montreal · New Delhi · Panama · Paris · San Juan
São Paulo · Singapore · Sydney · Tokyo · Toronto

Published by
McGRAW-HILL Book Company Europe
Shoppenhangers Road, Maidenhead, Berkshire SL6 2QL, England
Telephone 0628 23432
Fax 0628 770224

British Library Cataloguing in Publication Data
Farrow, David
    Mastering Finance and Accounting
    I. Title
    657
    ISBN 0–07–707833–0

Library of Congress Cataloging-in-Publication Data
Mastering finance and accounting / David A. Farrow.
    p.   cm.
    Includes index.
    ISBN 0–07–707833–0
    1. Accounting.   I. Title.
HF5635.F233   1994   94–18518
657–dc20   CIP

12345 CL 987654

Typeset by TecSet Ltd, Wallington, Surrey,
and printed and bound in Great Britain
by Clays Ltd, St Ives plc

Contents

vi   Contents

Preface

Whatever the ultimate aim of individual students, knowledge and competence stems from first acquiring a deep-rooted understanding. With this in mind, I have attempted to concentrate on the 'how to do it' aspect of topics rather than on theoretical discussion and to demonstrate the application of techniques within the whole accounting model.

While the sections on financing and cost and management accounting have been included primarily to address the needs of GNVQ and NVQ, they will also help other students to acquire a more rounded understanding of the financial framework in which business operates.

Finance and accounting is perceived by many to be dull and complex. I have attempted to explode those myths by writing a jargon-free text that flows through the subject matter in a natural progression to make for easy, and hopefully, enjoyable reading. Whether I have succeeded is, of course, for the reader to judge.

As well as covering the GNVQ and NVQ/SVQ finance elements, the book is suitable for students embarking on studies for the examinations of the following bodies:

- General Certificate of Secondary Education
- General Certificate of Education at 'A' Level
- Royal Society of Arts
- London Chamber of Commerce and Industry
- Association of Accounting Technicians
- The Institutes of Chartered Accountants
- Chartered Association of Certified Accountants
- Chartered Institute of Management Accountants
- Institute of Chartered Secretaries and Administrators

Competence in accounting can only grow out of continual and extensive practice. Traditional pen and paper methods are, without doubt, time consuming and somewhat tedious. To overcome this constraint, I have produced, together with a colleague and programming professional, Alec Danyshchuck, a computer-based training system that facilitates extensive hands-on practical exercises. Further details of the PC-based packages can be found at the back of this book.

My thanks go to Estelle and Anthea, without whose encouragement and practical support this book would not have been possible.

David Farrow

Section 1

Accounting 1

Unit 1

The fundamentals

Bookkeeping and accountancy — the different roles

The roles of bookkeeping and accountancy are often interpreted, quite wrongly, as being one and the same. This is not the case, and it is helpful at an early stage to understand the fundamental difference between the two.

- *Bookkeeping* is concerned with *recording precisely* what has happened when money or items of value move in or out of a business or, indeed, within the business itself. In the same way that a secretary uses shorthand to abbreviate the spoken word, the bookkeeper uses monetary shorthand to record events affecting the finances of a business. The bookkeeper does not make financial judgements or decisions but simply records what has actually taken place. Bookkeeping is, therefore, a precise and simple record of events.
- *Accountancy* is creative and subjective, requires judgements and decisions to be made. An accountant uses skill and knowledge to translate the bookkeeper's record into a concise and meaningful story which provides information understandable to the manager(s) of a business and acceptable to outside organizations such as the Inland Revenue, banks, etc.

Summary

Bookkeeping is the systematic recording of events using monetary shorthand. Accountancy translates the bookkeeping story into a short and comprehensive format for the owner(s) and manager(s) of a business and outsiders.

This is the format we shall follow in this study. We will first learn the rules and procedures of bookkeeping in order to write its story. We will then move on to accountancy and see how, with the application of knowledge and understanding, the bookkeeping story can be interpreted and presented in a comprehensible form.

An account — a concise understanding

Most people have 'tools of their trade' in order to carry out their work. A secretary has a typewriter or word processor, a taxi driver a cab. The bookkeeper has a book containing accounts in which he records events tracking the movement of money or value affecting a business. The book is more commonly known as a *ledger* but this should not confuse us. Ledger simply means a book in which accounts are kept. More importantly, we need to understand what an account is. Quite simply, we can imagine an account as being two facing pages within a book.

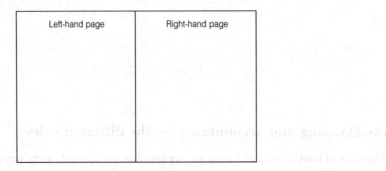

When we open a book at random there is a right-hand and left-hand page. This is precisely what an account is. The right-hand page is one side of an account and is used to record money or value *going out* while the left-hand page is the other side of the account which records money or value *going in*. For practical purposes, we can draw an account in a brief format which represents the two pages of a book.

All we have done is omit the vertical and bottom line of each page. For simplicity, this is the way in which accounts will be shown throughout this study, known as *T accounts*. We can, in our book, have as many accounts as we decide are necessary, open them as often as we wish and describe them in the best way we see fit as long as the description is readily understood.

For example, we will want to record money going into and out of our Bank Account. We may buy a vehicle for the business. To record these events we could open accounts as follows:

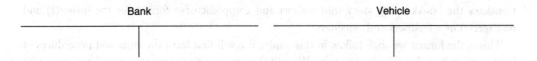

Eventually, our book will contain many accounts, each one used to record some aspect of financial events affecting the business. When we have finished recording all these events, the book will contain the full story of all the financial movements that the business has to keep track of. So far, we have referred to the movement of money or value as events. Now we can learn a piece of accounting terminology. Bookkeepers and accountants call such events *transactions*. From now on, we will understand a transaction to be money, or something of value, moving from or to the business or within the business.

Debits and credits — plain and simple

Let us straight away explode the myth that debits and credits are some complicated kind of formula, understood only by accountants. Debit simply means the left-hand page or left side of the account and credit the right-hand page or right side of the account. As you work on an account, think of your right hand being the credit side and your left hand being the debit side. So, understanding debits and credits is as easy as knowing your right hand from your left!

Let us now look at a transaction. In a transaction where there is movement of money or value, there is always a *giver* and a *receiver*. In other words, there are always two distinct aspects to any transaction: the giving and the receiving of money or value. Quite simply, it is these two aspects of every transaction that the bookkeeper records. This is done by entering the giving of money or value on the credit side (right-hand side) of the account. Conversely, the receiving of money or value is entered on the debit side (left-hand side). (*If you understand this then you understand the basic concept of double-entry bookkeeping.*)

This latter term, double-entry bookkeeping, warrants further explanation. Basically, the concept relies on the fact that there are two parties involved in every transaction — the giver and the receiver. In recording a transaction, the bookkeeper records the giving on the credit side and the receiving on the debit side of an account. Let us look at an example.

Assume that we write a cheque on our business bank account for £1000 and send it to a supplier called Regent Limited. To record this transaction we need two accounts — one to represent our bank account, the other to represent our supplier Regent Limited.

Bank	Regent Limited

It is our bank account which is giving up the money or value so we make a *credit* entry. Regent Limited is receiving the money so we make a *debit* entry.

Bank		Regent Limited	
	Regent Limited 1 000	Bank A/c 1 000	

Note: An entry in an account is cross-referenced to the account receiving the other entry.

From this understanding, two simple truths emerge:

1. For every credit entry there is a corresponding debit entry. Or, conversely, for every debit entry there is a corresponding credit entry.
2. When we have finished recording all the transactions and added up all the credit entries and debit entries, the two totals will be the same. In accounting terms, they are in balance. This is what is meant by 'balancing the books'.

The golden rules of bookkeeping and accountancy

Fortunately, the basic rules of bookkeeping and accountancy are few in number. However, they are of critical importance and must become ingrained in the memory of anyone practising these skills. Time spent making absolutely sure you know the rules and the concepts behind them, will be rewarded when we start the practical work.

1. There are two aspects to every transaction. The giving up of value or money and the receiving.
2. The giving up is recorded as a credit in an account and the receiving as a debit in an account.
3. For every credit entry there is a corresponding debit entry and, conversely, for every debit entry there is a corresponding credit entry.
4. If we add up all the credit entries and all the debit entries, the totals will be the same.

Now we will put these rules to the test by doing a short bookkeeping exercise:

Transaction 1   Paid a cheque, value £200, to a supplier E Worth & Co.
Thought process   We need an account to represent the giving up of £200. As the payment is being made by cheque the £200 will be taken out of our Bank Account. Therefore we need an account to represent the Bank. The money is being paid to E Worth & Co so we need an account to represent this supplier.

Action

Bank		E Worth & Co	

Thought process   It is our bank which is giving up the value so we must make a credit entry in the Bank Account. E Worth & Co are receiving the value so we must debit their account.

Action

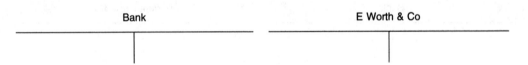

Bank		E Worth & Co	
	E Worth & Co 200	Bank 200	

Try now to apply the thinking process to the three following transactions so that you understand the bookkeeping entries that are illustrated:

Transaction 2   Wrote a cheque for £3000 for the purchase of a vehicle.
Transaction 3   Paid into the Bank, takings from sales of £6000.
Transaction 4   Paid rent of £500 by cheque.

Bank				E Worth & Co		
(3) Sales	6 000	E Worth & Co	200 (1)	(1) Bank	200	
		Vehicle	3 000 (2)			
		Rent	500 (4)			

Vehicles			Sales		
(2) Bank	3 000			Bank	6 000 (3)

Rent		
(4) Bank	500	

Now let us do a test to ensure the totals of our debit entries and credit entries are the same.

Account	Debit	Credit
Bank	6 000	
Bank		200
Bank		3 000
Bank		500
E Worth & Co	200	
Vehicle	3 000	
Sales		6 000
Rent	500	
	9 700	9 700

Perhaps without fully realizing it, we have just 'written' a simple set of accounts and proved the accuracy of our work. If you examine the four basic rules again, you will see that we have fully complied with their requirements.

Remember:

> *Credit — the giver, or value flowing out.*
> *Debit — the receiver, or value flowing in.*

If you understand these fundamental points then you understand the basis on which all book-keeping and accountancy entries, no matter how advanced, are made.

Unit 2

Writing the book

Opening an account

We have already noted that accounts can be opened as often as is necessary, so the accounts contained in our book can be as few or as many as we decide we need. We also know that each account has to be given a 'title' or description. Before we move on, we now need to consider the matter of account descriptions in a little more detail. In particular, we will look at certain types of account or groups of accounts and see how we can apply generally used descriptions. The advantage of doing this is that our account descriptions will conform to an established pattern and it will help us when we read accounts prepared by others.

Types of account

Money Accounts

Cash Account — transactions where we receive or make payments using actual currency.
Bank Account — transactions where we receive or make payments by cheque or through our Bank Account.
(In Unit 9 we will see how, in practice, these two accounts are usually combined but, for now, we will keep them separate.)

Sales Account

Sales Account — for recording the value of all sales made.

Expense Accounts

In Unit 3 we will be looking at these types of account in some detail but a little explanation will help us now, and later. Let us think in terms of running and maintaining a home. We could well be faced with making regular payments for rent, electricity, gas, telephone, etc. A business will have the same type of 'expenses' and many others. If we wanted an account to record the payment of rent payable to a landlord called Property Investments Ltd then we could open an account and describe it as Property Investments Ltd. The problem with doing so is that when we later want to read the accounts it may not be immediately obvious as to what the entries in the account represent. However, if we describe the account as Rent Account and record all payments to Property Investments Ltd in this account, we will overcome this problem. This is, in fact, how we describe 'expense' accounts — we describe what they are for, not to whom the payments are being made. Examples of these would be:

Rent Account — rent paid to a landlord.
Electricity Account — payments to Southern Electric for electricity consumed.
Gas Account — payments to British Gas for gas consumed.
Telephone Account — payments made to British Telecom for the cost of equipment rental and calls made

If in doubt with this type of transaction, ask yourself the question 'What is the payment for?' The answer will lead you to an appropriate account description.

Buying Accounts

When a business purchases something, it will normally be for one of two reasons:

1. It will purchase something it requires in order to run the business efficiently. The list of such items is virtually endless but examples would be: a vehicle with which to make deliveries; shelving on which to put stock; office furniture; office equipment. The business may buy its premises rather than rent them, etc.

   All these things that the business buys, and consequently owns, are called assets (we will be looking in more detail at these in Unit 3).

   The description we give these accounts is a description of what has been bought and consequently taken into ownership, e.g.

   Vehicle Account — purchased a vehicle from Rover Garage.
   Office equipment — purchased a computer for office use.
   Office equipment — purchased a fax machine for the office.

2. Some businesses will purchase materials to be made up into a finished product which can then be sold. As an example, think of a business making and selling chairs. It will buy timber from which to make the frame, foam to pad the seat and cloth to cover the seat. In other words, it will buy a stock of materials from which it can manufacture a product. All such buying transactions are entered in one account described as *Purchases Account*.

   Many businesses do not actually make anything, they just buy in products and resell them at a profit. As an example think of a shop selling clothes. This type of business will buy in the clothes from a manufacturer, add on its own profit and sell the clothes to its customers. The transaction of buying the clothes for resale would be entered in an account described as *Purchases Account*.

We are now starting to understand the distinction between these two main types of buying. Firstly, things the business needs to own in order *to operate* its business. These are technically called assets and accounts are opened to describe the asset, e.g. vehicle, building, office equipment, etc.

Secondly, the business will buy goods which it resells. These may be materials which go into making a product the business sells or they may be ready-made products. Anything bought for these purposes will be recorded in a *Purchases Account*.

Owner's Account

Almost certainly, the owner(s) of a business will have put money in to start the business. The owner(s) may also take money out for personal use so we need accounts to record these transactions.

Capital Account — owner putting money into the business
Drawings Account — owner taking money out of the business for personal use
(We will be covering these transactions and accounts in more detail on page 13.)

Bookkeeping — an illustration of monetary shorthand

Having looked at a little of the theory of bookkeeping, we can now practise the techniques. If the best route to learning is by actually doing, then from now on this, in the main, is how we will proceed.

We are now going to take a look at a situation where a new business is formed, sets itself up with premises, buys all the equipment it requires and then starts trading. We shall look at all these transactions and, from the information given, will write up the accounts.

As we look at each transaction, we will *analyse* each one and answer two basic questions:

1. What two accounts do we need to record the transaction?
2. (a) Which account is giving up value (credit)?
   (b) Which account is receiving the value (debit)?

Exercise

R Smith starts up in business as a hairdresser. He puts £10 000 of his own money into the business which is to be run from rented shop premises in the local High Street. The following lists details of all the business transactions during the first month of trading:

Transaction no.	Date	Transaction
1	1 May	R Smith pays £10 000 into the business Bank Account

Analysis: R Smith puts cash into business   Capital Account (*credit*)
Cash goes into business Bank Account   Bank Account (*debit*)

2	3 May	Purchases chairs, driers and other hairdressing equipment for £6500, paying by cheque

Analysis: Pays £6500 by cheque   Bank Account (*credit*)
Buys equipment (assets)   Equipment Account (*debit*)

3	4 May	Purchases a till, paying £300 by cheque

Analysis: Pays £300 by cheque   Bank Account (*credit*)
Buys till (asset)   Equipment Account (*debit*)

4	4 May	Pays one month's rent on the shop, £500 by cheque

Analysis: Pays £500 by cheque   Bank Account (*credit*)
Pays rent (expense)   Rent Account (*debit*)

5	8 May	Draws £50 in cash out of Bank Account, puts cash in till in order that customers can be given change

Analysis: Takes £50 out of the Bank   Bank Account (*credit*)
Puts cash in till   Cash Account (*debit*)

6	13 May	At the end of his first week's business, counts cash in till which totals £500. This means he has taken £450 from customers (he already had £50 cash float in the till)

Analysis: The giver, R Smith, gives up goods £450   Sales Account (*credit*)
Cash totalling £450 received by R Smith   Cash Account (*debit*)

7	16 May	Banks the previous week's takings of £450

Analysis: Takes £450 cash out of till   Cash Account (*credit*)
Pays cash into Bank   Bank Account (*debit*)

8	18 May	Pays window cleaner £20 by cheque

Analysis: Pays £20 by cheque   Bank Account (*credit*)
Pays for window cleaning   Cleaning Account (*debit*)

9	21 May	Counts cash in till at end of second week's trading

Analysis: Cash totals £750. This means his takings are £700 (£750 *less* £50 float)
The giver, R Smith, provides services £700   Sales Account (*credit*)
Cash £700 received by R Smith   Cash Account (*debit*)

Transaction no.	Date	Transaction
10	24 May	Banks the previous week's takings of £700

Analysis: Takes £700 out of till	Cash Account (*credit*)
Pays cash into Bank	Bank Account (*debit*)

11	29 May	Counts cash in till at end of third week's trading
		Cash totals £650. This means his takings are £600 (£650 *less* £50 float)

Analysis: The giver, R Smith, provides services £600	Sales Account (*credit*)
Cash £600 received by R Smith	Cash Account (*debit*)

12	29 May	Pays wages of £100 to a part-time assistant
		Payment is made by cash taken from the till

Analysis: Pay cash of £100	Cash Account (*credit*)
Payment is for wages (a service)	Wages Account (*debit*)

13	29 May	Takes £200 in cash from the till for his own personal use

Analysis: Takes £200 in cash	Cash Account (*credit*)
He is *drawing* cash for personal use	Drawings Account (*debit*)

Do be sure to think through each transaction and make sure you understand the analysis. When looking at any transaction, try to run through this kind of analysis in your mind. Now go through each transaction again, but this time trace the bookkeeping entries in the following set of accounts (numbers in parentheses in accounts refer to transaction numbers above).

R SMITH

Bank Account

(1)	1.5	Capital	10 000	3.5 Equipment	6 500 (2)
(7)	16.5	Cash	450	4.5 Equipment	200 (3)
(10)	24.5	Cash	700	4.5 Rent	500 (4)
				8.5 Cash	50 (5)
				18.5 Cleaning	20 (8)

Cash Account

(5)	8.5 Bank	50	16.5 Bank	450 (7)
(6)	13.5 Sales	450	24.5 Bank	700 (10)
(9)	21.5 Sales	700	29.5 Wages	100 (12)
(11)	29.5 Sales	600	29.5 Drawings	200 (13)

Capital

	1.5 Bank	10 000 (1)

Equipment

(2) 3.5 Bank	6 500	
(3) 4.5 Bank	300	

Rent

(4) 4.5 Bank	500	

Sales

	11.5 Cash	450 (6)
	21.5 Cash	700 (9)
	29.5 Cash	600 (11)

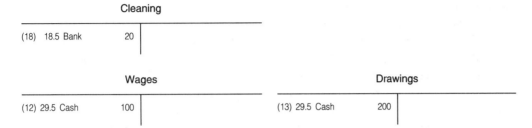

Cleaning

(18) 18.5 Bank 20	

Wages

(12) 29.5 Cash 100	

Drawings

(13) 29.5 Cash 200	

Capital Account made easy

The Capital Account is a topic which appears to cause confusion in the minds of many students. To avoid this situation, we are well advised to consider the matter in some detail.

When a business is started, there is obviously a need to have money available to purchase the various assets required in order to operate. We will see later that many businesses also require further investment after they have been operating for some time. The source of much of the investment is usually the owner(s) of the business, almost certainly so in the case of money invested to start a business. We will also discover, later in our studies, how the ownership of a business can be in the hands of one person (sole proprietor), shared among partners (partnership) or spread between many thousands of people (shareholders). For now, we will think in terms of a sole proprietor which will adequately illustrate the points that need to be made.

It will help us greatly if we try to think of the owner and the business as being two completely separate 'entities'. All this means is that if Mr Jones starts a business called Jones & Son, you have Mr Jones the man, and Jones & Son the business. The business Jones & Son is, in accounting terms, treated as something separate and apart from Mr Jones the man. It is Jones & Son, the business, which buys and sells goods, employs staff, owns the assets of the business, etc. When Mr Jones puts money into Jones & Son to start the business, he is effectively lending (or investing) his own *personal* money to a business called Jones & Son.

Another, more technical, way of saying this is that Mr Jones is investing his own *personal capital*. For its part, the business needs to record in an account the fact that Mr Jones has invested his capital in it.

Assuming the sum invested was £20 000 paid into the bank account of the business, the accounts and entries would be as follows:

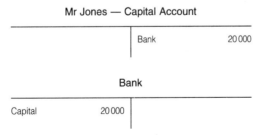

Mr Jones — Capital Account

	Bank	20 000

Bank

Capital	20 000	

The second point we have to understand is best illustrated by answering the question 'Why has Mr Jones invested in the business?' The simple answer is 'in the expectation of the business making profit for himself'. Why else would Mr Jones effectively have lent the £20 000, instead of investing his money in a Building Society or Bank Deposit Account, where he would receive interest on the sum invested? Instead, he chose to invest in the business, no doubt in the hope that it would make more profit for him than he would have received in interest by investing elsewhere. This gives us a clue as to what happens to the profits a business makes. They belong to the *owner* and represent the owner's reward on his or her investment in the business. The 'clever', technical way of expressing this is that 'Profits represent the return on the capital the owner has invested'.

The way we 'give' the owner(s) the profits of the business is to add any profit made to the sum already invested. If, in its first year of trading, Jones & Son made a profit of £5000 then, at the end of the year, the Capital Account would look like this:

Mr Jones — Capital Account

	Bank	20 000
	Profit for year	5 000

We can now readily see that, whereas at the start of trading the business 'owed' Mr Jones the £20 000 he invested, at the end of the first year it 'owes' him £25 000. It may be, that from time to time, Mr Jones will want to 'draw out' of the business some of the profit it has made, for his own personal use. When he does so, the money he takes will be charged to a Drawings Account. Say he writes a cheque on the business bank account payable to himself, then the entries would be:

Bank			Drawings	
	Mr Jones, Drawings	500	Bank	500

At the end of the year we could prepare a simple statement which details Mr Jones's position in relation to Jones & Son, and which shows the value of his investment. Using the previous examples, the statement would be:

Mr Jones — Capital Account

Capital at start of year	20 000	
Profit for year	5 000	25 000
Less: Drawings		500
Capital at end of year		24 500

Goods on credit

In the examples we have looked at so far, whenever a business has made a sale to a customer, the customer has paid in full for the goods or service at the time of receipt. Similarly, when the businesses have bought goods or services, they have paid for them in full at the time of receipt.

For a business, this is the ideal way to trade because it does not have to wait to be paid, and does not run the risk of not receiving payment.

Conversely, if the business is paying for all its purchases at the time of purchase then it will never owe money to anyone apart, that is, from the owner via the Capital Account as we saw in the previous section.

If, for convenience, we assume all payments and receipts are made in cash then the recording of selling or purchasing transactions is a simple, one stage, double-entry procedure:

Cash sale transaction

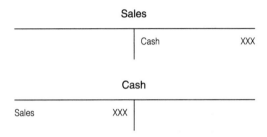

If we think of a supermarket, for example, this is precisely how its sales are made, cash at point of sale.

However, for the majority of businesses, life is not so simple. Many have to sell goods on credit, that is to say they supply goods on the understanding that the customer will pay for the goods at a later date. There are many reasons why a business will choose to, or has to, do business in this way but, basically they do so for one of two reasons or for both. Firstly, because it is the normal way of trading in their particular line of business and, secondly, because they supply customers who are some distance away, by delivering or sending the goods to the customer.

This type of trading, on credit, brings with it many problems. Firstly, it introduces the risk of not getting paid and, secondly, it creates a need for a bookkeeping system which tracks all sales made on credit and tells the business how much particular customers owe at any moment in time. (In Unit 10 we will see how a business attempts to keep moneys owed to it within acceptable levels and how, by doing so, tries to minimize the possibility of not being paid.)

The way in which bookkeeping records this type of transaction is by a two stage, double-entry procedure:

Stage 1 Records the sale on credit to a customer.
Stage 2 Records the payment received from the customer when the customer eventually pays.

Credit sales transaction

Stage 1

Sales				Name of customer		
	Customer	XXX		Sales	XXX	

The double entry to record the credit sale is Sales Account – *credit*, Customer Account — *debit*, unlike a cash sale which is Sales Account — *credit*, Cash Account — *debit*. The Customer Account now tells us that the business has supplied goods to the customer by way of a credit sale and at this time the customer has not paid. This means that the customer is in debt to the business — he is a *debtor* and will remain so until he pays. If we total all the customer accounts in our ledger which are in this position, we know how much, in total, all debtors owe to the company.

When the customer pays the sum due, we then move to Stage 2 of the double-entry procedure.

Stage 2

Customer				Bank		
Sales	XXX	Bank	XXX (1)	(2) Customer	XXX	

Here the customer has sent a cheque to pay his debt. We have therefore credited the customer (1) and debited the bank account (2). If we now look at the Customer's Account, we can see that the debit entry made when the goods were supplied, is now cancelled out by a credit entry made when the customer paid. The customer is no longer a debtor — the account is *clear*. This term 'clear' is one we use when both sides of an account are equal. It means there is no value in the account so it is clear. From all this, we can extract a simple but important fact:

> *An account bearing the name of a customer which has an uncleared debit entry is the account of a debtor — someone who owes money to the business.*

While a business may well sell goods on credit it will, almost certainly, buy goods from a supplier on an undertaking that it will pay at a later date. The bookkeeping procedure for recording such a buying transaction is essentially a mirror image of the selling transaction we have just looked at.

If a business buys goods in which it trades, and pays cash on receipt, the accounts and entries to record this one stage transaction will be:

Cash purchase transaction

Cash			Purchases		
	Purchases	XXX	Cash	XXX	

(In this example, a Purchase Account has been used because the goods were items bought in the course of trade, to be resold. If the items had been something the company needed to own in order to run its business, i.e. an asset, then of course the account would describe what had been bought, e.g. a vehicle.)

If, however, the business obtains goods on credit, then we have a two stage transaction:

Stage 1 Obtaining the goods on credit.
Stage 2 Paying for the goods at a future date.

The bookkeeping entries are:

Credit purchase transaction

Stage 1

Name of Supplier			Purchases		
	Purchases	XXX	Supplier	XXX	

Until the business pays the supplier, the Supplier's Account will have an uncleared credit entry — the supplier is a *creditor*, i.e. someone to whom the business owes money. When the supplier is eventually paid, we move to Stage 2 of the bookkeeping procedure. (We will assume payment is made by cheque.)

Stage 2

Bank			Supplier				
	Supplier	XXX (1)	(2) Bank	XXX	Purchases	XXX	

The entries are: (1) *credit* the Bank (giver); (2) *debit* the Supplier (receiver). The supplier is no longer a creditor as the account is now *clear*.

Again, from this example, we can extract another simple fact:

An account bearing the name of a supplier which has an uncleared credit entry is the account of a creditor — someone to whom the business owes money.

In many businesses, selling on credit, and buying on credit, is the normal method of trading. As we will see later, such is the volume of this type of trade that a large number of companies employ specialist staff whose prime task it is to account for and 'control' this type of transaction and debt.

We will now look at a number of transactions which include this type of trading on credit by a firm called Building Supplies Limited, who are merchants supplying the building trade:

Exercise

Transaction no.	Transaction	£
1	Purchased bricks on credit from Alpha Brick Manufacturing	6 000
2	Purchased a lorry on credit from Rover Garage	22 000
3	Sold goods for cash	80
4	Sold goods on credit to Quick Build Ltd	2 000
5	Sold goods on credit to R Fream & Sons	300
6	Purchased goods on credit from Timber Mills Ltd	11 000
7	Paid £22 000 to Rover Garage by cheque	
8	Received cheque from R Fream & Sons	300
9	Sold goods on credit to Dean Builders	3 500
10	Sold goods for cash	200
11	Purchased goods on credit from Quick Set Cement Ltd	4 000
12	Paid Alpha Brick Manufacturing £6 000 by cheque	

Try to trace each transaction in the following accounts:

Purchases

(1) Alpha Brick Man	6 000	
(6) Timber Mills Ltd	11 000	
(11) Quick Set Cement	4 000	

Alpha Brick Manufacturing

(12) Bank	6 000	Purchases	6 000 (1)

Lorry

(2) Rover Garage	22 000

Rover Garage

(7) Bank	22 000	Lorry	22 000 (2)

Quick Build Ltd

(4) Sales	2 000

R Fream & Sons

(5) Sales	300	Bank	300 (8)

Cash

(3) Sales	80
(10) Sales	200

Bank

(8) R Fream & Sons	300	Rover Garage	22 000 (7)
		Alpha Brick	6 000 (12)

Sales			Timber Mills Ltd		
	Cash	80 (3)		Purchases	11 000 (6)
	Quick Build Ltd	2 000 (4)			
	R Fream & Sons	300 (5)			
	Dean Builders	3 500 (9)			
	Cash	200 (10)			

Dean Builders			Quick Set Cement		
(9) Sales	3 500			Purchases	4 000 (11)

Let us now try to select creditor accounts:
(We are looking for Suppliers' Accounts which have uncleared credit entries.)

Timber Mills Ltd	11 000
Quick Set Cement	4 000
Total owed to creditors	15 000

Now we will select debtor accounts:
(Look for customer accounts which have uncleared debit entries.)

Quick Build Ltd	2 000
Dean Builders	3 500
Total owed by debtors	5 500

We can see that the accounts of: Alpha Brick Manufacturing; Rover Garage; R Fream & Sons are all cleared accounts.

> *Remember:*
> *Debit the customer to whom goods are sold on credit — debtor.*
> *Credit the supplier who supplies goods on credit — creditor.*

Balancing accounts — making the book readable

We are now well on our way to becoming proficient at recording transactions in the appropriate accounts. In other words, we have learnt the basics of 'writing the book'. However, like any book, our ledger is of little use if it cannot be read and understood. In this respect we have a problem. Let us illustrate it by looking at one example:

Bank				
R Jones	15 000	Vehicle	6 000
B Johnson	600	Rent	500
A Wright	1 300	Purchases	1 200
		Electricity	300
		Office Equipment	3 000
		J Clover	2 100

This account tells us many interesting things. For example, £15 000 has been received from R Jones; £600 from B Johnson; £1300 from A Wright. It also tells us that payments have been made for: a vehicle £6000; rent £500; goods purchased £1200, and so on.

What it does *not* tell us at a glance, is what the *balance* of the account is. By balance, we mean by how much the total of one side of the account exceeds the other. We should note that if the total of each side is the same, there is obviously no balance — the account is clear. We will soon see why it is important to know what the balance is for every account in our ledger. At this stage we need only appreciate that we need all these balances so that we can read the book.

We will now try to 'balance' the Bank Account we have just looked at:

Bank

R Jones	15 000	Vehicle	6 000	
B Johnson	600	Rent	500	
A Wright	1 300	Purchases	1 200	
		Electricity	300	
		Office Equipment	3 000	
		J Clover	2 100	
		Balance C/D	3 800	(1)
(2) TOTAL (2)	16 900	TOTAL	16 900	(2)
(3) Balance B/D	3 800			

Steps

1. Add up both sides of the account. We find the totals are:
   debit side £16 900; credit side £13 100.
2. The credit side is therefore £3800 less than the debit side (£16 900−£13 100).
3. Now insert the balancing figure (1) on the lowest side so as to make both sides the same. Describe this entry as Balance C/D.
4. Now total both sides to make sure our sums are correct (2). As we had hoped, we find both sides are now equal.
5. When we inserted the balancing figure of £3800 (1), we described it as Balance C/D (C/D means carried down). But we have only entered the figure on the credit side of the account. We know that in double entry bookkeeping, for every credit there must be a corresponding debit entry and vice versa. We can now complete the double entry by bringing the balance down on the debit side and describing the entry as Balance B/D (B/D meaning brought down).

We can now see at a glance that the balance of the Bank Account is £3800 which means that the business has £3800 in the bank.

Let us take another example:

Ream Paper Company

Bank	900	Purchases	900
Bank	670	Purchases	670
Bank	1 140	Purchases	1 140
		Purchases	460
		Purchases	880

After balancing, the account will look like this:

Ream Paper Company

	Bank	900	Purchases	900	
	Bank	670	Purchases	670	
	Bank	1 140	Purchases	1 140	
			Purchases	460	
(1)	Balance C/D	1 340	Purchases	880	
(2)	TOTAL	4 050	TOTAL	4 050	(2)
			Balance B/D	1 340	(3)

This is obviously a supplier's account and we can see how the first three credit entries for supplies received have all been 'cleared' by cheque payments. We can also see that the last two credit entries for supplies received have not yet been cleared and remain unpaid. The balance B/D is the total of these two credit entries. However, by balancing the account we can see at a glance that the total owed to the creditor (Ream Paper Company) is £1340.

Now let us take a set of accounts which have been balanced and see how the balances enable us to read quickly the bookkeeping story. For clarity, all the detailed entries in the accounts have been omitted and only the balance B/D on each account is shown:

Ledger of Cave Trading at 31 December 19– –

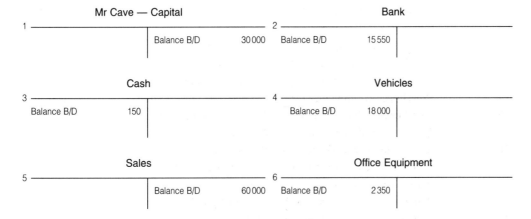

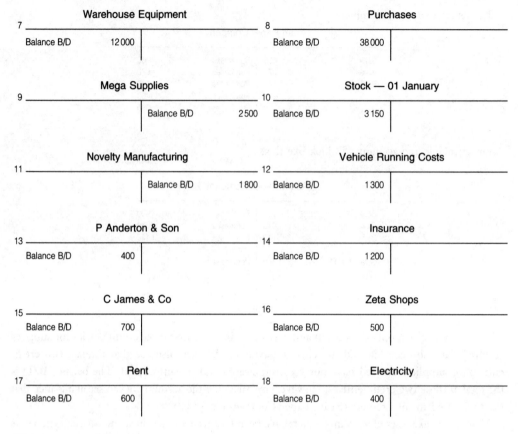

Warehouse Equipment				Purchases		
7				8		
Balance B/D	12 000			Balance B/D	38 000	

Mega Supplies				Stock — 01 January		
9				10		
		Balance B/D	2 500	Balance B/D	3 150	

Novelty Manufacturing				Vehicle Running Costs		
11				12		
		Balance B/D	1 800	Balance B/D	1 300	

P Anderton & Son				Insurance		
13				14		
Balance B/D	400			Balance B/D	1 200	

C James & Co				Zeta Shops		
15				16		
Balance B/D	700			Balance B/D	500	

Rent				Electricity		
17				18		
Balance B/D	600			Balance B/D	400	

The accounts tell us:

Account no.	Story
1	Mr Cave has invested personal capital of £30 000 in the business.
2	There is £15 550 in the bank.
3	There is £150 in cash.
4	Vehicles, costing £18 000, have been bought.
5	The business has sold £60 000 worth of goods.
6	Office equipment, costing £2350, has been bought.
7	Warehouse equipment, costing £12 000, has been bought.
8	The business has purchased trade goods costing £38 000.
9	£2500 is owed to a creditor — Mega Supplies.
10	The business started the year with stock worth £3150.
11	£1800 is owed to a creditor — Novelty Manufacturing.
12	It has cost £1300 to run the vehicles.
13	A debtor — P Anderton & Son — owes £400.
14	Insurance premiums have been paid costing £1200.
15	A debtor — C James & Co — owes £700.

16   A debtor — Zeta Shops — owes £500.
17   Rent of £600 has been paid.
18   Electricity costs of £400 have been paid.

Now we are actually starting to read accounts and can see how the balance (basically just one figure which sums up the whole account) helps us to read quickly. We can also extract more useful information. If, for example, we want to know how much in total Cave Trading owes to its creditors, then:

Account 9	2500
Account 11	1800
Total owed to creditors	4300

If, on the other hand, we want to know how much, in total, debtors owe to Cave Trading then:

Account 13	400
Account 15	700
Account 16	500
Total owed by debtors	1600

The Trial Balance — completing the bookkeeping story

In the last section we saw a set of balanced accounts. The accounts of Cave Trading on page 21 are a good example and we will now use these to learn about the next step towards translating the ledger accounts into a condensed and easily readable story. Let us start by reminding ourselves of how the balanced accounts looked:

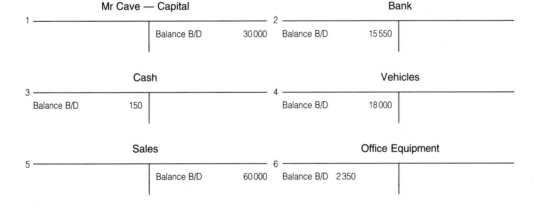

Ledger of Cave Trading at 31 December 19– –

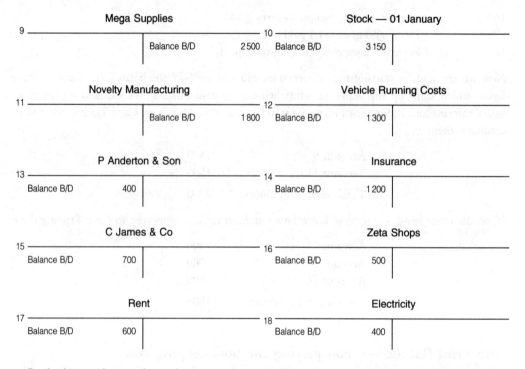

In the last section, we learnt how to read each individual account. But it is only by combining all the individual account stories that we will finally arrive at the *full story* of Cave Trading's business activity. Before we do this, however, let us remind ourselves of one of the 'golden rules' of bookkeeping we learnt in Unit 1: *If we add up all the credit entries and all the debit entries, the totals will be the same.*

Therefore, before we proceed, we need to test that the book (ledger) is in balance. You will remember that we did such a test in Unit 1. There, we listed all the debit entries and all the credit entries to prove that the total of both agreed. Because we have balanced each account, we do not now have to list each entry, only the balance on all accounts.

But why do such a test at all, when we know that in double-entry bookkeeping we always make corresponding credit and debit entries? The answer, quite simply, is to try and detect any errors made in the double entries and balancing of accounts. We can all make mistakes. We could, for example, when entering a transaction with a value of £100, make a correct entry on the credit side but, in error, enter it as £10 on the debit side. We could also make a mistake in calculating the balance on an account. We may even forget to make one part of a double entry altogether. Any mistakes like these mean that the ledger is not in balance. Or to put it another way, we have not 'balanced the books'.

The test we construct is technically called a *Trial Balance*. All we need do is list the accounts and enter the balances for each account in the appropriate column, debit or credit. The total of both columns should be the same.

In the following example, we see the Trial Balance of Cave Trading, constructed from the balanced accounts.

Cave Trading
Trial Balance 31 December 19– –

	Debit	Credit
Mr Cave — Capital		30 000
Bank	15 550	
Cash	150	
Vehicles	18 000	
Sales		60 000
Office equipment	2 350	
Warehouse equipment	12 000	
Purchases	38 000	
Mega Supplies		2 500
Stock 01 January	3 150	
Novelty Manufacturing		1 800
Vehicle running costs	1 300	
P Anderton & Son	400	
Insurance	1 200	
C James & Co	700	
Zeta Shops	500	
Rent	600	
Electricity	400	
Totals	94 300	94 300

If the Trial Balance does not balance then we must locate and rectify any errors. It is vital that this be done because the accuracy and ease with which 'final accounts' can be constructed from the Trial Balance will depend largely on its accuracy.

We should, however, be aware of the fact that the Trial Balance is not absolute proof of accurate bookkeeping. It is quite possible to make certain types of bookkeeping errors which the Trial Balance cannot detect. They are:

- *Errors of commission* — a debit or credit entry is made for the correct amount but in the wrong account.
- *Errors of omission* — both the credit and debit entry for a particular transaction are omitted.
- *Compensating errors* — where, for example, we might make a credit entry and a debit entry in the sum of £10, when the transaction value is £100.

Make sure that you now complete all the exercises in the following section. It is most important that you fully understand all aspects and techniques we have covered.

If you try to 'skimp' on the exercises you will inevitably find that, at a later stage, you will not have the depth of understanding so necessary to complete the later work.

Exercises

1. Open up relevant accounts and complete double entries for the following transactions.

   (a) Paid rent by cheque   £300
   (b) Sold goods on credit to A Andrews   £700
   (c) Sold goods on credit to L Long   £800
   (d) Purchased goods on credit from P Woods   £1200
   (e) Paid electricity account by cheque   £200
   (f) Banked cheque from A Andrews   £700
   (g) Sold goods for cash   £150
   (h) Sold goods on credit to C Beam   £350
   (i) Purchased goods on credit from P Woods   £750
   (j) Paid cash into the bank   £150

2. A Kempton started a business in July 19– –. From the following transactions: open up all necessary accounts; complete the double entries; balance the accounts; and complete a Trial Balance.

   July 01   Started by paying £10 000 into the business bank account.
        02   Bought goods on credit from J Jones £940 and P Clark £3400.
        03   Sold goods for cash £250.
        04   Banked £200 of the cash.
        05   Sold goods on credit to T Old £240.
        06   Sold goods on credit to H James £380.
        07   Bought goods on credit from J Jones £380.
        08   Purchased van for £2500 by cheque.
        12   Bought office furniture by cheque £800.
        14   Sold goods for cash £400.
        18   Sold goods on credit to S Simms £1300.
        19   Banked cash £380.
        22   Bought fixtures and fittings £3600, paying by cheque.
        24   Sold goods on credit to H James £500.
        26   Bought goods on credit from J James £390.
        27   Paid J James by cheque £940.
        29   Banked a cheque £320 from H James.
        31   Sold goods for cash £120.
        31   Banked cheque from T Old £240.

3. T Morgan opened a business on 01 September 19– –. From the following transactions of his first month of trading: open up accounts; balance the accounts; extract a Trial Balance.

   Sept 19– –
        01   Paid £15 000 personal capital into the business bank account.
        01   Bought fixtures and fittings by cheque £400.
        02   Purchased a van on credit from Harrow Motors £3500.
        04   Purchased goods from Traders Ltd £2800 on credit.
        05   Paid rent on warehouse £800 by cheque.
        06   Purchased goods £650 on credit from P Harris & Son.
        09   Sold goods on credit to P Parker £1500.
        12   Sold goods to R Rooney £600 on credit.

14   Paid insurances by cheque £450.
17   Sold goods for cash £900.
17   Took £400 for own personal use.
20   Bought goods on credit from Traders Ltd £1350.
22   Sold goods on credit to K Harper £1800.
24   Paid Traders Ltd £2800 by cheque.
26   Sold goods to P Parker £700 on credit.
28   Sold goods for cash £400.
28   Banked cheque from P Parker £1500.
30   Banked all cash held.

4. The following Trial Balance was extracted from the books of V Hearn & Co as at 31 August 19– –.

	Debit	Credit
Supply Services		3 400
Wright & Son	2 800	
Capital Account		10 000
Vehicle	4 000	
Fixtures and fittings	2 000	
Wages	8 000	
Electricity	400	
Insurances	300	
Rent	800	
Purchases	16 000	
Sales		24 000
Cash	100	
Bank	3 000	
	37 400	37 400

Open up all the ledger accounts and insert the balances from the Trial Balance as opening balances 01 September 19– –.

Next, complete the double entries for the following September transactions. Balance all accounts and extract a trial balance at 30 September 19– –.

September 19– –

02   Bought goods on credit from Supply Services £2000.
04   Paid a garage account for repair to vehicle £200 by cheque.
05   Sold goods for cash £800.
05   Paid cash into bank £700.
08   Paid rent by cheque £200.
10   Sold goods on credit to P Palmer £1800.
12   Paid Supply Services by cheque £3400.
13   Sold goods £2900 on credit to Wright & Son.
16   Banked cheque from Wright & Son £2800.
21   Bought goods from Supply Services £2600 on credit.
24   Paid electricity bill £100 by cheque.
26   Paid garage bill for petrol by cheque £100.
28   Banked cheque from P Palmer £1800.
28   Drew £900 cash from bank.
29   Paid wages in cash £1000.
30   Sold goods on credit to P Palmer £600.

Unit 3

Reading the book

Classifying accounts

In Unit 2 we constructed the Trial Balance of Cave Trading which looked like this:

Cave Trading
Trial Balance 31 December 19– –

	Debit	Credit
Mr Cave — Capital		30 000
Bank	15 550	
Cash	150	
Vehicles	18 000	
Sales		60 000
Office equipment	2 350	
Warehouse equipment	12 000	
Purchases	38 000	
Mega Supplies		2 500
Stock 01 January	3 150	
Novelty Manufacturing		1 800
Vehicle running costs	1 300	
P Anderton & Son	400	
Insurance	1 200	
C James & Co	700	
Zeta Shops	500	
Rent	600	
Electricity	400	
Total	94 300	94 300

Now we will rearrange the accounts listed in the Trial Balance into logical groupings to see if there is anything to be learnt from the Trial Balance.

In practice, we would not do this but it is a good way of preparing ourselves for the next stage of our study. If we fully understand the points we are now going to cover, then our future tasks will be easier to complete with confidence.

Cave Trading
Trial Balance at 31 December 19– –
Reorganized into logical account groups

Asset Accounts	Debit	Capital Accounts	Credit
Bank	15 550	Mr Cave — capital	30 000
Cash	150		
Vehicles	18 000		
Office equipment	2 350	*Liability Accounts*	
Warehouse equipment	12 000		
P Anderton & Son — debtor	400	Mega Supplies — creditor	2 500
C James & Co — debtor	700	Novelty Manufacturing — creditor	1 800
Zeta Shops — debtor	500		

Expense Accounts		Income Accounts	
Trading expenses:		Sales	60 000
Purchases	38 000		
Stock 01 January	3 150		
Operating expenses:			
Vehicle running costs	1 300		
Insurances	1 200		
Rent	600		
Electricity	400		
Total	94 300	Total	94 300

From this illustration many facts emerge but, before we look at what these might be, let us first remind ourselves of what the account groups represent:

- *Asset Accounts*   Assets are all the things that a business *owns*. In our example, we see money in the bank; cash held; vehicles and equipment owned; debts owed to the business by debtors. There is an old saying 'If you can kick it or count it, it's an asset'. (Whether debtors would take kindly to our kicking them is a dubious point.)
- *Expense Accounts*   These are subdivided into Trading Expenses which are the costs of buying the products which the business sells, or the costs of buying manufacturing materials. Operating Expenses are the day-to-day costs of running a business.
- *Liability Accounts*   These represent what the business *owes*. Sums owed to creditors are the prime example.

- *Capital Accounts*   The accounts show the sums invested in the business by the owner(s). Although we classify them as Capital Accounts they are really the same as Liability Accounts as they represent what the business *owes* to the owner(s).
- *Income Accounts*   These represent the sources of money coming into the business from selling its goods or services. We will see later that there can be other types of income, but sales is the main source.

Let us now search out the 'facts'. On examining the reorganized Trial Balance we discover:

- *Fact 1*   All Asset Accounts are *debit* balances.
           All Expense Accounts are *debit* balances.
- *Fact 2*   All Liability Accounts are *credit* balances (Liabilities here includes Capital Accounts).
           All Income Accounts are *credit* balances.
  Note: Look at Facts 1 and 2 above another way and we discover that:
  An account with a *debit* balance must be an asset or an expense.
  An account with a *credit* balance must be a liability or income.
- *Fact 3*   Debit   Credit
           Assets   Liabilities
             +   *equal*   +
           Expenses   Income

If we understand these basic facts then we are well equipped for what lies ahead.

Income and Expenditure Accounts v. Asset and Liability Accounts

These two types of account are equally important but very different. We will start by thinking of an average family and ask the questions:

1. 'How much can the family afford to save?'
2. 'How much is the family worth?'

To answer the first question, we need to find the difference between the income of the household and how much the family spends. We will take a situation which could be typical:

Income:	Husband — salary	15 000	
	Wife — wages	3 000	18 000
Expenses:	Mortgage repayments	3 500	
	Car loan repayments	1 500	
	Electricity	400	
	Heating costs	600	
	Clothing	800	
	Car running costs	1 000	
	Food and drink	2 500	
	Children's pocket money	500	
	Holidays	2 000	
	Entertainment and leisure	1 500	14 300
	Savings		3 700

Businesses exist to make profit and one of the prime purposes of bookkeeping is to enable the owner(s) of the business (and others) to see what, if any, profit has been made.

To do this, we follow essentially the same method we have just used for our family, the only change being that we do not call the difference between income and expenses savings, but profit.

We display the income and expenses in an account called the *Profit and Loss Account*. Profit and *loss* because, of course, if the expenses of the business are greater than its income it will make a loss. In its simplest form therefore, a Profit and Loss Account is:

Profit and Loss Account

Income	XXX
Less: Expenses	XXX
= Profit (or loss)	XXX

Let us go back to our family:

To answer the second question, 'How much is the family worth?', we can again look at what might be a typical situation:

Assets:	House value	60 000	
	Car	8 000	
	Furniture, TV, video, etc.	7 000	
	Money in the bank	1 000	76 000
Liabilities:	Mortgage on house	30 000	
	Car loan outstanding	4 000	
	Outstanding on credit cards	400	34 400
	Net worth		41 600

The owner(s) of a business similarly want to know what it is worth. Bear in mind, the net worth of the business will show whether the value of the owner(s) investment has grown or shrunk.

As with the Profit and Loss Account, we prepare a statement for the business using much the same method as we used for our family. Such a statement, produced for a business, is called a *Balance Sheet*.

Again, in a simple form, a Balance Sheet is:

Balance Sheet

Assets	XXX
Less: Liabilities	XXX
= Net worth of business	XXX

Notes:

1. The net worth of the business and the capital totals are the same, hence the term Balance Sheet.
2. The description of the statement is the Balance Sheet. Quite simply this is so because the Balance Sheet is *not* an account. It is only a listing of asset, liability and capital account balances. We will learn more of this later.
3. Because, unlike the Profit and Loss Account, the Balance Sheet is not an account, it is not part of the double-entry bookkeeping system.

Final Accounts — simply summaries

The term *final accounts* is used to describe the condensed story extracted from all the accounts in the ledger. This 'final' story is in two parts:

1. A Profit and Loss Account.
2. A Balance Sheet.

From what we have already learnt, we can construct a simple model to show the path to these 'final' statements:

Trial Balance/Balances		Destination
Debit	*Credit*	
Assets Expenses		Balance Sheet Profit and Loss
	Capital Liabilities Income	Balance Sheet Balance Sheet Profit and Loss

We can now see a most valuable role for the Trial Balance. It is the place where we collect all the ledger account balances and then, having proved the ledger is in balance, we can extract the balances and place them in the Balance Sheet or Profit and Loss Account. *The Balance Sheet and Profit and Loss Account are therefore simply summaries drawn from the account balances in the Trial Balance.*

The secret to initial success in constructing the Profit and Loss Account and Balance Sheet therefore depends on two skills:

1. Being able to decide which account balances in the Trial Balance represent:
   Asset Account
   Expense Account
   Capital Account
   Liability Account
   Income Account.
2. Knowing the final destination for each of the above categories of accounts, be it the Profit and Loss Account or Balance Sheet.

These are the skills we *must* practise. The speed and accuracy with which we can complete this process will count heavily in any examination or practical situation. It follows that the method we are about to explore will prove to be extremely useful. We are again going to take the Trial Balance of our old friend Cave Trading:

1. Allocate each balance to an account category using codes:
   A, Asset Account
   E, Expense Account
   C, Capital Account
   L, Liability Account
   I, Income Account.
2. Then allocate each to its final destination using codes:
   P, Profit and Loss Account
   B, Balance Sheet.

Before we start, consider these hints:

- First work *down* the debit column. We know that debit balances can only be:
  A = Asset Account
  E = Expense Account.
- Next work *down* the credit column. We know that credit balances can only be:
  C = Capital Account
  L = Liability Account.
  I = Income Account.

This method will help us to focus our minds more sharply.

Cave Trading

Trial Balance 31 December 19– –

	Debit £	Credit £	Category	Destination
Mr Cave — Capital		30 000	C	B
Bank	15 550		A	B
Cash	150		A	B
Vehicles	18 000		A	B
Sales		60 000	I	P
Office equipment	2 350		A	B
Warehouse equipment	12 000		A	B
Purchases	38 000		E	P
Mega Supplies		2 500	L	B
Stock 01 January	3 150		E	P
Novelty Manufacturing		1 800	L	B
Vehicle running costs	1 300		E	P
P Anderton & Son	400		A	B
Insurance	1 200		E	P
C James & Co	700		A	B
Zeta Shops	500		A	B
Rent	600		E	P
Electricity	400		E	P
Totals	94 300	94 300		

It is vitally important that you now complete all the exercises relating to this unit.

As you practise these skills you will soon find that you are starting to recognize categories of accounts very quickly and you will know, almost instinctively, their 'final' destinations.

Exercises

1. From the following list of balances, construct a Trial Balance. Remember that assets and expenses are debit balances and Capital, Liability and Income Accounts are credit balances.

	£
	£
Cash	100
Purchases	4 500
Owed to Suppliers Limited	1 200
Sales	9 000
Rent	800
Insurances	150
Capital	5 000
Owed by A Arnold	1 500
Owed to B Jones	800
Office equipment	5 500
Electricity	300
Owed by P Parker	600
Bank	2 550

Note The debit and credit totals should each be £16 000.

2. From a balanced ledger we have been given the total of all balances in each account category except Capital.

	£
All Liability balances total	3 000
All Asset balances total	14 000
All Income balances total	9 000
All Expense balances total	5 000

(a) What is the total of each side of a Trial Balance, produced from the above?
(b) What is the balance on the missing Capital Account?

3. On the following Trial Balance, first complete the Category column and then the Destination column.

Bean Trading
Trial Balance as at 31 March 19– –

	Debit	Credit	Category	Destination
	£	£		
Purchases	36 000		E	P
Vehicles	8 000		A	B
Daniel & Co		2 500	L	B
Rent	600		E	P
W Williams	1 800		A	B
Capital		10 000	C	B
Bank	2 300		A .	B
Insurances	300		E	P
Sales		40 000	I	P
Electricity	800		E	P
R Rowland	3 400		·A	B
T Trainer		700	L	B
	53 200	53 200		

4. The following list of balances has been taken from the ledger of Trojan Trading. In preparing the list, the balance on the Sales Account has been omitted. From the list:
   (a) Prepare a Trial Balance which of course includes the Sales Account balance.
   (b) Complete a category and destination column.

Account balances	£		
Rent	400 D	C	P
Vehicles	6 000 D	A	B
Purchases	32 000 D	E	P
Insurances	300 D	E	P
Wages	8 000 D	E	P
Vehicle running costs	1 500 D	E	P
Owed to R Reynold	2 400 C	L	B
Owed by K Darwin & Son	6 200 D	A	B
Sales	? C = 45,000		P
Electricity	600 D	E	P
Owed to E Ford & Co	1 600 C	L	P
Capital	11 000 C	C	B
Owed by G Goodwin	800 D	A	B
Bank	4 100 D	A	B
Cash	100 B	A	B
			B

60000   60,000

Unit 4

Developing the story

Trading profit and net profit

We are now ready to start formulating 'final' accounts which consist of the Profit and Loss Account and the Balance Sheet.

The Profit and Loss Account

We saw in Unit 3 how the Profit and Loss Account is essentially a simple statement:

Income	XXX
Less: Expenses	XXX
= Profit (or loss)	XXX

As we work through the detail of constructing the account, try to keep this fact clearly in your mind.

The account is actually split into two component parts:

1. The Trading part of the account where we determine the level of *gross profit* made by the business.
2. The Profit and Loss part of the account where we deduct all the operating expenses from the gross profit to arrive at the 'final' *net profit*.

The following illustration may help us to understand these two stages more clearly:

Trading and Profit and Loss Account

Stage 1	Trading part	(1) Income from sales	XXX
		(2) *Less*: Cost to the business of the goods sold	XXX
		(3) Gross profit	XXX
Stage 2	Profit and Loss part	(4) *Less*: Operating expenses	XXX
		(5) Net profit	XXX

Note   While, for convenience, we often refer to the account as the Profit and Loss Account, the correct title for a business which sells goods (i.e. trades) is the Trading and Profit and Loss Account.

Stage 1 The Trading part

Notes

(1) Income from sales. This is quite straightforward. The figure we want is the balance on the Sales Account in the Trial Balance.

(2) The cost to the business of the goods sold is an area which often causes students some difficulty. It need not, if we clearly understand the logic behind the method of arriving at the figure.

Take the cost of the stock of goods at the beginning of the year (Opening stock)	XXX
Then add stock purchased during the year (Purchases)	+XXX
	XXX
Then deduct the stock left at the end of the year (Closing stock)	−XXX
Result — Cost of goods sold	=XXX

Look at this again another way, using actual values. Let us take the Trial Balance of Cave Trading:

Cave Trading

Trial Balance 31 December 19– –

	Debit	Credit	Category	Destination
Mr Cave — Capital		30 000	C	B
Bank	15 550		A	B
Cash	150		A	B
Vehicles	18 000		A	B
Sales		60 000	I	P
Office equipment	2 350		A	B
Warehouse equipment	12 000		A	B
Purchases	38 000		E	P
Mega Supplies		2 500	L	B
Stock 01 January	3 150		E	P
Novelty Manufacturing		1 800	L	B
Vehicle running costs	1 300		E	P
P Anderton & Son	400		A	B
Insurance	1 200		E	P
C James & Co	700		A	B
Zeta Shops	500		A	B
Rent	600		E	P
Electricity	400		E	P
Totals	94 300	94 300		

Stock on 01 January is £3150. Purchases for the year are £38000. Now we will assume that after stocktaking, on 31 December, the stock (valued at cost price) was £2850.

Therefore: Cost of stock at start of year (Opening stock)	3 150
Plus: Cost of additional stock purchases during year (Purchases)	+38 000
It was possible, therefore, to sell stock which cost	41 150
But it was not all sold because at the end of the year there is unsold stock (Closing stock) which cost	− 2 850
Therefore, we actually sold stock which cost	38 300

In short, we have a situation where:

		Technical Terms
What we started with	=	Opening stock
plus		*plus*
What we bought	=	Purchases
less		*less*
What we have left	=	Closing stock
equals		*equals*
What we sold	=	Cost of goods sold

We can now prepare the Trading part of the Trading and Profit and Loss Account as it is normally presented.

In the case of Cave Trading, this is:

Trading Account

Sales		60 000
Less: Cost of goods sold:		
Opening Stock 01 January	3 150	
Plus: Purchases	38 000	
	41 150	
Less: Closing stock 31 December	2 850	38 300
Gross profit		21 700

You need to be totally familiar with this method of laying out the account and presenting the figures.

Stage 2 The Profit and Loss part

1. We start with the gross profit from the Trading Account.
2. All we now have to do is list the operating expenses (Expense Account balances shown in the debit column of the Trial Balance) and total them.

3. If we now deduct the total of the operating expenses from the gross profit, we have the net profit.

Gross profit	XXX
Less: Operating expenses	XXX
Equals: Net profit	XXX

We can now prepare the Profit and Loss part of the Trading and Profit and Loss Account for Cave Trading.

Profit and Loss Account

Gross profit		21 700
Less: Operating expenses:		
Vehicle running costs	1 300	
Insurances	1 200	
Rent	600	
Electricity	400	3 500
Net profit		18 200

Now we can combine the Trading Account and the Profit and Loss Account to arrive at the Trading and Profit and Loss Account which is the usual way of presenting the information:

Cave Trading
Trading and Profit and Loss Account for the year ended 31 December 19– –

Sales		60 000
Less: Cost of goods sold:		
Opening Stock 01 January	3 150	
Plus: Purchases	38 000	
	41 150	
Less: Closing stock 31 December	2 850	38 300
Gross profit		21 700
Less: Operating expenses:		
Vehicle running costs	1 300	
Insurances	1 200	
Rent	600	
Electricity	400	3 500
Net profit		18 200

There is now one other thing we have to do as far as items in the Trading and Profit and Loss Account are concerned. Remembering that this is a *proper account*, we must open an account in the ledger and do double entries to transfer the balances from each account we have used in preparing the Trading and Profit and Loss Account.

Sales				Purchases			
Trading A/c	60 000	Balance B/D	60 000	Balance B/D	38 000	Trading A/c	38 000

Vehicle running costs				Insurances			
Balance B/D	1 300	P & L A/c	1 300	Balance B/D	1 200	P & L A/c	1 200

Rent				Electricity			
Balance B/d	600	P & L A/c	600	Balance B/D	400	P & L A/c	400

Stock			
Balance (Stock 01 Jan)	3 150	Trading A/c	3 150
Trading A/c (Stock 31 Dec)	2 850		

(These entries are explained in detail later.)

Trading and Profit and Loss Account

Purchases	38 000	Sales	60 000
Vehicle running costs	1 300	Stock 31 December	2 850
Insurances	1 200		
Rent	600		
Electricity	400		
Stock (01 January)	3 150		
Balance C/D	18 200		
	62 850		62 850
		Balance B/D	18 200

As we would expect, the balance on the Trading and Profit and Loss Account is the same as the profit figure we produced in the presentation of the Trading and Profit and Loss Account.

Now let us have a closer look at the Stock Account to make sure we understand what has happened. At the start of the year (01 January) we had a Stock Account with a balance of £3150. No entries are made in this account during the year (additional stocks purchased during the year are entered in the Purchases Account) and at the end of the year the account looks like this:

Stock			
Balance (01 Jan)	3 150		

This is the opening stock for the year, which we transfer to the Trading Account part of the Trading and Profit and Loss Account (1).

		Stock			
Balance (01 Jan)	3 150	Trading A/c	3 150	(1)
(2) Trading A/c (Stock 31 Dec)	2 850			

Now we enter the stock at the end of the year — £2850 (2). The double entry for this is a credit in the Trading Account. The Stock Account now has a 'balance' of £2850 which represents an asset owned (stock) and therefore appears in the Balance Sheet. The closing stock of £2850 at 31 December is, of course, the opening stock for the following year at 01 January.

Note   Few, if any, examination questions will require you to do these entries to transfer balances to a Trading and Profit and Loss Account. Normally, all you will be expected to do is prepare the presentation of the Trading and Profit and Loss Account from the balances in the Trial Balance.

However, we should know that these entries have, in practice, to be made. Hopefully, by going through the procedure, it will also help us to understand better the formulation of the Trading and Profit and Loss Account presentation.

The Balance Sheet and why it is not an account

The Balance Sheet is merely a listing of those balances in the Trial Balance which represent the assets (things owned) or liabilities (owed) by a business. It is not an account, just a listing. The purpose of the listing is to ascertain the net worth of the business.

In laying out the Balance Sheet, the assets and liabilities are arranged in such a way that, apart from showing the net worth, other useful information is also produced. For this reason, a 'standard' layout has evolved and we are well advised to follow it.

In its simple form, omitting figures for clarity, the layout looks like this:

Balance Sheet as at . . .

Fixed assets:			
Detail			XXX
Detail			XXX
Current assets:			
Detail		XXX	
Detail		XXX	
Detail		XXX	
Less: Current liabilities:			
Detail	XXX		
Detail	XXX	XXX	
Working capital			XXX
Net worth			XXX
Financed by:			
Capital at start of year		XXX	
Plus: Profit for year		XXX	
		XXX	
Less: Drawings for year		XXX	
Capital at end of year			XXX

Now we will produce the Balance Sheet for Cave Trading using this layout. All we need do is extract the appropriate account balances from the Trial Balance and slot them in. However, we must remember that there are two account balances we have produced since the Trial Balance was drawn up and both must appear in the Balance Sheet. One is the net profit figure produced in the Trading and Profit and Loss Account, the other is the closing stock value as at 31 December.

Cave Trading

Balance Sheet as at 31 December— —

Fixed assets:

Warehouse equipment		12 000
Office equipment		2 350
Vehicles		18 000
		32 350

Current assets:

Stock 31 December	2 850	
Debtors	1 600	
Bank	15 550	
Cash	150	
	20 150	

Less: Current liabilities:

Creditors	4 300	
Working capital		15 850
Net worth		48 200

Financed by:

Capital 01 January — —	30 000	
Plus: Profit for year	18 200	
Capital 31 December — —		48 200

Before we look more closely at the detail of the Balance Sheet, let us first identify the most important information that it vividly portrays.

Much earlier in our study, we decided that one of the prime purposes of accountancy was to reveal the worth of the business to the owner(s) and others. The Balance Sheet certainly does that — in this example £48 200. It also shows how the business has acquired this net worth — in this case through the owner's investment of capital and the profits made by the business, totalling £48 200. This latter point is worthy of a little more explanation. We know that the profits made by the business belong to the owner(s), that is why they are added to his capital. In our example, the owner has not taken anything out of the business by way of drawings so the whole of his capital at the beginning of the year plus the profits for the year remain invested in the business at 31 December. This matter of leaving profits invested in a business is an important topic and one to which we will be returning in later units.

For the present, we will take a closer look at the detail of the Balance Sheet. We can see that in presenting the Balance Sheet, assets have been split into two distinct categories:

- Fixed assets
- Current assets.

Fixed assets

These are assets held for long-term use in the business. Examples would be land and buildings, plant and machinery, fixtures and fittings, office equipment, vehicles, etc. We can see that these assets are all things a business will need to keep in continuing ownership, if it is to go on trading year after year. Fixed assets are therefore held for long-term use in operating a business.

When listing the assets in a Balance Sheet, they should be listed in 'reverse order of liquidity'. The most liquid asset you can have is cash in the hand. Probably the next most liquid asset would be money in the bank, because we can quite easily draw cash out of a bank account. At the other end of the scale, a property would probably be the least liquid asset a business would possess. If it wished to dispose of the property, it would probably take longer to sell than other assets the business may own, e.g. vehicle. If we take what could be a representative, random sample of the types of fixed assets a business might own, we could have:

- Office equipment
- Vehicles
- Factory — tools and equipment
- Factory — machinery
- Land and buildings.

If we were to list these in reverse order of liquidity for balance sheet purposes, a sensible order would be:

Fixed assets:
    Land and buildings
    Factory — machinery
    Factory — tools and equipment
    Office equipment
    Vehicles.

Current assets

These are assets which a business expects to convert into cash in a relatively short period of time. Bearing this in mind, we can think of current assets as being cash or 'near cash'. The usual assets we could find under the heading of Current assets, listed in 'reverse order of liquidity', would be:

Current assets:
    Stock
    Debtors
    Bank
    Cash.

We can apply the description 'near cash' to stock and debtors because the stock can reasonably be expected to be sold within a relatively short time span and debtors are expected to pay to an agreed timescale.

Unlike fixed assets, the current assets of a business are continually changing as they support the trading activity. As every sale is made an item, or items, of stock is (are) used. If the sale is on credit, the total value of debtors is increased. When a debtor pays, the value of debtors is reduced but cash is increased. When payments are made to purchase new stock, or pay expense accounts, the bank balance is reduced. In this respect, current assets are 'working' to support the trading activity of the business. We will see, shortly, how current assets are measured against current liabilities to produce a most important piece of information.

Current liabilities

Liabilities, as we know, are those things a business owes. Just as assets are split into two categories (fixed assets and current assets), liabilities are also split into two categories. The categories are:

- Current liabilities
- Long-term liabilities.

Current liabilities are all the debts owed by a business which are due to be paid within a relatively short time span. In practice, it is usual to include any debt which is, or may be, payable within one year, as a current liability. Long-term liabilities are debts which are normally not due for payment within one year.

A debt to a bank is a good illustration of these points. A bank overdraft or a short-term loan of, say, six months, would be included in current liabilities whereas a long-term business loan of, say, five years, would be included as a long-term liability. We will be looking at long-term liabilities in later units and will see then how they are displayed in a Balance Sheet.

Working capital

For now, we will return to the matter of current assets and current liabilities because the relationship between the two is an important measure of the financial standing of a business. Let us again take a family situation. The family may own a house and a car but, if it had, say, £200 in the bank and was being pressed for payment of debts, say, credit card, telephone and electricity bills totalling £800, it would be in some difficulty. The business parallel of this is that if the current liabilities exceed current assets, it too will be in difficulty.

A business, therefore, will be working to ensure that its current assets exceed its current liabilities and the extent to which this is so is called *working capital*. If we refer back to the Balance Sheet of Cave Trading we see that the situation is:

Current assets	20 150
Less: Current liabilities	4 300
Working capital	15 850

The working capital is a measure of excess 'short-term' funds available to the business with which it can operate. In technical terms it is a *measure of liquidity*. This is an important matter to which we will be returning, and studying in greater depth, in later units.

Net worth

If we again refer to the Balance Sheet of Cave Trading, we can see that the *net worth* of the business is the total of fixed assets and working capital. In this case:

Fixed assets	32 350
Working capital	15 850
Net worth (of business)	48 200

Financed by

This section of the Balance Sheet shows the source of funding or investment, through which the business has acquired its 'net worth'. In the case of Cave Trading, the Balance Sheet clearly shows that the owner had £30 000 invested in the business at the start of the year and that the year's profit of £18 200 has been retained in the business to give the owner a total investment of £48 200 at the end of the year.

Summary

Unlike the Trading and Profit and Loss Account, the Balance Sheet is *not* an account. It is just a listing of the assets and liabilities of a business, arranged in such a way that the 'worth' of the business can be seen.

We can think of the Balance Sheet as being a 'snapshot' of the business at a particular moment in time. In the case of Cave Trading, where we have a Balance Sheet as at 31 December, we can equate the figures as representing the position of the business as at midnight on 31 December. If we assume that the firm opens for business the following day, and immediately receives a delivery costing £1000 from one of its suppliers (the supply being on credit) then the Balance Sheet immediately changes. Creditors will have increased by £1000 and the £1000 of supply has gone into stock. We can see, therefore, that the Balance Sheet situation is constantly changing.

The Trading and Profit and Loss Account and Balance Sheet we have looked at have been in a simple form. In the next unit, we shall see how reality is a little more complex. However, it is important to understand that, whatever the apparent complexities, the basic practice of double entry and final accounts production relies totally on the concepts we have covered.

In the next section, we will work carefully through the whole process of formulating simple final accounts. It is most important that you follow through all the entries to achieve a sound basis from which to move on. This is our opportunity to consolidate all that we have learnt to date.

Practical exercise — simple final accounts

From the following list of balances extracted from the Ledger of Key Trading we will:

1. Produce a Trial Balance.
2. Identify the destination of each balance.
3. Produce a Trading and Profit and Loss Account and Balance Sheet.

Note   To test our knowledge, we are not told whether a particular account balance is debit or credit.

Balances as at 31 December 19–3

Warehouse equipment	D	8 000	A
Vehicles running costs	D	2 200	E
Insurances	D	300	E
Wages	D	12 500	E
Capital	C	30 000	C
Debtors	D	8 300	E A
Rent	D	1 400	E
Purchases	D	54 000	E
Stock 01.01.19–3	D	9 000	A
Sales	C	73 000	I
Electricity	D	1 600	E
Bank	D	500	A
Cash	D	200	A
Creditors	C	7 000	L
Vehicles	D	12 000	A

We also know that the stocktake on 31 December 19–3 has valued the stock at £8500.

We will start by deciding to which category — Asset, Liability, Capital, Income or Expense— each account belongs. We can then decide whether an account has a debit or credit balance because we know:

- Assets — *debit* balance
- Expenses — *debit* balance
- Income — *credit* balance
- Liability — *credit* balance
- Capital — *credit* balance.

We can now make the appropriate note next to each account:

Balances as at 31 December 19–3		Category	Balance
Warehouse equipment	8 000	Asset	DR
Vehicles running costs	2 200	Expense	DR
Insurances	300	Expense	DR
Wages	12 500	Expense	DR
Capital	30 000	Capital	CR
Debtors	8 300	Asset	DR
Rent	1 400	Expense	DR
Purchases	54 000	Trading expense	DR
Stock 01.01.19–3	9 000	Asset	DR
Sales	73 000	Income	CR
Electricity	1 600	Expense	DR
Bank	500	Asset	DR
Cash	200	Asset	DR
Creditors	7 000	Liability	CR
Vehicles	12 000	Asset	DR

Now we can prepare the Trial Balance:

Key Trading
Trial Balance as at 31 December 19–3

	DR	CR	Destination
Warehouse equipment	8 000		B
Vehicles running costs	2 200		P
Insurances	300		P
Wages	12 500		P
Capital		30 000	B
Debtors	8 300		B
Rent	1 400		P
Purchases	54 000		T
Stock 01.01.19–3	9 000		T
Sales		73 000	T
Electricity	1 600		P
Bank	500		B
Cash	200		B
Creditors		7 000	B
Vehicles	12 000		B
	110 000	110 000	

Closing stock of £8500 T & B

Notes

1. In practice, it is now sensible to 'tick off' against the appropriate destination letter, as each balance is placed in the final accounts.
2. Remember:
   (a) the closing stock figure goes in the Trading Account and in the Balance Sheet;
   (b) the profit calculated in the Profit and Loss Account balances up the Balance Sheet by being added to the Capital Account.

Key Trading

Trading and Profit and Loss Account for the year ended 31 December 19–3

Sales		73 000
Less: Cost of goods sold:		
Opening stock 01.01.19–3	9 000	
Purchases	54 000	
	63 000	
Less: Closing stock 31.12.19–3	8 500	54 500
Gross profit		18 500
Less: Expenses:		
Vehicles running costs	2 200	
Insurances	300	
Wages	12 500	
Rent	1 400	
Electricity	1 600	18 000
Net profit		500

Balance Sheet as at 31 December 19–3

Fixed assets:		
Warehouse equipment		8 000
Vehicles		12 000
		20 000
Current assets:		
Stock 31.12.19–3	8 500	
Debtors	8 300	
Bank	500	
Cash	200	
	17 500	
Less: Current liabilities:		
Creditors	7 000	
Working capital		10 500
Net worth		30 500
Financed by:		
Capital 01.01.19–3	30 000	
Plus: Profit for year	500	
Capital 31.12.19–3		30 500

It is now important that you complete *all* the exercises in the next section.

Exercises

1. (a) From the following information, prepare the Trading section of Rota Trading's Trading and Profit and Loss Account as at 31 March 19–2 so as to show gross profit.

	DR	CR
Stock 01.04.19–1	8 000	
Sales		55 000
Purchases	36 000	

The stock on hand at 31.03.19–2 cost £6500.

(b) Now complete the Profit and Loss section of Rota Trading's Trading and Profit and Loss Account, using the following information, so as to show net profit.

	£
Wages	7 000
Vehicles running costs	2 400
Rent	600
Electricity	450
Advertising costs	1 600
Insurances	300

Note Retain your workings and answer as these link in with the next exercise.

2. *Note* To complete this exercise, you require your workings and answer to Exercise 1. From the following information, and your answer to Exercise 1, construct a Balance Sheet for Rota Trading as at 31.03.19–2.

	Debit	Credit
Vehicle	8 000	
Debtors	13 000	
Creditors		9 000
Warehouse equipment	4 000	
Bank	2 550	
Cash	200	
Capital		15 000
Bank loan		5 100

Helpful hints:

(a) You require the closing stock figure and net profit figure from the Trading and Profit and Loss Account to complete a Balance Sheet.

(b) Neither figure appears in the Trial Balance so students consistently forget them when trying to construct a Balance Sheet. Strive to remember this and you will save yourself a lot of trouble.

3. From the following Trading and Profit and Loss Account and Balance Sheet, construct the Trial Balance from which they were drawn.

Note   You may think it odd to work backwards, but this will really develop your skills.

Lots Trading
Trading and Profit and Loss Account for the Year Ended 31.03.19–3

Sales		60 000
Less: Cost of goods sold		
Opening stock 01.04.19–2	5 000	
Plus: Purchases	40 000	
	45 000	
Less: Closing stock 31.03.19–3	3 000	42 000
Gross profit		18 000
Expenses:		
Rent	600	
Wages	11 000	
Vehicles running costs	800	
Advertising	1 600	14 000
Net profit		4 000

Balance Sheet as at 31.03.19–3

Fixed assets:		
Equipment		8 000
Vehicle		12 000
		20 000
Current assets:		
Stock	3 000	
Debtors	5 000	
Bank	2 000	
	10 000	
Less: Current liabilities:		
Creditors	4 000	
Working capital		6 000
Net profit		26 000
Financed by:		
Capital 01.04.19–2	22 000	
Plus: Profit for year	4 000	
Capital 31.03.19–3		26 000

Helpful hint   Think carefully about which stock figure goes in the Trial Balance.

4. From the following information for Capp Trading:
   (a) Prepare a Trial Balance as at 31.12.19–1.
   (b) Prepare a Trading and Profit and Loss Account.
   (c) Prepare a Balance Sheet.

Ledger balances	£
Bank	1 750
Creditors	5 000
Cash	100
Rent	650
Debtors	6 400
Vehicle	7 000
Vehicle running costs	800
Wages	12 000
Stock 01.01.19–1	6 000
Capital	15 000
Miscellaneous expenses	2 300
Office equipment	3 000
Sales	80 000
Purchases	60 000

The stock on hand at 31.12.19–1 was £6500

Unit 5

Accountancy — a creative exercise

We are now going to venture into the arena of accountancy. Here, we will have the opportunity to bring our basic knowledge to bear on practical problems. We will be in an area where we have to start making decisions about how we should represent certain events which affect the financial picture presented by a business.

It is important that the Trading and Profit and Loss Account and Balance Sheet portray as accurate and fair a view of a business's profitability and net worth as possible. However, for reasons we are about to explore, the accounts we have produced so far — for example Cave Trading — while being an accurate representation of the result of all the bookkeeping entries can be adjusted to give a much fairer and accurate picture. By studying the kind of adjustments which are usually made, we will be embarking on the pursuit of accountancy skills.

Prepayments and accruals

Let us start by assuming that a business has its year end on 31 December 19–1 and that it pays rent of £450 quarterly in advance on the 1st day of March, June, September and December. Let us assume that in the Trial Balance, we have a debit for rent paid of £2100. We can see immediately that in the Profit and Loss Account we should only be charging rent of £1800 — four quarters @ £450 = £1800. What, in fact, has happened is that rent has been paid on 1 December 19–1 covering the three months December 19–1, January 19–2 and February 19–2. In other words, rent has been paid in advance for two months beyond the end of the financial year. If the rent is £450 per quarter (three months), then the monthly rent is £450 ÷ 3 = £150. The payment in advance is therefore £300 (two months × £150). We must therefore find some way of excluding £300 of rent when we charge rent for the year 19–1 in the Profit and Loss Account. Let us start by looking at the Rent Account:

	Rent	
Balance B/D	2 100	

To do a double entry to take out the advance payment of £300, we credit the account with the advance payment, which is technically called a 'prepayment'.

Rent

Balance B/D	2 100	Prepayment	300

The balance on the Rent Account is now £1800 and this is the amount which should be properly charged to the Profit and Loss Account. Before doing this, however, we first need to complete the double entry for the prepayments. This is done by 'jumping' a couple of lines and bringing the prepayment down on the opposite side of the account, ready for the following year (to which the prepayment belongs).

Rent

Balance B/D	2 100	Prepayment C/D	300
Prepayment B/D	300		

Now, in order to complete the year 19–1 part of the account, all we need do is transfer the year 19–1 balance to the Profit and Loss Account.

Rent

Balance B/D	2 100	Prepayment C/D	300	
		Profit and Loss A/c	1 800	(1)
	2 100		2 100	
19–2 Prepayment B/D	300			

The double entry to (1) is, of course, a debit for rent of £1800 in the Profit and Loss Account. The prepayment of £300 is an *asset* as at 31 December and must appear in the Balance Sheet under Current assets. It is an asset because it is money paid in advance. (If the advance payment had not been made, the money would still be in the bank.) Students continually forget this when preparing the Balance Sheet and as a consequence it will not balance. The same is true of the other adjustments we are going to explore in this unit. To try to control this problem, in Unit 6 we will be looking at a method of working in assignments and examinations which can help avoid such omissions.

Accruals

Having looked at prepayments (payments in advance) let us now consider the opposite situation. Where we should have a charge for some expense in, say, year 19–1 the bill has not been paid.

Consequently, no entries appear in the 19–1 accounts. This is, in practice, a far more common occurrence than prepayments.

Let us take a situation where the Electricity Company raises its bills quarterly in arrears. In other words, a bill received for electricity at the end of February, would be for electricity consumed during the months of December, January and February.

Now consider a business whose electricity account at the end of year 19–1 is

Electricity

Balance B/D	2 200	

and the last electricity bill paid was for electricity consumed up to the end of November 19–1. Clearly, we need to include an account for December (19–1) but we have a problem. The bill covering this period will not be received until some time in February. In the circumstances, all we can do, apart from reading the meter(s) late in December, is to estimate a reasonable sum to be put into the accounts to represent December's consumption. There are many ways we may choose to do this, but the simplest, perhaps, is to take the account balance of £2200 which represents actual bills paid for the 11 months January to November. If we divide £2200 by 11, we see that the *average* monthly charge is £200. We therefore need to add £200 to the account in order that the charge for electricity in the Profit and Loss Account is a more reasonable representation of the year's total. Let us do that first:

Electricity

Balance B/D	2 200	
Accrual 19–1	200	

Notice that we call the entry an 'accrual'. In technical terms, we are accruing for an expense which we know has actually been incurred but which will be paid for at a later date. We can see that the amount to be charged for the year is now £2400. First, we need to complete the double entry for the accrual. This is done by bringing the accrual down on the opposite (credit) side of the account.

Electricity

Balance B/D	2 200		
Accrual 19–1	200		
		Accrual 19–2	200

In order to complete the year 19–1 part of the account, all we need do is transfer the year 19–1 total of £2400 to the Profit and Loss Account.

Electricity

Balance B/D	2 200	Profit and Loss A/c	2 400	(1)
Accrual 19–1	200			
	2 400		2 400	
		Accrual 19–2	200	

The double entry to (1) is, of course, a debit for electricity of £2400 in the Profit and Loss Account.

The accrual brought down of £200 is a *liability* as at 31 December (an account owed) and *must* appear in the Balance Sheet under Current liabilities.

In any examination or assignment requiring the production of a Profit and Loss Account and Balance Sheet, there will, almost certainly, be a requirement to make adjustments for prepayments and accruals. This is an area therefore with which we need to be fully conversant. Let us return to our old friend Cave Trading. We will start with the Trial Balance but this time we have to make certain adjustments:

Cave Trading
Trial Balance 31 December 19– –

	Debit	Credit	Category	Destination
Mr Cave — Capital		30 000	C	B
Bank	15 550		A	B
Cash	150		A	B
Vehicles	18 000		A	B
Sales		60 000	I	T
Office equipment	2 350		A	B
Warehouse equipment	12 000		A	B
Purchases	38 000		E	T
Mega Supplies		2 500	L	B
Stock 01 January	3 150		E	T
Novelty Manufacturing		1 800	L	B
Vehicle running costs	1 300		E	P
P Anderton & Son	400		A	B
Insurance	1 200		E	P
C James & Co	700		A	B
Zeta Shops	500		A	B
Rent	600		E	P
Electricity	400		E	P
Totals	94 300	94 300		

Adjustments:

1. Rent is payable at £200 per quarter in arrears but the rent for the quarter October to December 19–1 has not been paid.
2. Vehicle running costs includes a payment for a Road Fund Licence which cost £300 for the period September 19–1 to August 19–2.
3. Electricity bills have been paid for electricity consumed up to 31 October 19–1. It is estimated that the electricity to December 19–1 will cost a further £100.

Action required:

1. Provide an accrual for unpaid rent of £200
   Debit rent account £200
   Credit rent account (accrual) £200
2. Licence costs £25 per month. Eight months have been paid in advance, £25 × 8 = £200
   Credit vehicle running costs account £200
   Debit vehicle running costs account (prepayment) £200
3. Provide an account for unpaid electricity of £100
   Debit electricity account £100
   Credit electricity account (accrual) £100

Rent

Balance B/D	600		
Accrual 19–1	200	Profit and Loss A/c	800
	800		800
		Accrual 19–2	200

Vehicle running costs

Balance B/D	1300	Prepaid 19–1	200
		Profit and Loss A/c	1 100
	1 300		1 300
Prepaid 19–2	200		

Electricity

Balance B/D	400		
Accrual 19–1	100	Profit and Loss A/c	500
	500		500
		Accrual 19–2	100

The revised Trial Balance will now be:

Cave Trading
Trial Balance 31 December 19– –

	Debit	Credit	Category	Destination
Mr Cave — Capital		30 000	C	B
Bank	15 550		A	B
Cash	150		A	B
Vehicles	18 000		A	B
Sales		60 000	I	P
Office equipment	2 350		A	B
Warehouse equipment	12 000		A	B
Purchases	38 000		E	P
Mega Supplies		2 500	L	B
Stock 01 January	3 150		E	P
Novelty Manufacturing		1 800	L	B
Vehicle running costs	1 100		E	P
P Anderton & Son	400		A	B
Insurance	1 200		E	P
C James & Co	700		A	B
Zeta Shops	500		A	B
Rent	800		E	P
Electricity	500		E	P
Prepayment (1)	200		A	B
Accruals (2)		300	L	B
Totals	94 600	94 600		

Note Prepayments and accruals are totalled under headings (1) and (2).

The revised Trading and Profit and Loss Account and Balance Sheet will now be:

Cave Trading
Trading and Profit and Loss Account for the year ended 31 December 19– –

Sales		60 000
Less: Cost of goods sold:		
Opening Stock 01 January	3 150	
Plus: Purchases	38 000	
	41 150	
Less: Closing stock 31 December	2 850	38 300
Gross profit		21 700
Less: Operating expenses:		
Vehicle running costs	1 100	
Insurances	1 200	
Rent	800	
Electricity	500	3 600
Net profit		18 100

Cave Trading
Balance Sheet as at 31 December 19– –

Fixed assets:

Warehouse equipment		12 000
Office equipment		2 350
Vehicles		18 000
		32 350

Current assets:

Stock 31 December	2 850	
Debtors	1 600	
Prepayment	200	
Bank	15 550	
Cash	150	
	20 350	

Less: Current liabilities:

Creditors	4 300	
Accruals	300	
	4 600	
Working capital		15 750
Net worth		48 100

Financed by:

Capital 01 January 19–	30 000	
Plus: Profit for year	18 100	
Capital 31 December 19–		48 100

The problems and treatment of doubtful debts

An important task for businesses which sell goods or services on credit is to ensure that all debts owed by debtors do in fact get paid. The systems used to control this important function are commonly referred to as *credit control* procedures which we will be looking at, in some detail, in Unit 10. All we need to appreciate now is that in spite of credit control procedures, almost inevitably some debts will not be paid.

Bad debts

Firstly, let us look at a situation where it is known for certain that the debt owed by a particular debtor cannot be collected. It is a 'bad debt'. This could happen for a variety of reasons. For example, the debtor may have 'disappeared' and cannot be traced or become bankrupt, with no possibility of paying his or her debt(s). In such circumstances, the debt will have to be 'written off'. Let us take an example where a business has a debtor, Ford & Co, who owe £2000 and it is certain that the debt is 'bad' (unrecoverable). The accounting entries would be:

Ford & Co				Bad Debts		
Balance B/D	2 000	Bad debts	2 000 (1)	(1) Ford & Co	2 000	

The double entry shown (1) closes the account of the debtor — Ford & Co — and transfers the debt to a Bad Debts Account. As we will see later, the Bad Debt Account is charged to the Profit and Loss Account.

Doubtful debts

We have already seen that it is necessary to produce final accounts so that they give as 'true and fair a view' of a business as is possible. In order to do this, we should be very cautious when preparing a Profit and Loss Account or Balance Sheet and must avoid overstating profit or the worth of the business. If we have reason to believe that something has happened, or will happen, which will affect the financial situation of the business, then we should make provision for such an event in the accounts before we produce the final accounts.

In this context, we need to consider carefully the likelihood of some debts not being paid. The treatment of bad debts is straightforward and, as we have seen, they are 'written off'. However, we should provide for the fact that almost certainly some other debts will *eventually* prove to be irrecoverable. We cannot write them off because we do not know for certain which debts will eventually fall into the bad debts category. What we can *do* is try to assess what value of the total debt owed by all debtors may eventually prove to be uncollectable and make provision for this. Let us look at an illustration.

Assume that a business has total debtors of £105 000 at the end of its financial year 19–1. Of this, one debt of £5000 is known to be 'bad' and needs to be written off. Of the rest, it is felt that two particular debts, one of £1000 and another of £3000, will almost certainly prove to be uncollectable but the business is still trying to recover them so they cannot be written off. Looking back on the history and experience of bad debts in the business, it would also be sensible to provide for 3 per cent of all debts eventually becoming 'bad'. At the end of the previous year, the business had made a provision for 'doubtful debts' of £4500.

Before we do anything, the relevant accounts in the ledger would be:

Debtors			Provision for Doubtful Debts	
Balance B/D	105 000		Balance B/D 19–0	4 500

Action required

1. Write off as bad debt £5000.
2. Make a doubtful debts provision for:
   (a) two 'specific' debts of £1000 + £3000 = 4000.
   (b) 3 per cent of all other debtors calculated as follows:

Total debtors	105 000
Bad debts written off	5 000
	100 000

Two debts provided for			
(a) above	4 000		
3 per cent 'general' provision on	96 000	=	2 880
Total provision for doubtful debts required		=	6 880
Provision already in accounts at start of year		=	4 500
Additional provision to be made this year — 19–1		=	2 380

Note In calculating a 'general' provision we *must* first deduct 'specific' provisions (if any) otherwise we will be 'double counting' these debts.

Let us now look at the accounting entries:

1. Writing off the bad debt:

Debtors				Bad Debts		
Balance B/D	105 000	Bad debts	5 000	Debtors	5 000	Profit and Loss A/c 5 000 (1)
		Balance C/D	100 000			
	105 000		105 000			
Balance B/D	100 000					

Note The Bad Debts Account is written off by a double entry in the Profit and Loss Account (1).

2. Provision for doubtful debts:
   Account at start of year:

Provision for Doubtful Debts			
		Balance B/D	4500

Provide an 'extra' £2380

Provision for Doubtful Debts			
Balance C/D (19–1)	6 880	Balance B/D	4 500
		Profit and Loss A/c	2 380 (1)
	6 880		6 880 (2)
		Balance B/D (19–2)	6 880

Notes

(1) The double entry to provide the 'extra' provision is a *credit* in the Provision for Doubtful Debts Account as shown and a *debit* in the Profit and Loss Account.
(2) The balance of £6880 on the Provision for Doubtful Debts Account is effectively an estimate of the amount by which the real value of debtors can expect to be reduced. It is shown in the Balance Sheet as a deduction from the total of debtors.

To illustrate these points:

The Profit and Loss Account will include the entries:

Profit and Loss Account

Bad debts	5 000	
Provision for doubtful debts	2 380	

Note   At the start of the year, £4500 had already been provided for doubtful debts, therefore this year we only need to charge against profits the 'extra' £2380 required to increase the provision to £6880.

HEALTH WARNING

A common mistake made by students is to put the total provision in the Profit and Loss Account. All you charge against the current year's profit is any extra provision required. We need to be absolutely clear on this point.

In the Balance Sheet, the total provision for doubtful debts is shown as a deduction from debtors as follows:

Current assets:
Debtors	100 000	
Less: Provision for doubtful debts	6 880	93 120

Note   *Here* we use the total provision for doubtful debts. The Balance Sheet now tells us that the *total debt* owed by debtors is £100 000. However, *of this*, £6880 may prove uncollectable so a 'conservative value' of this asset (debtors) is £93 120.

Assets are wearing out

In this section, we will look at the loss in value of fixed assets caused by the passage of time, and the effect of wear and tear.

Let us start by taking the example of a family car. If the car cost £8000, then it may be reasonable to assume that after one year's ownership, its value (what it could likely be sold for) could have *depreciated* to £6000. This depreciation of £2000 is a loss to the owner in the value of the asset (the car), caused by the fact that the car is now 12 months older and has had 12 months' wear and tear on the engine, brakes, etc. In accounting terms we define depreciation as 'the recovery of the original cost of an asset over its working life'.

Most of the fixed assets of a business will similarly depreciate in value and we need to recognize this fact in the accounts. We need to ensure that two things happen:

1. Depreciation (loss in value) is charged against any profits made. In this context, the depreciation is an expense of having owned and used the asset during the trading year.
2. If the Balance Sheet is to give a 'true and fair' view of the worth of the business, then assets need to be shown at their 'depreciated' value. If this pattern is followed, year on year, the value of these assets will reduce until eventually an asset will have little, if any, value. It is important to draw a distinction here. The cost price of an asset is the full original cost paid for the asset. The term 'book value', often used in business circles, refers to the current depreciated value of an asset as it appears in the accounts.

Before we can do any accounting entries, we have to work out the yearly depreciation to be charged. There are, in fact, two main ways of doing this:

- Straight line method
- Reducing balance method.

Straight line method of calculating depreciation

This method relies on calculating a fixed annual sum by which an asset will be depreciated. Let us take an example.

A business buys a machine for its factory at a cost of £13 000. It is estimated that the machine will have a useful life span of six years, at the end of which it may be able to be sold for about £1000. The technical term for this estimate of what the machine may realize at the end of its useful life is *residual value*.

The calculation would be:

Cost	13 000
Less: Estimated residual value	1 000
Net cost	12 000

$$\frac{12\,000}{6 \text{ years}} = £2000 \text{ annual depreciation}$$

Reducing balance method of calculating depreciation

Use of this method means that the depreciation charged against profit reduces year on year. The main justification for using this method is that each year, as the machine wears out, more and more will be spent on maintaining and repairing it. The fact that each year the depreciation 'cost' of using the machine is reducing, will help balance out the annually increasing repair costs.

We can illustrate this graphically:

Let us take the same machine we used in the straight line method and apply the reducing balance method using an annual rate of depreciation of 30 per cent.

Net cost 12 000	Calculation	Depreciation	Book value
End of year 1	12 000 × 30%	3 600	8 400
2	8 400 × 30%	2 520	5 880
3	5 880 × 30%	1 764	4 116
4	4 116 × 30%	1 235	2 881
5	2 881 × 30%	864	2 017
6	2 017 × 30%	605	1 412

Helpful hint   There is a way of calculating what percentage should be applied so as to reduce the book value to precisely the estimated residual value at the end of the estimated life span. However, it will only serve to confuse at this time and, in any event, most examination questions will only ask for a given percentage to be used to calculate depreciation for a particular year. *Whichever method* of calculating the annual depreciation is used, the *accounting entries are the same* and are as follows:

- Accounts *before* adjusting for depreciation in the current year:

Plant and Machinery		Provision for Depreciation	
(1) Balance B/D 60 000		Balance B/D 24 000 (2)	

Notes

1. The depreciation is put in a separate account called 'Provision for Depreciation'. We will soon see why.
2. The accounts tell us that we have plant and machinery which cost £60 000 (1). To the end of the previous year, depreciation of £24 000 has been provided (2).

- We will now take the usual examination approach. We are told that plant and machinery is to be depreciated at 20 per cent on cost. The depreciation to be charged is therefore £60 000 × 20 per cent = £12 000.
- *Accounting entries*

Plant and Machinery		Provision for Depreciation	
Balance B/D 60 000			Balance B/D 24 000
	Balance C/D 36 000		Profit and Loss A/c 12 000 (3)
	36 000		36 000
			Balance B/D 19–1 36 000

Notes

1. The Plant and Machinery Account is left showing the original cost of £60 000. In the Balance Sheet the *total* depreciation provided to date of £36 000 is deducted to show a 'net book value' of £24 000.
2. The year's provision is added into the Provision for Depreciation Account, the double entry being in the Profit and Loss Account (3).

Before we leave this section, it is important to realize that provisions for depreciation are based on estimates. It follows, therefore, that the depreciation charged against profits and the net book value of fixed assets are themselves only the result of calculations based on estimates. When reading and interpreting accounts, we should not imply any greater degree of accuracy attaching to these figures than can be expected from an estimating process. What we can say is, that provided a reasonable basis of estimating has been used, the accounts will give a 'truer and fairer' view than if no attempt to provide depreciation had been made.

Unsold stock — a necessary burden

We have already seen how, in the Trading part of the Trading and Profit and Loss Account, the value of closing stock is used as part of the calculation of cost of goods sold. We also know that the closing stock of one year is also the opening stock of the following year. It follows that the way in which the stock is valued is an important element in giving a true and fair view of the profits and worth of a business.

Valuing the stock really presents two problems:

1. Determining, with a high degree of accuracy, what volume of different types of stock is held.
2. Deciding what cost should be applied to different types of stock to arrive at a fair valuation.

The answer to the first problem is that a comprehensive stocktake is carried out. Every item of stock is identified into categories, and numbers of items are physically counted. From this exercise, a stock list is drawn up which can then be costed and added to give a total stock value. A business therefore carries out a stocktake on the last day of its financial year and its auditors will want to do 'spot checks' on the accuracy of this exercise. We have all seen a notice 'Closed for Stocktaking' — now we know what it means.

Knowing what stock we have is one thing, knowing how to value the stock is another matter altogether and this is the second problem. There are a number of alternatives available in deciding what cost to apply to stocks.

For now, all we need to appreciate is that stock is valued at cost price, subject to one restriction. If the realizable value of the stock (what it can be sold for) sinks below what the stock cost, the lower figure should be used. This could happen if, for example, a product in stock became relatively obsolete in the face of a much improved version of the product coming on to the market. In these circumstances, a business may well have to sell the product at below cost, just to dispose of the stock. This can happen quite easily in high-tech industries, where products are developed and improved quickly. In such an event, a 'true and fair view' can only be obtained by valuing such stock at what it will have to be sold for, which is less than cost.

The overriding rule is therefore: *Stock is valued at the lower of cost or realizable value.*

HEALTH WARNING

Stock is never valued above cost.

In exercises and examinations, the closing stock figure to be used is normally given so we do not have to worry too much. However, it is not unknown for crafty examiners to say, for example:

> Closing stock is valued as follows:
> | | |
> |---|---|
> | At selling price | £30 000 |
> | At cost price | £20 000 |

You *cannot* use a valuation *above cost* so you use the £20 000 valuation. Students then worry because they have been given information they are not using. *Do not worry*, the selling price valuation is a 'red herring'.

Value added tax (VAT)

Taxation takes many forms. Income tax is perhaps the best known. For the majority of employees, it is deducted from salaries and wages under the PAYE system. We will be looking at this in detail in Unit 14. From the Government's point of view, it is a very efficient form of taxation, as the tax is deducted by the employer who then pays the employee net of tax. Administration of the PAYE system is a considerable burden on employers for which they receive no financial compensation.

Whatever the burden on businesses of operating the PAYE system, collecting and accounting for value added tax (VAT) is, perhaps, even more onerous. VAT is a sales tax which has to be levied on every single item a business sells. The only exception is where goods are zero rated. For reasons we will soon understand, a business, in order to comply with VAT regulations, must record the VAT charged to customers on every sale made and VAT paid on every purchase from suppliers. Even in the case of zero rated goods, the business still has to be able to supply statistical information. The requirement to charge, record and account for VAT is a statutory duty placed on businesses by government, and the penalties for non-compliance are severe. Whereas the Inland Revenue administers the PAYE system, it is the Customs and Excise Authority that administers VAT.

VAT is a powerful weapon in the armoury of a government wishing to raise more revenue from taxation. Not only can the rate of VAT be changed, but the range of goods or services subject to VAT can also be altered. This places on businesses the additional burden of keeping in touch with changing regulations and, if necessary, changing printed documentation, systems and procedures.

Accounting for VAT

There are two opposite sides to the VAT equation for businesses.

1. VAT has to be charged on sales and the VAT charged has to be accounted for. This tax on sales is known in VAT terminology as an *output tax*.
2. VAT paid by a business on the supplies it receives has also to be accounted for. This tax 'suffered' on purchases is known as *input tax*.

This information is required in order that a mandatory return can be completed. On its return, a business has to declare the total of output tax collected and the total of input tax paid. The business also has to pay to Customs and Excise, the excess of VAT collected (output tax) over VAT paid (input tax). Conversely, if input tax exceeds output tax, the Customs and Excise will refund the difference. There are strictly enforced deadlines for submission of the periodic VAT returns and payment of any amount due.

It is important that we understand that VAT is not part of a business activity. By this, we mean that in accounting for VAT, the business is merely acting as a tax collector on behalf of government and all VAT accounting entries must be separate and readily identifiable.

Let us look at this in practice and start by taking a straightforward sale of goods for £100 ignoring VAT. The accounts could be:

Sales			Bank		
	Bank	100	Sales	100	

Now let us look at the same transaction but this time we will include VAT at an assumed rate of 20 per cent. The sale price is now £100 + 20 per cent = £120.

We also need a separate account for VAT:

Sales			Bank		
	Bank	100	Sales	120	

VAT		
	Bank	20

We can see at this stage, that the VAT Account represents a liability to Customs and Excise. When the business eventually pays over the VAT to Customs and Excise, the accounts are:

Sales			Bank		
	Bank	100	Sales	120	VAT	20

VAT		
Bank	20	Sales	20

We can now clearly see that the sales income and cash received from the sale of £100 is exactly the same as it would have been had VAT not been charged. The business has merely collected the tax and paid it over to government.

The description of the tax — *value added* — is interesting. Let us take another example to illustrate the meaning of this description.

A business purchases an item on credit for £100 plus VAT @ 20 per cent from Jackson & Son (1). It then sells the item on credit to Bean & Co for £150 plus VAT @ 20 per cent (2).

	Purchases			Jackson & Son	
(1) Jackson & Son	100			Purchases	120 (1)

	VAT		
(1) Purchases	20	Sales	30 (2)

	Sales			Bean & Co	
	Bean & Co	150 (2)	(2) Sales	180	

If we now examine the VAT Account, we can see that the liability to Customs and Excise is £10. That is the difference between the output tax and the input tax of £20. The difference between the selling price of £150 and the purchase price of £100 is deemed to be the 'value added' by the business. The tax on this 'value added' of £50 @ 20 per cent is, of course, £10. The same £10 the business will pay over to Customs and Excise to clear the VAT liability.

Exercises

1. A photocopier was purchased on 01 January 19–4 at a cost of £2000.

   You are to:
   Calculate, to the nearest £, the annual depreciation charge on the photocopier for the years ended 31 December 19–4; 19–5; 19–6; 19–7, on the following basis:

   (a) Straight line method.
   (b) Diminishing balances method at 60 per cent p.a.

2. Bean Engineering purchased a drilling machine on 01 April 19–4 for £112 000.

   The firm estimates that the machine will have a useful life span of four years, at the end of which it is expected that about £12 000 could be obtained on the second-hand market.

   The firm's year end is 31 December.

   You are to:
   Calculate the yearly depreciation on the machine for the financial years 19–4; 19–5; 19–6; 19–7; 19–8 on the following basis:

   (a) Straight line method.
   (b) Diminishing balance method at 40 per cent p.a.

3. Holgate Ltd charges depreciation on a pro rata basis each year.
   On 01 October 19–4, Holgate purchased two machines costing £1550 each. The cost of installing the machines was £770 and the machines were eventually taken into use on 01 April 19–5.
   Depreciation is charged on a straight line basis from the date the machines start to operate. They have an expected life span of 10 years with no residual value.
   The firm's year end is 30 September.

A further, similar machine was bought for £2800 and taken into use on 01 July 19–4. It has the same expected life span and no residual value.

You are to:
Calculate the depreciation to be provided on the three machines for the year ended 30 September 19–4 and 19–5.

4. In March 19–3, the trial balance of Tops Traders included the following balances:

	Debit	Credit
Debtors	12 360	
Provision for doubtful debts		410
Bad debt recovered (from D Dean)		970

It is also revealed that:

(a) The debt of D Dean had been written off in the year ended 31 March 19–2.
(b) The following debts are to be written off:

C Cryer	210
B Bean	50

(c) The provision for doubtful debts is to be 2 per cent of debtors.

Required:

(i) Complete the Provision for Doubtful Debts Account for the year ended 31.03.19–3.
(ii) Show the entries to be made in the Profit and Loss Account for these events.
(iii) Show the relevant entries which will appear in the Balance Sheet.

5. Carr & Son was established on 1 January 1993 to manufacture a single product using a machine which cost £400 000. The machine is expected to last for four years and then have a scrap value of £52 000. The machine will produce a similar number of goods each year and annual profits before depreciation are expected to be in the region of £200 000. It has been suggested that the machine should be depreciated using either the straight line method or the reducing balance method. If the latter method is used, it has been estimated that an annual depreciation rate of 40 per cent would be appropriate.

Required:

(a) Calculations of the annual depreciation charges and the net book value of the fixed asset at the end of 1993, 1994, 1995 and 1996 using:
   (i) the straight line method
   (ii) the reducing balance method.
(b) A discussion of the differing implications of these two methods for the financial information published by Carr & Son for the years 1993 to 1996 inclusive. You should also advise management which method you consider more appropriate, bearing in mind expected profit levels.

6. Imagine that you have been engaged to complete a set of year-end accounts for a business.
   The bookkeeper has presented you with a Trial Balance extracted from the ledger after all accounts have been balanced. No work has been done by the bookkeeper on any of the usual period-end adjustments you would expect to see before final accounts are produced.

Required:
Write a report identifying each adjustment you might expect to make and describing briefly the reason(s) for each adjustment.

Unit 6

Presenting accounts

Trial Balance to final accounts — the practical way

So far, we have covered the basics of double-entry bookkeeping and seen how simple final accounts are formed from all the ledger balances. Having covered the normal adjustments required to some of the balances, we can now look to producing 'final accounts' which reflect, not only the balances produced by bookkeeping, but also the accounting adjustments we have explored.

This exercise lies at the root of many examination questions or assignments which confront students. Before we look at how the adjustments might be handled, within the constraints of an examination, let us first look at how, in practice, an accountant might tackle the job.

We will start, as might many examination questions, with a given Trial Balance and a list of required adjustments. From the information given:

Alpha Products
Trial Balance as at 31 December 19–1

	Debit	Credit
Capital		80 000
Drawings	12 000	
Vehicles	60 000	
Trade creditors		40 000
Trade debtors	37 000	
Stock 1 January 19–1	18 000	
Rent	15 400	
Telephone	1 800	
Postage	300	
Electricity	2 100	
Bank	22 000	
Returns inwards	4 000	
Returns outwards		2 500
Provisions for doubtful debts		900
Purchases	220 000	
Sales		370 000
Plant and equipment	157 000	
Discounts received		6 000
Provision for depreciation:		
Vehicles		15 000
Plant and equipment		37 000
Bank charges	1 800	
Totals	551 400	551 400

We are told that:

1. (a) A bad debt of £2000 is to be written off.
   (b) The provision for doubtful debts is to be 3 per cent of debtors.
2. There are unpaid bills for electricity £200, telephone £300.
3. Rent is payable at £3300 per quarter, and has been paid to the end of February 19–2.
4. Stock valuation 31 December 19–1:
   | at selling price | £28 000 |
   | at cost price | £16 500. |
5. Depreciation is to be provided on cost:
   | Plant and equipment | 10 per cent |
   | Vehicles | 20 per cent. |

1. Debtors
   (a) Bad debt write off £2000

<table>
<tr><td colspan="3" align="center">Bad Debts</td><td colspan="3" align="center">Debtors</td></tr>
<tr><td>Debtors</td><td>2 000</td><td>Profit and Loss A/c   2 000</td><td>Balance B/D</td><td>37 000</td><td>Bad debts   2 000
Balance C/D   35 000</td></tr>
<tr><td></td><td></td><td></td><td></td><td>37 000</td><td>37 000</td></tr>
<tr><td></td><td></td><td></td><td>Balance B/D</td><td>35 000</td><td></td></tr>
</table>

(b) Provision of 3 per cent for doubtful debtors

Debtors	37 000	
Bad debts	2 000	
	35 000 × 3 per cent =	1 050
	Already provided	900
	Extra provision required	150

<table>
<tr><td colspan="2" align="center">Provision for Doubtful Debts</td><td colspan="2" align="center">Profit and Loss Account</td></tr>
<tr><td>Balance C/D   1 050</td><td>Balance B/D   900
Profit and Loss A/c   150</td><td>Bad debts   2 000
Prov. for doubtful debts   150</td><td></td></tr>
<tr><td>1 050</td><td>1 050</td><td></td><td></td></tr>
<tr><td></td><td>Balance B/D   1 050</td><td></td><td></td></tr>
</table>

2. Unpaid bills: electricity £200; telephone £300

<table>
<tr><td colspan="2" align="center">Electricity</td><td colspan="2" align="center">Telephone</td></tr>
<tr><td>Balance B/D   2 100
Accrual   200</td><td>Profit and Loss A/c   2 300</td><td>Balance B/D   1 800
Accrual   300</td><td>Profit and Loss A/c   2 100</td></tr>
<tr><td>2 300</td><td>2 300</td><td>2 100</td><td>2 100</td></tr>
<tr><td></td><td>Accrual   200</td><td></td><td>Accrual   300</td></tr>
</table>

<table>
<tr><td colspan="2" align="center">Profit and Loss Account</td></tr>
<tr><td>Bad debts</td><td>2 000</td></tr>
<tr><td>Prov. for doubtful debts</td><td>150</td></tr>
<tr><td>Electricity</td><td>2 300</td></tr>
<tr><td>Telephone</td><td>2 100</td></tr>
</table>

3. Rent paid in advance
   Rent is £3300/3 = £1100 per month.
   Rent in advance January, February 19–2 = 2 × £1100 = £2200.

Rent				Profit and Loss Account		
Balance B/D	15 400	Prepayment	2 200	Bad debts	2 000	
		Profit and Loss A/c	13 200	Prov. doubtful debts	150	
				Electricity	2 300	
	15 400			Telephone	2 100	
			15 400	Rent	13 200	
Prepayment	2 200					

4. Closing stock 31 December 19–1

Stock				Trading Account		
Stock 1 Jan 19–1	18 000	Profit and Loss A/c	18 000	Stock 1 Jan 19–1	18 000	Stock 31 Dec 19–1 16 500
Stock 31 Dec 19–1	16 500					
Profit and Loss A/c						

5. Provision for depreciation

Prov Depn Vehicles				Prov Depn Plant and Machinery		
Balance C/D	27 000	Balance B/D	15 000	Balance C/D	52 700	Balance B/D 37 000
		Profit and Loss A/c	12 000			Profit and Loss A/c 15 700
	27 000		27 000		52 700	52 700
		Balance B/D	27 000			Balance B/D 52 700

Profit and Loss Account

Bad debts	2 000	
Provision for bad debts	150	
Electricity	2 300	
Telephone	2 100	
Rent	13 200	
Provision for depreciation:		
Vehicles	12 000	
Plant and equipment	15 700	

Having completed all the adjustments we can now complete the Trading Account, Profit and Loss Account and Capital Account in the ledger.

Trading Account

Stock 01 January 19–1	18 000	Stock 31 December 19–1	16 500
Returns inwards	4 000	Returns outwards	2 500
Purchases	220 000	Sales	370 000
Gross profit			
Profit and Loss A/c	147 000		
	389 000		389 000

Profit and Loss Account

Bad debts	2 000	Gross profit:	
Provision doubtful debts	150	Trading A/c	147 000
Electricity	2 300	Discounts received	6 000
Telephone	2 100		
Rent	13 200		
Prov for depreciation:			
Vehicles	12 000		
Plant and equipment	15 700		
Postage	300		
Bank charges	1 800		
Net profit:			
Capital A/c	103 450		
	153 000		153 000

Capital

Drawings	12 000	Balance B/D	80 000
		Net profit:	
Balance C/D	171 450	Profit and Loss A/c	103 450
	183 450		183 450
		Balance B/D	171 450

Drawings

Balance B/D	12 000	Capital A/c	12 000

If we now extract the remaining 'live' ledger balances, we can produce a revised trial balance:

Alpha Products
Revised Trial Balance as at 31 December 19–1

	Debit	Credit
Capital		171 450
Vehicles	60 000	
Trade creditors		40 000
Trade debtors	35 000	
Provision for doubtful debts		1 050
Plant and equipment	157 000	
Provision for depreciation:		
Vehicles		27 000
Plant and equipment		52 700
Accruals:		
Electricity 200		
Telephone 300		500
Prepayment (Rent)	2 200	
Stock 31 December 19–1	16 500	
Bank	22 000	
Totals	292 700	292 700

From this Trial Balance, we can easily produce a Balance Sheet. To produce the Trading and Profit and Loss Account, all we need do is extract the information from the Trading Account and the Profit and Loss Account in the ledger, and present the information in the standard format. The procedure we have followed, of entering all the adjustments in the actual ledger accounts and producing the ledger Trading Account and Profit and Loss Account, is the comprehensive procedure to be followed in practice. Most textbooks do not cover the detailed procedures simply because in an examination we have to deploy short cuts in producing the Trading and Profit and Loss Account and Balance Sheet from a Trial Balance.

There is, however, a great deal to be gained from students working through the full procedure so as to understand better the short cut methods and to be familiar with real working applications.

Your time spent thinking through and working through the detail will not be wasted!

Having looked at the detailed, practical way of producing final accounts from a Trial Balance we now need to look at short cut methods which can be used in assignment and examination work. We will cover two methods:

- *Extended Trial Balance.* This method could well be required in assignment work and indeed does have a real practical application, as we shall see.
- *Examination method.* We will explore possible ways of moving from the Trial Balance to final accounts without doing any intermediate documentation. Such drastic short cuts may well be required if working to tight time constraints in an examination.

Extended Trial Balance

This involves taking the Trial Balance produced from the original ledger account balances. Next to the Trial Balance are two columns for adjustment to be entered — debit and credit. Then we have a debit and credit column representing the Trading and Profit and Loss Account and, finally, a debit and credit column for the Balance Sheet. The advantage of this method is that we can see, on one document, the whole story developing and mistakes are more readily identified. Producing the actual presentations of the Trading and Profit and Loss Account and Balance Sheet is really a straightforward copying of the proven figures on to a standard layout. External accountants, brought into a business to produce final accounts, often use this method. The client business can then do the various entries in the actual ledger accounts at a later date.

Alpha Products
Extended Trial Balance as at 31 December 19–1

Ledger Balances	Trial Balance Debit	Trial Balance Credit	Adjustments Debit	Adjustments Credit	Trading/P and L A/c Debit	Trading/P and L A/c Credit	Balance Sheet Debit	Balance Sheet Credit
Capital		80000						80000
Drawings	12000						12000	
Vehicles	60000						60000	
Trade creditors		40000						40000
Trade debtors	37000			2000 (1)			35000	
Stock 1 January 19–1	18000				18000			
Rent	15400			2200 (3)	13200			
Telephone	1800		300 (2)		2100			
Postage	300				300			
Electricity	2100		200 (2)		2300			
Bank	22000						22000	
Returns inwards	4000				4000			
Returns outwards		2500				2500		
Provision for doubtful debts		900		150 (1)				1050
Purchases	220000				220000			
Sales		370000				370000		
Plant and equipment	157000						157000	
Discounts received		6000				6000		
Provision for depreciation:								
Vehicles		15000		12000 (5)	12000			27000
Plant and equipment		37000		15700 (5)	15700			52700
Bank charges	1800				1800			
Bad debts			2000 (1)		2000			
Increase bad debts provision			150 (1)		150			
Accruals				500 (2)				500
Prepayment			2200 (3)				2200	
Stock 31 December 19–1			16500 (4)			16500 (4)	16500	
Totals	551400	551400			291550	395000	304700	201250
Net profit					103450			103450
Grand totals					395000	395000	304700	304700

Notes

(1) Writing off a bad debt of £2000.
(2) Adjusting the provision for doubtful debts to £1050. (£900 had already been provided in previous year(s) and we are now providing an extra £150. This increase in the provision is charged against profit in the Profit and Loss Account but the whole provision of £1050 is shown in the Balance Sheet.)
(3) Creating accruals for unpaid expenses.
(4) Inserting closing stock.
   Note   The accounting double entry is debiting the Stock Account (adjustment column) and crediting the Trading Account. Remember, the Balance Sheet is not an account and not part of the double-entry system. The entry in the Balance Sheet column is merely a listing of the ledger account balance.
(5) Providing depreciation for the year.
   Note   The depreciation for the current year is charged against profit in the Profit and Loss Account but the total provision to date is shown in the Balance Sheet.

Examination short cuts

Clearly, if we were working to time deadlines in an examination, we would not have time to draft a complete extended Trial Balance. What we require is a short cut method of noting the effects of the various adjustments to the original Trial Balance in such a way that we can confidently progress straight on to the presentation of the Trading and Profit and Loss Account and Balance Sheet.

Individuals can develop their own schemes of working but the following suggestion may be helpful:

1. Calculate required adjustments as necessary.
2. Where an adjustment alters a balance in the Trial Balance, as shown on the examination paper, cross out the original balance and note the revised figures.
3. Where the adjustments require a 'new' account to accommodate an entry, list the accounts and entries on a separate sheet.
4. Allocate every balance with:
    T   Trading Account
    P   Profit and Loss Account
    B   Balance Sheet.
   This process can save time and 'brain strain' when selecting and placing items.
5. Prepare the Trading and Profit and Loss Account and Balance Sheet from the amended Trial Balance on the examination question paper and account entries on the separate sheet. Tick each item off as you select it and place it in the Trading and Profit and Loss Account or Balance Sheet.

EXAMINATION PAPER

Alpha Products
Trial Balance as at 31 December 19–1

	Debit	Credit
Capital		80 000
Drawings	12 000	
Vehicles	60 000	
Trade creditors		40 000
Trade debtors	37 000	
Stock 1 January 19–1	18 000	
Rent	15 400	
Telephone	1 800	
Postage	300	
Electricity	2 100	
Bank	22 000	
Returns inwards	4 000	
Returns outwards		2 500
Provision for doubtful debts		900
Purchases	220 000	
Sales		370 000
Plant and equipment	157 000	
Discounts received		6 000
Provision for depreciation:		
Vehicles		15 000
Plant and equipment		37 000
Bank charges	1 800	
Totals	551 400	551 400

We are told that:

1. (a) A bad debt of £2000 is to be written off.
   (b) The provision for doubtful debts is to be 3 per cent of debtors.
2. There are unpaid bills for electricity £200, telephone £300.
3. Rent is payable at £3300 per quarter, and has been paid to the end of February 19–2.
4. Stock valuation 31 December 19–1:
   at selling price   £28 000
   at cost price   £16 500.
5. Depreciation is to be provided on cost:
   Plant and equipment   10 per cent
   Vehicles   20 per cent.

Examination paper
Alpha Products
Trial Balance as at 31 December 19–1

		Debit	Credit
B	Capital		80 000
B	Drawings	12 000	
B	Vehicles	60 000	
B	Trade creditors		40 000
B	Trade debtors	(1) 35 000 ~~37 000~~	
T	Stock 1 January 19–1	18 000	
P	Rent	(4) 13 200 ~~15 400~~	
P	Telephone	(3) 2 100 ~~1 800~~	
P	Postage	300	
P	Electricity	(3) 2 300 ~~2 100~~	
B	Bank	22 000	
T	Returns inwards	4 000	
T	Returns outwards		2 500
B	Provision for doubtful debts		~~900~~ 1 050 (2)
T	Purchases	220 000	
T	Sales		370 000
B	Plant and equipment	157 000	
P	Discounts received		6 000
	Provision for depreciation:		
B	Vehicles		~~15 000~~ 27 000 (6)
B	Plant and equipment		~~37 000~~ 52 700 (6)
P	Bank charges	1 800	
	Totals	551 400	551 400

We are told that:

1. (a) A bad debt of £2000 is to be written off.
   (b) The provision for doubtful debts is to be 3 per cent of debtors.
2. There are unpaid bills for electricity £200, telephone £300.
3. Rent is payable at £3300 per quarter, and has been paid to the end of February 19–2.
4. Stock valuation 31 December 19–1:
   at selling price   £28 000
   at cost price   £16 500.
5. Depreciation is to be provided on cost:
   Plant and equipment   10 per cent
   Vehicles   20 per cent.

SEPARATE WORKING SHEET

(1) Bad debts Written off.   £2 000   P
(2) Prov For doubtful debts.   £150   P
(3) Accruals. Electricity £200, Telephone £300 = £500   B
(4) Prepayment. Rent £2 200   B
(5) Closing stock.   £16 500   TB
(6) Prov for depreciation:
            Plant and equipment £15 700   P
            Vehicles   £12 000   P

Trading and Profit and Loss Account and Balance Sheet

Construction of the formal Trading and Profit and Loss Account is a relatively straightforward task, provided we are familiar with the 'standard' layout. There is much to be gained from practising drafting out the layout without figures, until you can readily form it from memory. The same is true of the Balance Sheet. If you have the layout committed to memory, and marked each balance with a T, P or B, then you only have to concentrate on picking up the figures and slotting them in. Now we can present the Trading and Profit and Loss Account and Balance Sheet.

Alpha Products
Trading and Profit and Loss Account for the year ended 31 December 19–1

Sales		370 000	
Less: Returns inwards		4 000	366 000
Less: Cost of sales			
Stock 01 January 19–1		18 000	
Plus: Purchases	220 000		
Less: Returns outwards	2 500	217 500	
		235 500	
Less: Stock 31 December 19–1		16 500	219 000
Gross profit			147 000
Discounts received			6 000
			153 000
Less: Expenses:			
Bad debts		2 000	
Provision for doubtful debts		150	
Electricity		2 300	
Telephone		2 100	
Rent		13 200	
Provision for depreciation:			
Vehicles	12 000		
Plant and equipment	15 700	27 700	
Postage		300	
Bank charges		1 800	49 550
Net profit			103 450

Notes
1. Returns inwards and outwards are deducted from sales and purchases respectively to give net sales and net purchases.
2. Income, other than trading income (in this case discounts received), is added to gross profit before deduction of expenses.

Alpha Products
Balance Sheet as at 31 December 19–1

Fixed assets:	Cost	Provision for depreciation	Net book value
Plant and equipment	157 000	52 700	104 300
Vehicles	60 000	27 000	33 000
	217 000	79 700	137 300

Current assets:			
Stock 31 December 19–1		16 500	
Trade debtors	35 000		
Provision for doubtful debts	1 050	33 950	
Prepayment		2 200	
Bank		22 000	
		74 650	
Less: Current liabilities:			
Trade creditors	40 000		
Accrued expenses	500	40 500	
Working capital			34 150
Net worth			171 450
Financed by:			
Capital 01 January 19–1	80 000		
Net profit for year	103 450	183 450	
Less: Drawings		12 000	
Capital 31 December 19–1			171 450

Notes
1. Fixed assets show original cost, provision for depreciation and net book value.
2. Provision for doubtful debts is deducted from debtors to show the best estimate of the value of debtors.
3. Prepayments appear under Current assets and accruals under Current liabilities.

Exercises

1. The following was the Trial Balance of CAL Trading at its year end on the 30 September 19–3. The owner of the business now wishes to have accounts produced monthly and you are to produce the accounts at the end of the first month of trading in the new financial year.

	£	£
Capital account		30 360
Vehicles	28 800	
Fixtures and fittings	16 400	
Bank loan		26 340
Debtors:		
C Jones	3 970	
P Peters	2 840	
J Harris	4 210	
Provision for doubtful debts		520
Bank	9 630	
Stock	14 360	
Creditors:		
Supply Co		5 490
ABC Supplies		2 700
Provision for depreciation:		
Vehicles		11 520
Fixtures and fittings		3 280
	80 210	80 210

During the month of October, the following transactions were completed:

(a) Paid rent by cheque £630.
(b) Paid for servicing of vehicle by cheque £180.
(c) Banked cheque from C Jones £3970.
(d) Sold goods on credit to D Dean & Son £8410.
(e) Purchased goods on credit from Supply Co £4930.
(f) Cash sales totalling £12 340.
(g) D Dean returned damaged goods value £330.
(h) Paid salaries totalling £2660.
(i) Paid Supply Co by cheque £5490.
(j) Purchased goods on credit from Trade Factors £5240.
(k) Repaid bank loan £3000.

You are to prepare a Trading and Profit and Loss Account for the month of October 19–3 and a Balance Sheet as at 31 October 19–3, after making the following provisions and adjustments:

(l) The provision for doubtful debts is to be increased to £1000.
(m) Vehicles are to be depreciated by 2.5 per cent and fixtures and fittings by 1 per cent.
(n) The proprietor had drawn £2000 from the bank for his own use.

Stock at 31 October 1993 was valued at £13 400.

2. The following Trial Balance has been taken from the books of R Kearn at the year ended 30 September 19–3.

R Kearn — Capital		35 000
Vehicles	26 000	
Fixtures and fittings	13 000	
Drawings	14 500	
Electricity	2 100	
Insurances	900	
Sales/Purchases	86 000	158 000
Stock 01.10.19–2	9 300	
Telephone	2 400	
Rent	8 000	
Miscellaneous expenses	3 800	
Bank — current	6 250	
Bank — deposit	30 800	
Debtors	14 700	
Creditors		12 900
Provision for doubtful debts		150
Provision for depreciation:		
Vehicles		6 500
Fixtures and fittings		5 200
	217 750	217 750
Stock	8 700	

Prepare a Trading and Profit and Loss Account and Balance Sheet as at 30 September 19–3, using the extended Trial Balance technique, after adjusting for the following:

(a) Expenses accrued: insurances £200; miscellaneous expenses £460.
(b) Rent paid in advance £600.
(c) Depreciation to be provided (straight line)
    Vehicles   25 per cent.
    Fixtures and fittings   20 per cent.
(d) Provision for doubtful debts to be 3 per cent of debtors.

3. The following Trial Balance has been extracted from the books of J Jones as at 31 December 1992

Capital		29 000
Sales and purchases	61 000	100 000
Sales returns and purchase returns	2 000	4 000
Debtors and creditors	20 000	7 000
Land and buildings at cost	40 000	
Plant (cost and depreciation provision at 1 January 1992)	50 000	22 000
Long-term loan		30 000
Stock at 1 January 1992	15 000	
Administration expenses	12 000	
Distribution expenses	10 000	
Bank account		8 000
Sundry account (see Note (ii) below)		10 000
	210 000	210 000

Notes

(i) Closing stock is £18 000 at cost.

(ii) The bookkeeper was not quite sure how to complete the double entry for a cash receipt and has temporarily credited it to a 'sundry account'. The amount received was:
Further capital introduced   £8000.

(iii) Plant is depreciated over 10 years on a straight line basis with nil residual value. Land and buildings are not depreciated.

(iv) The long-term loan was received on 1 October 1992. Interest payable on this loan is at the rate of 12 per cent per annum, payable at half-yearly intervals in arrears. The first interest payment is due on 31 March 1993.

(v) Administration expenses include a payment of £1200 for insurance premiums up to 28 February 1993.

(vi) By mistake, Mr Jones's drawings of £5000 for the year have been charged to administration expenses.

Required:

Prepare Mr Jones's Profit and Loss Account for the year to 31 December 1992 and his balance sheet at that date.

4. A Trial Balance extracted from the books of Ream Trading at 31.12.19–2 reveals the following information:

Capital and drawings	6 000	59 800
Sales and purchases	52 000	108 000
Returns in and out	2 000	800
Stock	23 000	
Vehicles and provision for depn	50 000	20 000
Fixtures and fittings and prov for depn	40 000	8 000
Rent	2 600	
Electricity (3 quarters)	3 900	
Insurances	1 200	
Salaries	24 000	
Telephones	2 900	
Debtors and prov for doubtful debts	16 400	300
Creditors		13 900
Bank	6 800	
Bank loan		20 000
	230 800	230 800

You are to prepare a Trading and Profit and Loss Account and Balance Sheet as at 31.12.19–2 after making the following adjustments:

(a)   Vehicles are to be depreciated at 20 per cent.
Fixtures and fittings are to be depreciated at 10 per cent.
(b)   The following accruals and prepayments are to be provided:
(i) Rent at £200 per month is paid to 31.01.19–3
(ii) Electricity
(iii) £300 for telephone charges, unbilled at 31.12.19–2
(iv) The insurances paid included a premium for the proprietor's house insurance of £150.
(c)   Bad debts of £1400 are to be written off against profit and the provision for doubtful debts is to be 3 per cent of debtors.
(d)   Closing stock has been valued at £18 700.

Unit 7
Interpreting accounts and judging performance

The main purpose of producing final accounts is to provide information to the owner(s) of a business and to interested parties such as the Inland Revenue, banks and others providing financing, creditors, etc.

We have already seen that the accounts do, at first glance, reveal some important information:

- Trading and Profit and Loss Account:
  — Gross profit.
  — Net profit.
- Balance Sheet:
  — Fixed assets employed in the business. Availability and extent of working capital.
  — Net worth (net assets employed).
  — Capital employed in the business.

This information, though useful, is somewhat limited. It does not, for example, tell us whether any profit being made is at an acceptable level. It does not tell us whether the profit made for the owner(s) represents an acceptable level of reward on his (their) investment, nor does it tell us whether the business is doing better or worse than other similar businesses, some of whom may be competitors.

We need to be able to take figures from the final accounts and refine them in such a way that they reveal even more information about the performance of the business and its financial standing. The method we use to do this is commonly referred to by the rather grand title of *ratio analysis*: a description probably conjured up to strike dread in the hearts of students who no doubt perceive the exercise as involving high level mathematical calculations. We need have no such fears! In fact, the methods used are simple provided we grasp the basic concepts which are illustrated in the following example:

Say we are told that a business has made a net profit of £20 000. We can conclude from this that the business has at least made a profit (which is, of course, infinitely better than making a loss) but could we really say much more?

If we are then told that the sales of the business were £125 000 and that the owner has £100 000 invested, can we make more use of the net profit figure? Yes, we can.

If we relate the net profit to sales, then we can get a measure of profitability:

$$\text{Net profit } \frac{20\,000}{125\,000} \times 100 = 16 \text{ per cent}$$

This measure of profitability could be extremely useful for many reasons:

1. If the owner had set selling prices and managed the business with the intention of attaining 20 per cent, he did not achieve his target.
2. If it is known what level of net profitability is made by similar businesses and competitors, the result can be compared.
3. We can see that every £1 of sales generated £0.16 (16p) of net profit.

We know that the owner has £100 000 invested in the business and it is reasonable to suppose that he could have invested his money in a bank or building society, rather than in a business which inevitably involves a higher degree of risk. Let us assume he could have taken this safer option and invested his money at, say, 6 per cent interest.

Now let us see what rate of return he got on his business investment.

$$\text{Net profit } \frac{20\,000}{100\,000} \times 100 = 20 \text{ per cent}$$

The owner may well feel that the 'extra' 14 per cent is a good reward for the additional risk taken. However, if the return on the business had been 8 per cent, he may have concluded that the extra 2 per cent was not sufficient compensation for the risk taken.

This brief illustration demonstrates how easily we can extract figures from final accounts and convert them into very useful information and indicators. The methods all involve taking one figure and measuring it against another.

We will now run through all the most commonly used basic measures we are likely to encounter. The measures involved are:

- Profitability:
  - Gross profit percentage
  - Net profit percentage.
- Return on investment.
- Liquidity:
  - Working capital ratio
  - Acid test.
- Control of working capital:
  - Control of stocks
  - Control of debtors
  - Control of creditors.

We will use the following abbreviated Trading and Profit and Loss Account and Balance Sheet of Quick Trade as the set of final accounts to be analysed.

Quick Trade
Trading and Profit and Loss Account for the year ended 31 December 19–1

Sales			242 000 (2)
Less: Cost of goods sold:			
Opening stock	17 000 (10)		
Purchases	155 000	172 000	
Less: Closing stock		15 000	157 000 (9)
Gross profit			85 000 (1)
Less: Expenses:			
Distribution costs		13 000	
Administrative expenses		25 000 (4)	
Advertising costs		5 000	43 000
Net Profit			42 000 (3)

Balance Sheet as at 31 December 19–1

Fixed assets			223 000
Current assets:			
Stock	15 000 (8)		
Debtors	28 000 (11)		
Bank	9 000	52 000 (6)	
Less: Current liabilities:			
Creditors		13 000 (7)	
Working capital			39 000
Net worth			262 000
Financed by:			
Capital 1 January 19–1		220 000 (5)	
Profit for year		42 000	
Capital 31 December 19–1			262 000

Profitability

Gross profit percentage

By using this measure, we determine the gross profit percentage obtained from sales.

$$\frac{\text{Gross profit}}{\text{Sales}} \times 100 = \text{Gross profit percentage return}$$

(1)
(2) $\dfrac{85\,000}{242\,000} \times 100 = 35.1$ per cent

The gross profit percentage is useful for:

- seeing if the gross return used when setting prices has been achieved
- comparing with similar businesses and competitors
- showing us that the gross profit on every £1 of sales was 35.1p.

Net profit percentage

This measures net profit against sales.

$$\frac{\text{Net profit}}{\text{Sales}} \times 100 = \text{Net profit per cent}$$

(3)
(2) $\dfrac{42\,000}{242\,000} \times 100 = 17.4$ per cent

The net profit percentage is useful for:

- comparison with similar businesses and competitors
- telling us that the net profit on every £1 of sales was 17.4p.
- showing the impact of operating expenses on gross profit.
  Gross profit was 35.1 per cent of sales and net profit 17.4 per cent.
  Expenses are therefore accounting for 17.7 per cent of sales income (35.1 per cent − 17.4 per cent).

We could, if we wished, break this analysis down even further. For example, we can measure how much of sales income is absorbed by a particular expense. Let us look at administrative expenses:

(4)
(2) $\dfrac{25\,000}{242\,000} \times 100 = 10.3$ per cent

Administrative costs are therefore absorbing 10.3p of every £1 of sales income. If we did this for all expenses we could construct an interesting table:

Proportion of £1 of sales income

Cost of goods sold	64.9%	64.9p
Distribution costs	5.4%	5.4p
Administration cost	10.3%	10.3p
Advertising cost	2.0%	2.0p
Net profit	17.4%	17.4p
TOTAL SALES INCOME	100.0%	£1.00

Return on investment

This measure will enable the owner(s) of the business to decide whether the business, by way of profit, is giving an adequate return on investment(s). They will be looking to see to what extent they are being rewarded for risk.

$$\frac{\text{Net profit}}{\text{Investment}} \times 100 = \text{Return on investment}$$

(3)
(5) $\quad \dfrac{42\,000}{220\,000^*} \times 100 = 19.1 \text{ per cent}$

Note   We have used the capital invested at the start of the year. There is some controversy over whether the capital invested at the start of the year or the end of the year should be used. As the profits we use in the measure have been earned during the year, it seems logical to use the capital investment on which the year's trading started.

It is a matter for the owner(s) to judge whether the 19.1 per cent return is adequate for investing their money and taking the risk element.

Liquidity

Like individuals, a company has to be able to pay its debts as and when they fall due for payment. In order to do this it needs to have cash available when required. This may seem a very obvious statement but it does help us to understand why some businesses, even if they are trading profitably, can run into a financial crisis. If such a company tries to expand too quickly, and invests too much in increasing its fixed assets and stocks, it can find itself short of cash. This situation is technically called *over-trading*. This is an important point, because it highlights the fact that profitable as well as unprofitable businesses can become insolvent (unable to pay debts when they become due). From this, we can see that profitability and cash flow are two different things. Businesses exist to make profit but even the most profitable need to manage their cash situation very carefully. It is useful therefore to have indicators with which to assess liquidity.

Working capital ratio

This measures the extent to which current assets cover current liabilities.

$$\frac{\text{Current assets}}{\text{Current liabilities}} = \text{Working capital ratio}$$

(6) $\quad \dfrac{52\,000}{13\,000} = 4.1$

The figures from our example show that the current assets cover the current liabilities 4 times. In other words, *quick trade* has £1 of current liabilities for £4 of current assets.

This would certainly be seen as a very healthy situation. There is strictly no 'ideal ratio' but between 1.5 : 1 and 2 : 1 is a generally accepted level.

There is, however, a serious limitation to the viability of this measure. The measure is supposedly one of liquidity but just how liquid are all our current assets, stock in particular? One answer is that it depends on the type of business. Food retailers, for example, may turn over their stock weekly, whereas it may take furniture retailers three months to turn over their stock.

In these circumstances, stock is a far more liquid asset to the food retailer than to the person selling furniture. However, should we apply this idea of liquidity to stocks at all? The answer could be no, for one very simple reason. For businesses that trade by selling goods, their ability to trade depends on having a stock of goods to sell. If they have no stock they cannot trade. Therefore, they must always carry a level of stock and consequently always have cash tied up in that stock. Any cash tied up in this stock is not available to pay creditors. Of course, they need to be efficient in not tying up more cash in stocks than is necessary for the business to operate efficiently and we will look at measuring this aspect shortly.

If we accept that stocks are not a truly liquid asset, then we must exclude them if we want a tighter measurement of liquidity. The next measurement seeks to do precisely that.

Liquidity ratio (commonly known as the acid test)

$$\frac{\text{Current assets } - \text{ Stocks}}{\text{Current liabilities}} = \text{Liquidity ratio}$$

(6)
(7) $\dfrac{52\,000 - 15\,000}{13\,000}$ (8) $= 2.8 : 1$

In our example, the 'liquid assets' cover current liabilities 2.8 times. In other words, there is £2.80 of liquid assets available to cover every £1 of current liabilities. As a general rule, we would want this ratio to be at least 1 : 1. However, we should be aware that, for example, many large supermarkets do operate on less than 1 : 1.

Controls on working capital

We have now got a better appreciation of just how important working capital and liquidity are to any business.

However, in looking at measures of these we have used the total of *all* current assets and liabilities. (All current assets *less* stock in the case of the acid test.) But, for example, current assets is made up from constituent parts — stock, debtors, cash, etc. If we are to control each part, which contributes to the overall working capital and liquidity ratios, we need to be able to measure how effectively a business manages its stocks, debtors and creditors.

Control of stocks

We have already seen how important it is that stocks are efficiently managed and are 'turned over' on a regular basis. We have also seen how the turnover period will vary markedly according to the type of business. However, if we can measure how long, on average, it takes, we can at least compare the results with previous years and with other similar businesses. We can express stock 'turnover' as the number of times stock has been turned over in a year.

$$\frac{\text{Cost of goods sold}}{\text{Average stock}}$$

The cost of sales figure (Cost of goods sold) can be readily taken from the accounts but we have no figure in the accounts for average stock. This is calculated by adding Opening stock and Closing stock and dividing the result by 2. From our example we have:

$$17\,000\ (10) + 15\,000\ (8) = 32\,000 \div 2 = 16\,000$$

We can now calculate the stock turnover for our example:

$$\frac{\text{Cost of goods sold}}{\text{Average stock}} \quad \frac{157\,000}{16\,000} = 9.81 \text{ times}$$

If we wish, we can express the turnover in months or weeks using the following formula:

months $12 \div$ stock turnover
weeks $52 \div$ stock turnover

e.g.   months $12 \div 9.81 = 1.22$ months
       weeks $52 \div 9.81 = 5.3$ weeks

Control of debtors

Most businesses trading on credit do so on the basis of requiring payment within 30 days, and the efficiency with which a business collects its debts has a critical impact on its liquidity.

The average payment period can be calculated as follows:

$$\frac{\text{Trade debtors}}{\text{Turnover (sales)}} \times 365 \text{ days} = \text{Average days for payment}$$

Using our example:

(11) $\dfrac{28\,000}{242\,000} \times 365 = 42$ days
(2)

or

$$\frac{28\,000}{242\,000} \times 52 \text{ weeks} = 6 \text{ weeks}$$

Control of creditors

We can assess the average period taken for paying creditors in a manner similar to the one used for debtors.

Exercises

1. The following summarized information relates to a business for the year to 31 December 19–1.

Trading and profit and loss account for the year to 31 December 19–1

	£000	£000
Sales:		
Cash	200	
Credit	600	800
Less:		
Opening stock	80	
Purchases	530	
	610	
Less:		
Closing stock	70	540
Gross profit		260
Expenses		205
Net profit for the year		55

Balance Sheet at 31 December 19–1

	£000	£000
Fixed assets:		
Fixtures and fittings	1000	
Less: Depreciation	450	550
Current assets:		
Stock	70	
Debtors	120	
Cash	5	
	195	
Less: Current liabilities		
Creditors	130	65
		615
Capital		
As at 1 January 19–		410
Net profit for the year	55	
Less: Drawings	50	
		5
		415
Bank loan		200
		615

Required:

(a) Based on the above information, calculate six accounting ratios.

(b) List what additional information you would need in order to undertake a more detailed analysis of the business.

2. Able and Baker are traders. Both trade in a similar range of goods. Their Profit and Loss Accounts and Balance Sheets for the same year are as follows:

Profit and Loss Accounts for the year

	Able		Baker	
	£000	£000	£000	£000
Sales		600		800
Cost of goods sold		450		624
		150		176
Administrative expenses	64		63	
Sales expenses	28		40	
Depreciation provided:				
Equipment	10		20	
Vehicles		102	5	128
		48		48

Balance sheets as at end of year

	Able		Baker	
	£000	£000	£000	£000
Assets:				
Buildings		29		47
Equipment and vehicles		62		76
Stock		56		52
Debtors		75		67
Bank balance		8		—
		230		242
Liabilities:				
Creditors	38		78	
Bank balance	—	38	4	82
Capital		192		160

Required:
Compare the performance and financial position of the two businesses, supporting your findings with ratios and noting what further information you would need before reaching firmer conclusions.

3.   Summarized accounts of P Cannon for the years 19–1 and 19–2 are as follows:

Trading and Profit and Loss Account for the year ended 31 December

	19–1		19–2
	£000	£000	£000
Sales	200		280
Less: Cost of sales	150		210
Gross profit	50		70
Less: Administration expenses	38	46	
General expenses	—	4	50
Net profit	12		20

Balance Sheet as at 31 December

	19–1	19–2		19–1	19–2
	£000	£000		£000	£000
Capital — P Cannon	130	191	Fixed assets, at cost Less: depreciation	110	140
Creditors	15	12	Stock	20	30
Bank	10	—	Debtors	25	28
			Bank	—	5
	155	203		155	203

Stock at 01 January 19–1 was £50 000

Required:
Calculate the following ratios for 19–1 and 19–2:
(a) Gross profit percentage
(b) Stock turnover
(c) Net profit percentages
(d) Acid test
(e) Working capital ratio
(f) Return on investment.

Unit 8

Accounting for cash

Whenever we use the term 'cash' in accounting, we tend to be referring not only to actual cash in hand but also to cheque payments and receipts. Set in this context, the vast majority of business transactions involve the payment or receipt of cash. Even sales and purchases on credit result in a cash transaction when the debtor pays or the creditor is paid. Recording cash payments and receipts is therefore a major part of accounting within any business and, for reasons of security and the prevention of fraud, one to which maximum care and supervision must be given. In many organizations, where large volumes of cash transactions take place, it is not unusual to employ a cashier, whose main task is to make and receive payments and to record all these cash transactions. For all these reasons, the importance of cash accounting cannot be over-emphasized and we really do need to be conversant with the process and procedures.

The Cash Book

In our study so far, we have had a cash and bank account within our Nominal Ledger and this has been a convenient way of working through exercises. In practice, however, the cash and bank accounts are normally kept in a separate book called the Cash Book. This is so for a number of reasons, but primarily because the accounts contain a large number of detailed transactions and, by taking them out to a separate record the nominal ledger is kept to manageable proportions. However, it is important to recognize that the Cash Book, although kept separate, is part of the nominal ledger and of the double-entry system. Another benefit of maintaining a separate book is that it can be entered up independently of the nominal ledger.

The most common form of Cash Book is the two column, with a cash and bank column on the debit (receipts) and credit (payments) side. The following example is a typical layout:

Date	Detail	Folio	Cash	Bank	Date	Detail	Folio	Cheque Number	Cash	Bank

Note   The folio column is used to enter the page number of the account in the main ledger where the double entry is made.

Let us now look at an example of how transactions would be entered in such a Cash Book where the balances, as at 31 March, were Cash £198 and Bank £12 240.

Transactions

1	April 01	Paid Bloom Ltd £930 by cheque number 436791.
2	03	Banked cash takings from sales £380.
3	04	Paid VAT to Customs & Excise by cheque £1316.
4	08	Banked a cheque from P Jones for his February Account £2100.
5	11	Paid for stationery by cash £132.
6	14	Paid by cheque for vehicle repair to ABC Garage £420.
7	18	Drew cash from bank £700.
8	19	Paid wages by cash £630.
9	20	Banked a cheque from Alco Ltd for their March Account £4300.
10	24	Paid Supplies Ltd by cheque £3900.
11	26	Paid electricity bill by cheque £310.
12	28	Banked cheque for March Account from Jackson & Son £2600.
13	29	Paid rent £800 by cheque.
14	29	Banked cheque from Taylors Ltd for their March Account £3400.
15	30	Paid salary by cheque £1400.

Cash Book

Date	Detail	Folio	Cash	Bank	Date	Detail	Cheque Number	Folio	Cash	Bank
01.04	Balances B/D		198	12 240						
03.04	Sales			380	01.04	Bloom Ltd	436791			930
08.04	P Jones			2 100	04.04	Customs & Excise	792			1 316
18.04	Cash from Bank	c	700		11.04	Stationery			132	
					14.04	ABC Garage	793			420
					18.04	Bank to cash (1)	794	c		700
20.04	Alco Ltd			4 300	19.04	Wages			630	
					24.04	Supplies Ltd	795			3 900
28.04	Jackson & Son			2 600	26.04	Electricity	796			310
29.04	Taylors Ltd			3 400	29.04	Rent	797			800
					30.04	Salary	798			1 400
					30.04	BALANCE C/D (2)			136	15 244
	TOTAL		898	25 020		TOTAL			898	25 020
01.05	BALANCES B/D		136	15 244						

Notes

(1) When cash is drawn from the bank, the double entry is credit bank, debit cash. C in the folio column stands for contra entry.
(2) The columns are balanced in the usual way.

There are many alternative ways in which the Cash Book can be laid out — it depends on personal preferences. However, it is worth noting a common variation. It is not unusual to see a discount received and discount allowed column, in addition to the cash and bank columns. This type of three-column Cash Book enables the *totals* of discounts received or allowed to be posted to the respective discount accounts in the main ledger and, of course, entries in the individual debtor and creditor accounts complete the double entry.

Petty cash and imprest systems

There are many instances in a business where small amounts of actual cash are often expended on relatively small purchases or payments. Buying stamps, paying the window cleaner, paying a taxi fare, etc., would be good examples of such payments. All these can pass through the Main Cash Book and in small businesses often do. However, if all these small transactions are kept out of the Main Cash Book, then this important record is restricted in size and kept more manageable. This is achieved by recording such 'petty' transactions in a separate record called the 'Petty Cash Book'.

There are many advantages to this system:

1. The Main Cash Book is not overloaded with 'small entries'.
2. The Petty Cash Book can be maintained by someone other than the person maintaining the Main Cash Book.
3. It is now possible to make cash available for small purchases within departments of a business. (This can reduce significantly the need for staff to 'visit' the accounts department for small payments.)

The imprest system

Where petty cash is kept, and the records maintained by someone other than the accountant or cashier, then it is usual for the petty cash to be operated under an *imprest system*. Under such a system, the imprest holder (person maintaining the petty cash) has an agreed fixed amount of cash, often referred to as a 'float'.

Let us say an imprest holder has an agreed float of £100. On the first day of a petty cash accounting period (which could be a week or a month) the imprest holder will have £100 in cash available. During the course of the accounting period, payments will be made and of course the amount of actual cash held will diminish. However, at any time the imprest holder can produce cash plus paid receipts which in total amount to £100. At the end of the accounting period, the payments made are totalled and if, say, the imprest holder totals the payments made to £85, then there should be paid receipts totalling £85 and £15 held in cash. A reimbursement of the £85 paid out will bring the cash holding back to £100.

There are a number of advantages to be gained from operating an imprest system:

1. A responsible person can carry out 'spot checks' on the petty cash very easily. At any time, the paid receipts and cash held should total to the value of the imprest.
2. The imprest holder can only spend up to the total of the agreed float in any one petty cash accounting period.
3. It discourages theft, as only relatively small sums are involved and the imprest holder cannot accumulate a large amount of cash by drawing direct from the bank.
4. The Petty Cash Book has to be kept up to date because cash paid is not reimbursed until the Petty Cash Book is written up and the total of expenditure ascertained.
5. The practice of 'loans and subs' from petty cash is discouraged as a full account is made at the end of every period and, in any event, any loans or subs made may leave the imprest holder short of cash to meet legitimate payments.

Analysis of petty cash

It is usual for a Petty Cash Book to contain a number of appropriately headed columns, into which frequent payments of certain types of expense are analysed. The column descriptions should relate to particular types of expenditure accounts used in the Nominal Ledger. Examples might be: postage; travel expenses; cleaning; stationery, etc. It is usual to have a column for VAT paid and one headed 'MISC' (miscellaneous) to accommodate payments which do not readily identify with the 'standard' column descriptions. The following illustration is fairly representative:

Cash received	Date	Detail	Folio	Cash paid	Vat	Office sundries	Staff travel	Cleaning	Postage	Misc

Note At the end of each period, the *total* of each column is posted to the appropriate expense account in the Nominal Ledger. This reduces the number of entries that would otherwise be made in the expense account if each payment was posted separately.

Double entries

There are basically two ways petty cash can be treated:

1. As part of the main ledger, albeit a separate record.

2. The ledger can contain a 'Petty Cash Control Account' and the actual Petty Cash Book is a subsidiary record from which an analysis of expenditure can be taken.

We will look briefly at how each system would deal with the following transactions:

1	Started with a cash float of	£100		6	Pens and pencils	£6
2	Postage stamps	£8		7	Postage stamps	£8
3	Envelopes	£4		8	Photocopier paper	£24
4	Taxi fare	£14		9	Mileage allowance	£9
5	Window cleaning	£20		10	Float reimbursement	

As part of the double-entry system

Main Cash Book

Date	Detail	Cash	Bank	Date	Detail	Cash	Bank
					xxxx xxxxxx		xxxx
					xxxxxx xxxxxxx		xxxx
				31.01	Petty cash	93 (1)	

Petty Cash Book

Cash recvd	Date	Detail	Cash paid	Postage	Stationery	Travel	Cleaning	Misc
100	01.01	Balance B/Fwd						
		Stamps	8	8				
		Envelopes	4		4			
		Taxi	14			14		
		Window cleaning	20				20	
		Pens and pencils	6		6			
		Stamps	8	8				
		Photocopier paper	24		24			
		Mileage allowance	9			9		
93(1)	31.01	Reimbursement	93	16	34	23	20	
		Balance C/D	100					
193			193					
100				(2)	(3)	(4)	(5)	

Nominal Ledger

Postage		Stationery	
(2) Petty Cash Book	16	(3) Petty Cash Book	34

Travel		Cleaning	
(4) Petty Cash Book	23	(5) Petty Cash Book	20

Note the numbered double entries.

As a subsidiary record of a Petty Cash Control Account

Main Cash Book

Date	Detail	Cash	Bank	Date	Detail	Cash	Bank
					XXXX XXXXXX		XXXX
					XXXXXX XXXXXXXXX		XXXX
				31.01	Petty Cash	93 (1)	

Nominal Ledger

Petty Cash Control Account

01.01	Balance B/D	100	Payments January per Petty Cash Book:	
			Postage	16 (2)
			Stationery	34 (3)
			Travel	23 (4)
			Cleaning	20 (5)
31.01	Reimbursement (1)	93	Balance C/D	100
		193		193
01.02	Balance B/D	100		

Postage		Stationery	
(2) Petty Cash Control	16	(3) Petty Cash Control	34

Travel		Cleaning	
(4) Petty Cash Control	23	(5) Petty Cash Control	20

Notes

(i) The numbered double entries.

(ii) The payments totals shown in the Petty Cash Control Account (numbered (2)–(5)) are taken from the Petty Cash Book which is a subsidiary record. The Petty Cash Book is written up in the same way as in the previous example.

We have seen that one of the advantages of running petty cash through a separate Petty Cash Book, and operating under an imprest system, is that the maintenance of petty cash can be moved out to user departments. It follows that often in this situation the imprest holder is a person without any financial training or skills. A set of detailed instructions on how to operate the system can therefore be of immense value.

Let us imagine that we have recently been appointed to the post of Accounts Office Manager with SKB Products Limited. We have decided that for the first time Petty Cash Accounts are to be run under an imprest system operated by nominated imprest holders in the Sales Office and the Production and Distribution Department. We are to draft a set of operating procedures for the guidance of the nominated imprest holders.

The following document is a specimen of such a set of procedures. Work through the document so as to reinforce what you already know about petty cash accounting.

Specimen procedure

SKB Products Limited
Petty Cash Procedure

This procedure has been laid down for guidance of imprest holders operating company Petty Cash Accounts. Any queries or problems should be referred immediately to the Accounts Office Manager.

Paragraph	Content
1	Records, supporting vouchers and security
2	Imprest
3	Recording petty cash transactions
4	Month-end procedures
5	Reimbursement of month's cash payments
6	Balancing the Petty Cash Account
7	Analysis of expenditure
8	Filing of each month's records

Appendix	Specimen
A	Monthly petty cash account sheet
B	Petty cash voucher

Anytown
3 January 19– –

Petty Cash Accounting

1. *Records, supporting vouchers and security*
   (a) Petty Cash Account. The recording of petty cash transactions is to be carried out on 'monthly petty cash account sheets' a specimen of which is to be found in Appendix A.
   (b) Petty cash vouchers. In all but the most exceptional circumstances, all claims for reimbursement of petty cash expenditure must be supported by a receipt for the purchase made. The actual claim consists of a fully completed 'petty cash voucher' to which the purchase invoice must be attached. A specimen of the petty cash voucher is to be found in Appendix B.
   (c) All petty cash and vouchers against which reimbursements have been made are to be kept in the petty cash box. When not in use, the petty cash box is to be kept in a locked drawer of the fire-proof cabinet in the General Office.
   (d) The Accounts Office Manager will carry out periodic spot checks of the cash held. At any time, the value of cash and 'paid' vouchers in the petty cash box should total £100 (the value of the petty cash 'imprest').
   (e) A list of authorized signatures for petty cash expenditure should be held by the Petty Cashier.

2. *Imprest*
   Petty cash is organized on the imprest system. This means that the holder of the petty cash will, at all times, be able to account for a £100 holding either in cash, paid vouchers or a combination of both. On the 1st of every month the imprest holder will have £100 in cash. During the course of a month, cash will be paid out against petty cash vouchers. On the last day of each month, the Accounts Manager will reimburse the imprest holder with cash in exchange for the month's paid vouchers. Consequently, on the 1st day of the next month the imprest holder will again start the month with £100 in cash.

3. *Recording of petty cash transactions*
   (a) All petty cash receipts and payments are to be recorded on the month's petty cash account sheet — see Appendix A.
   (b) Appendix A is a specimen petty cash account sheet on which sample entries have been made.
   (c) Particular attention should be paid to VAT. VAT shown on any petty cash voucher must be recorded in the column headed VAT — this is important because the company can reclaim any VAT paid.
   (d) Any expenditure which cannot be readily identified as fitting into the analysis columns office sundries to postage should be allocated to the last column headed 'Misc'.
   (e) Each petty cash voucher is given a consecutive folio number and that folio number is entered on the petty cash account sheet.

4. *Month-end procedure*
   On the last working day of each month three tasks are to be completed:
   (a) Petty cash expended throughout the month is to be reimbursed to the imprest holder (see 5 below).
   (b) The imprest holder is to 'balance' the Petty Cash Account (see 6 below).

(c) The analytical columns of VAT to Misc are to be totalled and must, in total, equal the total of cash expended in the month (as above; see 7 below).

5. *Reimbursement of month's cash payments*

All payments made during the month have been entered, in folio number order, on the month's account sheet. These payments are now totalled. The Accounts Office Manager will, on sight of the month's account sheet and supporting petty cash vouchers, refund in cash to the imprest holder the value of the paid petty cash vouchers. This will reinstate the petty cash holding to £100 in cash.

6. *Balancing the Petty Cash Account*

(a) On the next available line of the 'Details' column of the month's account sheet the imprest holder will enter the description 'Imprest reimbursement' and, in the Cash receipts column will enter the sum reimbursed as in 5 above.

(b) On the next available line of the 'Details' column of the month's account sheet the imprest holder will enter the description 'Balance C/Fwd' and in the Cash paid column will enter the total of cash held which is, of course, £100.

(c) On the next available line of the 'Details' column of the month's account sheet the imprest holder will enter the description 'Totals' and in the cash receipts and cash paid columns will enter the total of those columns. Both columns will total to the same amount. The 'Balance C/Fwd' figure of £100 becomes the opening entry on the following month's account sheet described as 'Balance B/Fwd'.

7. *Analysis of expenditure*

On the same line of the account sheet that totals were entered in 6 (c) above, a total will be entered for each column from VAT to Misc. The final check is to ensure that when all the column totals of 'VAT' to 'Misc' are added together, the resultant sum is the same as the sum reimbursed and entered in the accounts sheet as in 6(a) above.

8. *Filing of each month's records*

Each month's completed petty cash account sheet and supporting petty cash vouchers will be filed in a document wallet annotated as Petty Cash Account . . . . .19– –.

The completed wallets will be retained in the same locked drawer of the fire-proof cabinet as the current petty cash and documents are retained in. At the end of each financial year the year's Petty Cash Accounts and supporting documents will be required for accounting and audit purposes.

Exercises

1. Write up a two-column Cash Book from the following and balance the Cash Book as at 30 November 19–3:

19–3

Nov. 01	Balance brought forward from last month: cash £105.00; bank £2164.00
03	Cash sales £605.00
05	Took £500.00 out of the cash till and paid it into the bank
06	A Bean paid us by cheque £230.00
07	We paid for postage stamps in cash £60.00
08	Bought office equipment by cheque £314.00
10	We paid J Jones by cheque £50.00
12	Received rates refund by cheque £72.00
14	Withdrew £250.00 from the bank for business use
15	Paid wages in cash £239.00
17	Paid motor expenses by cheque £57.00
20	T Trent lent us £200.00 in cash
22	R Rogers paid us by cheque £112.00
26	We paid general expenses in cash £16.00
30	We paid insurance by cheque £19.00

2. Write up a two-column Cash Book from the following and balance off as at 31 March 19–3:

19–3

Mar 01	Balances brought down from last month: cash in hand £56.00: cash in bank £2680.00
03	Paid rates by cheque £156.00
04	Paid for postage stamps in cash £5.00
06	Cash sales £318.00
07	Cash paid into bank £60.00
09	We paid: T Tom by cheque £75.00; R Rivers in cash £2.00
11	P Priest pays us £150.00, £100.00 by cheque and £50.00 in cash
16	Cash drawings by proprietor £50.00
19	K Prim pays by cheque £79.00
23	Withdrew £200.00 from the bank for business use
26	Paid deposit on van £250.00 by cheque
29	Paid rent by cheque £40.00
30	Cash sales paid direct into the bank £21.00

3. Write up a two-column Cash Book from the following and balance off as at 31 May 19–3:

19–3
May 01   Started business with capital in cash £100.00 and bank £400.00
   03   Paid rent by cash £10.00
   04   I Ivor lent us £500.00, paid by cheque
   05   We paid B Cline by cheque £6.00
   08   Cash sales £98.00
   09   T Thomas paid us by cheque £62.00
   11   We paid D Dean in cash £22.00
   12   Cash sales paid direct into the bank £53.00
   14   T Anson paid us in cash £65.00
   16   We took £50.00 out of the cash till and paid it into the bank account
   18   We repaid I Ivor £100 by cheque
   21   Cash sales paid direct into the bank £214.00
   25   Paid motor expenses by cheque £12.00
   27   Withdrew £100.00 cash from the bank for business use
   31   Paid wages by cash £104.00

4. The following is a summary of the petty cash transactions of A Trading for September 19–3

Sept 01   Received from cashier £300.00 as petty cash float

		£
03	Postage	18.00
04	Travelling	12.00
06	Cleaning	19.00
08	Petrol for delivery van	22.00
09	Stationery	17.00
12	Travelling	25.00
13	Cleaning	18.00
14	Postage	5.00
17	Travelling	8.00
19	Stationery	9.00
19	Cleaning	28.00
22	Postage	13.00
25	Delivery van 3000 mile service	46.00
26	Petrol	18.00
28	Cleaning	21.00
28	Postage	15.00
30	Petrol	14.00

Required:
(a) Rule up a suitable Petty Cash Book with analysis columns for expenditure on cleaning, motor expenses, postage, stationery and travelling.
(b) Enter the month's transactions.

5. Betty Jackson keeps her petty cash on the imprest system, the interest being £25. For the month of April 19–2, her petty cash transactions were as follows:

		£
April 01	Petty cash balance	1.13
02	Cash from bank to restore imprest	23.87
04	Bought postage stamps	8.50
09	Paid for refreshments	2.35
11	Paid travel costs	1.72
17	Bought stationery	0.72
23	Received cash for personal telephone call	0.68
26	Bought petrol	10.00

(a) Enter the above transactions in a suitably analysed Petty Cash Book and balance the Petty Cash Book at 30 April.
(b) On 01 May Betty Johnson received an amount of cash from the cashier to restore the imprest. Enter this transaction in the Petty Cash Book.

6. The Old Trading Company maintains a Petty Cash Account on the imprest system. On the first day of each month, the petty cash is restored to its agreed imprest balance of £100.
At 30 April 19–5, the petty cash held stood at £23.40.
During May 19–5, the following petty cash transactions have to be accounted for:

Date 19–7		£
May 01	Cash received to restore imprest	to be inserted
01	Travel costs	0.46
02	Stationery	2.35
04	Travel costs	0.30
07	Postage stamps	1.70
07	Trade journal	0.95
08	Travel costs	0.64
11	Envelopes	1.29
12	Tea and coffee	5.42
14	Parcel postage	3.45
15	Travel cost	1.42
15	Newspapers	2.00
16	Photocopier repair	16.80
19	Stamps	1.50
20	Drawing pins	0.38
21	Train fare	5.40
22	Photocopier paper	5.68
23	Tea and coffee	3.07
23	Correction fluid	1.14
25	Wrapping paper	0.78
27	String	0.64
27	Tea and coffee	1.75
27	Newspapers	0.46
28	Computer disks	13.66
30	Travel costs	2.09
June 01	Cash received to restore imprest	to be inserted

Required:
Complete the Petty Cash Account for the period 01 May to 01 June 19–5 and balance the account at 30 May 19–5. The account should have suitably totalled analytical columns into which all expenditure should be allocated.

Appendix A   Example

PETTY CASH

MONTH _____   SHEET NO _____

RECEIPTS		DATE	NO	PAYMENTS	TOTAL	VAT	POSTAGE	SUNDRIES	TRAVEL	MISC
TOTAL										
			TOTALS							
			ACCOUNT NUMBER		2200	5007	5016	5001	5009	

112

Appendix B

PETTY CASH	Date	No	
Item(s)		£	p
Example			
	VAT		
	TOTAL		
Authorized by:	Signature:		

Unit 9

Keeping your eyes on the bank

Checking statements

We have seen already how a large proportion of transactions by any business are payments made by cheque and receipts of cash and cheques paid into the Bank Account. We also know that all such payments and receipts are recorded in the business Cash Book. The Cash Book therefore becomes the record of what is happening within the Bank Account. Meanwhile, the bank is keeping its own record of payments and receipts of the business and periodically sends a *Statement of Account* showing all the cheques that have been paid, all the deposits the business has made and the balance of cash or overdraft the business has with the bank.

Banks, like any other organization, can make mistakes so it is important that their statements of account are checked against business records — the Cash Book. We will soon see that there are also other reasons, apart from mistakes, why the bank statement must be carefully checked.

This process of checking is the first stage of performing a *bank reconciliation*. The checking process, like the bank reconciliation itself, is a straightforward task and, if carried out methodically and carefully, will not cause any difficulty. *During the checking process we are only concerned with items in the Cash Book and on the Bank Statement which agree.* Having identified these, and they are the majority of entries, then we can forget them. Let us now look at a typical checking process.

The ABC Co has just received its bank statement for the month ended 31 January 19– –. The bookkeeper sets about checking the statement against the firm's Cash Book.

Western Bank Plc
Statement of Account ABC Company Sheet No 20

Jan	Particulars	Debit	Credit	Balance
01	Balance B/Fwd			5000.00
03	548976	134.90		4865.10
08	548977	341.76		4523.34
10	SO Bingham Council	68.00		4455.34
10	Counter Credit		846.20	5301.54
16	548979	59.20		5242.34
17	548978	84.30		5158.04
20	Bank Charges	28.90		5129.14
21	Counter Credit		512.10	5641.24
26	548975	210.48		5430.76
29	SO Southern Electric	150.00		5280.76
31	548981	9.47		5271.29
31	Credit Transfer — Beams Ltd		209.60	5480.89

Cash Book

Jan	Detail	£	p	Jan	Cheque	Detail	£	p
01	Balance B/D	5000	00	01	548975	Ream & Co	210	48
				01	548976	Greens Garage	134	90
				03	548977	Anderson & Co	341	76
				09	548978	Preen Ltd	84	30
				09	548979	Duplo Ltd	59	20
				09	548980	P Anderson	39	40
10	Deposit	846	20	10	548981	Freeman Ltd	9	47
				19	548982	A Potter	16	90
21	Deposit	512	10	21	548983	L Jones & Sons	148	30
				30	548984	Bonds Ltd	52	84
				31		BALANCE C/D	5260	75
31	TOTAL	6358	30	31		TOTAL	6358	30

Recommended checking procedure

1. Take each entry in the payments column of the Cash Book and try to locate the same cheque number and amount in the debit column of the bank statement, e.g. the first payment in the Cash Book payment column is cheque number 548975 — £210.48. The same cheque number and amount appear on the bank statement (4th line from the bottom).
2. Put a tick next to the amount in the Cash Book and on the bank statement. We have no further interest in this item as it appears in both records and both entries match precisely.
3. Continue to do this with every item in the payment column of the Cash Book.
4. When you have finished you will have some entries in the payments column of the Cash Book that you have not ticked because they did not appear on the bank statement. Do not worry about the unticked items at this stage.
5. Now go to the receipts column of the Cash Book and locate the corresponding entries in the credit column of the bank statement, again ticking the matched items.
6. Again, ignore any unticked items at this stage.

The following page shows this process having been completed. What we have done is match items on the bank statement with entries in the Cash Book. From now on, we can ignore the matched (ticked) items completely as they are of no further consequence. We now have to look at what is to be done about the unmatched (unticked) items.

This illustration shows how the bank statement and the Cash Book will look after the checking process has been completed. We can clearly see that the unticked items represent the unmatched transactions which we will deal with in the next section.

Bank Statement

Western Bank Plc
Statement of Account   ABC Company   Sheet No 20

Jan	Particulars	Debit	Credit	Balance
01	Balance B/Fwd			5000.00 ✓
03	548976	134.90 ✓		4865.10
08	548977	341.76 ✓		4523.34
10	SO Bingham Council	68.00		4455.34
10	Counter Credit		846.20 ✓	5301.54
16	548979	59.20 ✓		5242.34
17	548978	84.30 ✓		5158.04
20	Bank Charges	28.90		5129.14
21	Counter Credit		512.10 ✓	5641.24
26	548975	210.48 ✓		5430.76
29	SO Southern Electric	150.00		5280.76
31	548981	9.47 ✓		5271.29
31	Credit Transfer — Beams Ltd		209.60	5480.89

Cash Book

Jan	Detail	£	p	Jan	Cheque	Detail	£	p
01	Balance B/D	✓5000	00	01	548975	Ream & Co	210	48 ✓
				01	548976	Greens Garage	134	90 ✓
				03	548977	Anderson & Co	341	76 ✓
				09	548978	Preen Ltd	84	30 ✓
				09	548979	Duplo Ltd	59	20 ✓
				09	548980	P Anderson	39	40
10	Deposit	✓846	20	10	548981	Freeman Ltd	9	47 ✓
				19	548982	A Potter	16	90
21	Deposit	✓512	10	21	548983	L Jones & Sons	148	30
				30	548984	Bonds Ltd	52	84
				31		BALANCE C/D	5260	75
31	TOTAL	6358	30	31		TOTAL	6358	30

Accounting for differences

Remember, we can ignore the matched items. We are now only concerned with the unmatched items (unticked). These unmatched items can be summarized as:

Bank Statement

Jan	Detail	Debit	Credit
10	SO Bingham Council	68.00	
20	Bank Charges	28.90	
29	SO Southern Electric	150.00	
31	Credit Transfer — Beams Ltd		209.60

Cash Book

Jan	Cheque	Detail	£	p	Jan	Cheque	Detail	£	p
					09	548980	P Anderson	39	40
					19	548982	A Potter	16	90
					21	548983	L Jones & Sons	148	30
					30	548984	Bonds Limited	52	84

Let us now consider the *unmatched* items:

Cash Book

None of these four cheques has, as yet, gone through the bank and been paid (if they had, they would have appeared on the bank statement). We can expect that the firms to whom the cheques were sent will eventually pay them in to their bank accounts and they will then appear on a future bank statement (probably the next statement that the ABC Company receives). We need do nothing more about these unpaid cheques at this stage.

Bank statement

The item on 10 January, like that on 29 January, represents a standing order payment which the bank has paid. Provided we are satisfied that the ABC Company has authorized these standing order payments, all we need to do is enter them in the Cash Book to make it agree with the bank statement.
Action: Enter in Cash Book (Payment column).
The item on 20 January represents a charge the bank has made for operating the Bank Account. The item is not entered in the Cash Book because we did not know of the charge until we received the bank statement.

Action: Enter in Cash Book (Payment column).

The item on 31 January represents a sum of money Beams Limited has paid into our Bank Account by credit transfer. We did not know about this receipt until we received the bank statement, consequently it does not appear in the Cash Book.

Action: Enter in Cash Book (Receipts column).

We now enter these items in the Cash Book because they are legitimate payments and receipts.

Cash Book

Jan	Cheque	Detail	£	p	Jan	Cheque	Detail	£	p
31		BALANCE B/D	5260	75	10		SO Bingham Council	68	00
					20		Bank Charges	28	90
		Credit Transfer	209	60	29		SO Southern Electric	150	00
							BALANCE C/D	5223	45
			5470	35				5470	35
Feb 01		BALANCE B/D	5223	45					

The only remaining unmatched items between the Cash Book and the bank statement are the four cheques we discovered during the checking procedure. In the next section, we will see how we use this information to complete a reconciliation between the Cash Book and bank statement.

Before leaving this section, however, we must remember to make the double entries for the items we have added to the Cash Book in the appropriate accounts.

Reconciling your books to the bank statement

This actually means explaining the difference between the balance in the Cash Book and the balance shown on the bank statement. The accepted way of doing this is to start with the Cash Book balance. The differences (unmatched items) are then listed and the resulting figure is the bank statement balance. In the case of our example, this would be done as follows:

Bank Reconciliation

Balance as per Cash Book		5223.45
Add: Cheques not yet paid		
548980	39.40	
548982	16.90	
548983	148.30	
548984	52.84	257.44
Balance as per bank statement		5480.89

*Deciding whether to add or subtract unmatched items is a problem which frequently causes confusion, if not panic.

If we examine the problems closely, we should see the rationale to be applied in solving the problem.

In our example, the Cash Book includes four cheque payments which are not yet shown on the bank statement. In order to reconcile the two, we must therefore adjust the Cash Book balance in such a way that the revised balance will be the same as it would have been had the cheques not been written. We do this by 'adding back' the value of the cheques to the Cash Book balance.

However, *if the Cash Book balance is overdrawn* we have to do exactly the opposite. This means 'deducting' unpaid cheques from the Cash Book balance. Students should be acutely aware of these two opposite approaches as examiners have a nasty habit of introducing overdrawn balances in examination questions. The following rules apply:

Bank Reconciliation

Cash Book — *debit balance*	*Add*	Cheques not yet paid
	Deduct	Deposits into the bank not shown on the bank statement
Cash Book — *credit balance*	*Deduct*	Cheques not yet paid
	Add	Deposits into the bank not shown on the bank statement

HEALTH WARNING

The system we have just covered is the proper procedure followed in a real working situation. However, some examiners do have a nasty habit of divorcing themselves from reality by trying to make a reconciliation more complicated than it need be. They do this by asking for a bank reconciliation statement to be prepared without any adjustment to the Cash Book. If this happens, the first rule is do not panic. *The second rule is just carry on, after the checking process, with preparing a reconciliation statement. The only difference is that you will have more 'unmatched' items to include and consequently more to think about.*

Let us use this approach for the reconciliation we have just done.

Balance as per Cash Book			
(*Note* original Cash Book balance)			5260.75
Add:			
Cheques not yet paid		257.44	
Credit transfer — Beams Ltd		209.60	467.04
			5727.79
Deduct:			
SO Bingham Council		68.00	
Bank charges		28.90	
SO Southern Electric		150.00	246.90
Balance as per bank statement			5480.89

Bank reconciliation: summary of procedure

1. *Checking.* Tick every matching entry in the Cash Book and on the bank statement.
2. *Accounting.* Enter in the Cash Book any unticked items appearing on the bank statement provided they are legitimate payments or receipts.

   Remember to do the appropriate double entries for these items in the accounts.
3. *Unmatched items.* Mark or list the remaining unmatched items for easy reference.
4. *Reconcile.* Prepare a bank reconciliation statement. This is done by starting with the Cash Book balance. Adjust the Cash Book balance by any unmatched (unticked) items to arrive at the bank statement balance.
5. *Retain.* The bank reconciliation should be carefully filed as it will be needed when doing the following month's reconciliation. Some bookkeepers copy the bank reconciliation on the appropriate page of the Cash Book as a permanent record, which is a sensible procedure.

Exercises

1. The bank statement for the month of May 19–3 is:

19–3		Debit £	Credit £	Balance £	
May 01	Balance			5197	O/D
07	P Paine	122		5319	O/D
15	Cheque		244	5075	O/D
19	D Roach	208		5283	O/D
22	Cheque		333	4950	O/D
30	K Kettering — Giro Credit		57	4893	O/D
31	Rates — Standing Order	49		4942	O/D
31	Bank charges	28		4970	O/D

The Cash Book for May 19–3 is:

19–3		£	19–3		£
	Dr			Cr	
May 14	L Leo	244	May 01	Balance B/F	5197
20	M Norman	333	05	P Paine	122
29	A Mather	160	29	D Roach	208
31	Balance C/D	5280	30	L Searle	490
		6017			6017

Required:
(a) Write the Cash Book up to date.
(b) Draw up a bank reconciliation statement as at 31 May 19–3.

2. Jill James wishes to reconcile her bank statement for August 19–4 with her Cash Book. Extracts of both are as follows:

Bank Statement

Date		Payments £	Receipts £	Balance £
August 19–4				
01	Balance		_previous month_	1051.29
02	236127	210.70		842.59
03	Giro Credit		192.35	1034.94
06	236126	15.21		1019.73
06	Charges	12.80		1006.93
09	236129	43.82		963.11
10	427519	19.47		943.64
12	236128	111.70		831.94
17	Direct Debit	32.52		799.42
20	Sundry Credit		249.50	1048.92
23	236130	77.87		971.05
23	236132	59.09		911.96
25	Giro Credit		21.47	933.43
27	Sundry Credit		304.20	1237.63
30	236133	71.18		1166.45

Cash Book

Date August	£	Date August	Cheque No.	£
01	827.38	05	128	111.70
02	192.35	10	129	43.82
18	249.50	16	130	87.77
24	304.20	18	131	30.00
30	192.80	20	132	59.09
		25	133	71.18
		30	134	52.27
	1766.23			1766.23

Required:
Prepare a reconciliation statement reconciling the Bank Statement balance at 30 August to the Cash Book balance at the same date.

3. The summarized Cash Book for Blake & Co as at 30 November 19–3 is as follows:

Cash Book

	£		£
Opening balance B/D	1 407	Payments	15 520
Receipts	15 073	Closing balance C/fwd	960
	16 480		16 480

In preparing a bank reconciliation, it is found that:
(a) Bank charges of £35 shown on the Bank Statement have not been entered in the Cash Book.
(b) A cheque drawn for £47 has been entered in error as a receipt.
(c) A cheque for £18 has been returned by the bank marked 'refer to drawer', but no entry has been made in the Cash Book.
(d) The Cash Book opening balance should have been £1470.
(e) Three cheques for £214, £370 and £30 have not yet been presented.
(f) A deposit of £1542 has not yet been credited to the account by the bank.
(g) The bank has debited a cheque for £72, which is not a company cheque. This is a bank error and will be corrected.
(h) The bank statement has an overdrawn balance of £124.

Required:
(i) Make adjustments to the summarized Cash Book.
(ii) Prepare a bank reconciliation as at 30 November 19–3.

4. At the end of his financial year (31 May 19–4), Peter Cook has a balance in his Cash Book of £894.68 debit. On checking his bank statement, you discover the following:
(a) Cheque 176276, dated 06 May 19–4 for £310.84, had been written in the Cash Book as £301.84. The bank statement entry was, of course, correct.
(b) Bank charges of £278.66 had not been entered in the Cash Book.
(c) A cheque for £29.31, paid into the Bank Account on 14 May 19–4, had been returned 'refer to drawer' and debited on the bank statement. No entry has been made in the Cash Book, other than the original debit.
(d) Cheques totalling £1895.60 had been paid into the Bank Account on 30 May 19–4 but do not appear on the bank statement.
(e) The bank statement shows a standing order payment of £150 which has not been entered in the Cash Book.
(f) Cheques totalling £395.80 had been sent to creditors on 28 May 19–4, but none appears on the bank statement.

Required:
(i) Prepare a bank reconciliation statement as at 31 May 19–4, starting with the Cash Book balance of £894.68.
(ii) Write up the Cash Book so that the closing balance is the figure to be included in P Cook's Balance Sheet.

Unit 10

Sharing the workload

In our study up to this point we have thought of all the accounts of a business being contained in one ledger. For a small business, where only one person works on the accounts, this method is feasible. However, if we think of a business with, say, 2000 customers, to whom sales are made on credit and 200 suppliers who supply on credit, then we can see problems emerging.

- The ledger containing accounts for each customer and supplier as well as other accounts, such as assets, expenses, etc., would be impossibly large.
- A business of this size would, almost certainly, need to have more than one person working on the accounts at any one time.
- If the accounts were 'out of balance', then finding errors would be a mammoth task.

In practice, therefore, the ledger is normally split into at least three different ledgers:

1. *The Sales Ledger*. Sometimes called the Debtors' Ledger, contains the personal accounts of all debtors.
2. *The Purchase Ledger*. Sometimes called the Creditors' Ledger, contains the personal accounts of all creditors.
3. *The Nominal Ledger*. Sometimes called the Impersonal Ledger, contains all the expense accounts and asset and liability accounts other than individual trade debtors and creditors. It will usually also include a Sales Ledger Control Account and a Purchase Ledger Control Account. These accounts contain totals of all the individual entries made in the Sales Ledger and Purchase Ledger. In other words, the balance on the Sales Ledger Control Account will show the total amount owed by all debtors. Similarly, the Purchase Ledger Control Account balance shows the total amount owed to suppliers (creditors). A Trial Balance can therefore be drawn up from the Nominal Ledger without recourse to the Sales or Purchase Ledgers.

An illustration of the relationships may be helpful:

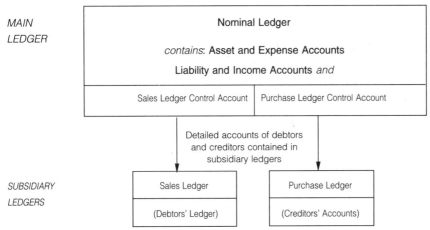

We can see the advantages of this arrangement:

1. The Nominal Ledger is manageable. By taking all the individual debtors' and creditors' accounts out into their own ledgers, we have greatly restricted the size of the Nominal Ledger.
2. We can now have staff working on the Sales and Purchase Ledgers independently of the Nominal Ledger and the person who maintains it.
3. The balances on the Sales and Purchase Ledger Control Accounts are the figures to which the Sales and Purchase Ledger clerks must balance. For example, the sum total of all the debtor account balances in the Sales Ledger must agree with the balance on the Sales Ledger Control Account.
4. Locating errors is much easier. For example, if errors have been made in entering transactions in debtors' accounts, the errors are within the Sales Ledger and will prevent the Sales Ledger balancing with the Sales Ledger Control Account. However, a Trial Balance can still be extracted from the Nominal Ledger and final accounts produced. In the Trial Balance and final accounts we only want the *total* of debtors and creditors and these are the balances on the Sales Ledger Control Account and Purchase Ledger Control Account, within the Nominal Ledger.

Day Books and Journal

Before we examine control accounts and their operation in detail, we will review other subsidiary records which allow record keeping to be dispersed among a number of staff and so facilitate sales and purchase ledger accounting.

These records, or books, are commonly known as 'Books of Prime Entry'. They are not part of the double-entry system but assist the process and reduce the number of entries required in the Nominal Ledger.

Sales Day Book or Sales Journal

When goods are sold on credit, an invoice is made out and sent to the customer and a copy of the invoice kept. From the copy invoice, details are then entered into a Sales Day Book (more recently referred to as a Sales Journal). The Day Book is merely a 'diary' of all supplies on credit and normally shows: the date of supply; the name of the customer (debtor); the invoice reference number; a folio reference (the page of the sales ledger where the debtor's account is located) and the amount.

Sales Day Book				
Date	Customer	Invoice	Folio	£
April 01	J Cooper	14561	SL 5	600.00
April 13	P Fearn	14562	SL 14	1250.00
April 25	D Dean	14563	SL 11	1960.00
	Entered in		NL 28	3810.00

From this subsidiary record, two important double entries can be made:

1. The total of sales for a period can be credited to the Sales Account in the Nominal Ledger. In this case, £3810 into the Sales Account found on page 28 of the Nominal Ledger (folio reference NL 28). We can see that as only the totals are being posted periodically then the number of entries in the Nominal Ledger is kept to a minimum.
2. The sales invoice value can be debited to the customer's (debtor's) account in the Sales Ledger. In our example, *debit* J Cooper £600 in folio SL 5 (Sales Ledger page 5).

Sales Returns Book or Sales Returns Journal

For many reasons goods sold may be returned. They may be faulty, or the wrong type supplied, etc. Again, a 'diary' record similar to the Sales Day Book is kept but this time it records 'credit note' details for the returned goods. A credit note has the opposite effect to an invoice in that it is credited to the customer's account thereby reducing the amount owed.

Sales Returns Book				
Date	Customer	Credit note	Folio	£
April 20	P Fearn	814	SL 14	180.00
April 27	R Rogers	815	SL 17	70.00
	Entered in		NL 29	250.00

From this record, the following double entries can be made:

1. The total of the returns for a period can be debited to a Sales Returns Account (often known as Returns in) in the Nominal Ledger. In this case, £250 is debited to the Sales Returns Account found on page 29 of the Nominal Ledger.
2. The credit note value can be credited to each customer's account in the Sales Ledger. In this example, *credit* P Fearn £180 in folio SL 14 (Sales Ledger page 14).

Purchases Day Book — Purchases Journal

This works in a similar fashion to the Sales Day Book except, of course, it is recording purchases.

Purchases Day Book				
Date	Supplier	Supplier's invoice	Folio	£
April 02	R Dukes & Co	3496	PL 4	600.00
April 11	K Rendall	1047	PL 13	850.00
April 20	Suppliers Ltd	A/241	PL 8	1150.00
	Entered in		NL 24	2600.00

Double entries from this record are:

1. The total of the purchase for a period is debited to the Purchases Account in the Nominal Ledger. In this case, £2600.00 into the Purchases Account located on page 24 of the Nominal Ledger.
2. The invoice value is credited to each supplier's (creditor's) account in the Purchase Ledger. In this example: *credit* R Dukes & Co £600.00 in folio PL 4 (Purchase Ledger page 4).

Purchases Returns Book or Purchases Returns Journal

When goods are returned to a supplier for any reason, a debit note should be sent to the supplier to advise that his account is being debited with the value of the returned goods. Details of the supplier and debit notes are entered in a Purchases Returns Book.

Purchases Returns Book				
Date	Supplier	Debit note	Folio	£
April 09	P Porter	194	PL 18	180.00
April 12	R Dukes & Co	195	PL 4	150.00
	Entered in		NL 25	330.00

The double entries are:

1. The total of returns for a period are credited to a Purchases Returns Account in the Nominal Ledger. In this case, £330.00
2. The debit note value is debited to the supplier's (creditor's) account in the Purchase Ledger, e.g. *debit* P Porter £180.00 in page 18 of the Purchase Ledger.

Helpful hints   The inclusion of sales and purchases returns in examination questions is common practice and they do trouble many students. They need not, if we understand that:

(Sales — *credit balance*) − (Sales returns — *debit balance*)
(Purchases — *debit balance*) − (Purchases returns — *credit balance*)

Example: *Extract from Trial Balance*

	Debit	Credit
Sales		50 000
Sales returns (Returns in)	2 000	
Purchases	30 000	
Purchases returns (Returns out)		1 200

In a Trading and Profit and Loss Account the returns accounts are displayed as:

Trading and Profit and Loss Account

Sales		50 000	
Less: Sales returns		2 000	48 000
Less: Cost of goods sold:			
Opening stock (say)		1 000	
Purchases	30 000		
Less: Purchases returns	1200	28 800	
		29 800	
Less: Closing stock (say)		900	
			28 900
Gross profit			19 100

The Sales Ledger and the Sales Ledger Control Account

We have seen already that the Sales Ledger contains all the debtor (customer) accounts. In some businesses, the number of debtor accounts could run into thousands and in these circumstances, the ledger may be split down so that individual clerks can look after certain parts (customers). For example, Clerk 1 may look after that part of the ledger which contains customers in an alphabetical listing A–E. Clerk 2 may look after G–L, and so on. There are many ways in which the ledger could be divided up and many forms in which it may be kept. Up to now, we have thought of a ledger as a book containing accounts but we now need to broaden our understanding. A ledger can be a collection of accounts maintained in a variety of forms. They could be in a book; kept on separate index cards; computer listings, etc. However, in whatever form they are kept, the purpose is still to maintain a record of what each debtor owes and to be able to total all the individual debtors' account balances to agree with the balance on the Sales Ledger Control Account.

We can therefore think of the Sales Ledger Control Account in the Nominal Ledger as being one huge debtors' account. By entering the *totals* of all transactions affecting debtors into the account, then this account shows us, at any time, the total owed by all debtors. The same is true of the Purchases Ledger Control Account which will show at any time the total owed to all creditors. For the purpose of producing a Trial Balance and final accounts, we only need the totals of all debtors and creditors which are the balances on the Sales Ledger and Purchase Ledger Control Accounts.

The details of each individual debtor and creditor account are kept in the Sales Ledger and Purchase Ledger respectively. The accuracy of these ledgers is checked by balancing the totals of all accounts in each ledger with the balance on the respective Control Account in the Nominal Ledger.

By employing this method, we ensure that the Nominal Ledger contains all the information required to produce a set of 'balanced accounts' from which final accounts can be produced. We have taken all the mass of detail about each individual debtor and creditor out of the Main (Nominal) Ledger into subsidiary ledgers where they can be worked on and maintained by the appropriate clerks. We can now explore the detailed working of these systems and see how they also allow us to exercise some important financial controls.

Sales Ledger and its Control Account

Let us take a simple example to see how the system works:

Transactions

		Sales on Credit	Returns	Cash Received
1	Able Company	3 600		
2	Green Limited	2 100		
3	Able & Company		300	
4	Baker & Son	6 400		
5	Able & Company			3 300
6	Black Limited	1 800		
7	Redline Limited	1 200		
8	Baker & Son			4 000
		15 100	300	7 300

Nominal Ledger

Sales Ledger Control Account

Sales	15 100	Returns inwards	300
		Bank	7 300
		Balance C/D	7 500
	15 100		15 100
Balance B/D	7 500		

Sales Ledger

Able & Company

Sales	3 600	Returns	300
		Bank	3 300
	3 600		3 600

Green Limited

Sales	2 100

Baker & Son

Sales	6 400	Bank	4 000
		Balance C/D	2 400
	6 400		6 400
Balance B/D	2 400		

Black Limited

Sales	1 800

Redline Limited

Sales	1200

If we now list and add the balances of the debtor accounts within the Sales Ledger, the total should balance with the Sales Ledger Control Account in the Nominal Ledger.

Green Limited	2100
Baker & Son	2400
Black Limited	1800
Redline Limited	1200
Total	7500

We can see that they do, in fact, balance.

This is, of course, only a brief illustration, using a few debtor accounts. However, the system would work in exactly the same way if the debtor accounts numbered hundreds or even thousands.

The Purchase Ledger and the Purchase Ledger Control Account

The Purchase Ledger and its Control Account system operate in exactly the same way as that of the Sales Ledger and its Control Account except, of course, the entries are reversed.

We can therefore move straight to an illustration.

Transactions

		Purchase on Credit	Returns	Cash Paid
1	Jones & Son	3 900		
2	Cable Limited	2 600		
3	Bryants	4 800		
4	Jackson & Spear	1 700		
5	Ream Limited	800		
6	Cable Limited		200	
7	Jones & Son			3 900
8	Steelman & Company	3 600		
9	Bryants		600	
10	Cable Limited			2 400
		17 400	800	6 300

Nominal Ledger

Purchase Ledger Control Account

Returns	800	Purchases	17 400	
Bank	6 300			
Balance C/D	10 300			
	17 400		17 400	
		Balance B/D	10 300	

Purchase Ledger

Jones & Son

Bank	3900	Purchases	3900

Cable Limited

Returns	200	Purchases	2600
Bank	2 400		
	2 600		2 600

Bryants

Returns	600	Purchases	4 800
Balance C/D	4 200		
	4 800		4 800
		Balance B/D	4 200

Jackson & Spear

		Purchases	1 700

Ream Limited			Steelman & Company	
Purchases	800		Purchases	3600

If we now list the creditor balances we have:

Bryants	4 200
Jackson & Spear	1 700
Ream Limited	800
Steelman & Company	3 600
	10 300

The total of the creditor accounts at £10 300 balances with the Purchase Ledger Control Account.

Exercise in sales and purchase accounting

Let us now look at quite an extensive exercise which takes in the use of:

- Day Books
- Control Accounts
- Sales and Purchase Ledgers

Try to track each entry carefully.

Transactions (April 19–1)

1	April 02	Bought on credit from Suppliers Ltd, goods costing £4000, *less* a trade discount of 25 per cent.
2	04	Sold goods on credit to Bood Ltd for £2800.
3	07	Sold goods on credit to Reed & Co £3500, *less* a trade discount of 20 per cent.
4	09	Purchased goods on credit from Harris & Son £6200.
5	11	Paid Suppliers Ltd by cheque after deducting a cash discount of 5 per cent.
6	15	Sale on credit to Porters Ltd £7300.
7	17	Porters Ltd returned damaged goods £800.
8	19	Paid Suppliers Ltd in full by cheque.
9	23	Purchased goods on credit from Rowlands & Sons £3100.
10	23	Reed & Co returned goods £400.
11	24	Returned goods to Harris & Co £600.
12	24	Received cheque from Reed & Co in full settlement of their account.
13	25	Sold goods on credit to Simons Ltd £2400.
14	28	Bought goods from Suppliers Ltd for £3600, *less* a trade discount of 25 per cent.
15	30	Sold goods to Vickers Ltd on credit £3300.

Day Books

Sales Day Book

Date	Debtor	Invoice number	Amount	
04 April	Bood Ltd	12345	2 800	
07 April	Reed & Co	12346	2 800	(1)
15 April	Porters Ltd	12347	7 300	
25 April	Simons Ltd	12348	2 400	
30 April	Vickers Ltd	12349	3 300	
			18 600	

Sales Returns Day Book

Date	Debtor	Credit note	Amount
17 April	Porters Ltd	873	800
23 April	Reed & Co	49	400
			1 200

Purchases Day Book

Date	Creditor	Invoice number	Amount	
02 April	Suppliers Ltd	8439/1	3 000	(1)
09 April	Harris & Son	49873	6 200	
23 April	Rowlands & Sons	18439	3 100	
28 April	Suppliers Ltd	8441/8	2 700	(1)
			15 000	

Note (1) Net figure after deducting trade discount.

Purchases Returns Day Book

Date	Creditor	Credit note	Amount
24 April	Harris & Co	319	600

Note
(1) Trade discount is deducted and only the *net* figure is entered in the Day Books and Accounts.

Nominal Ledger

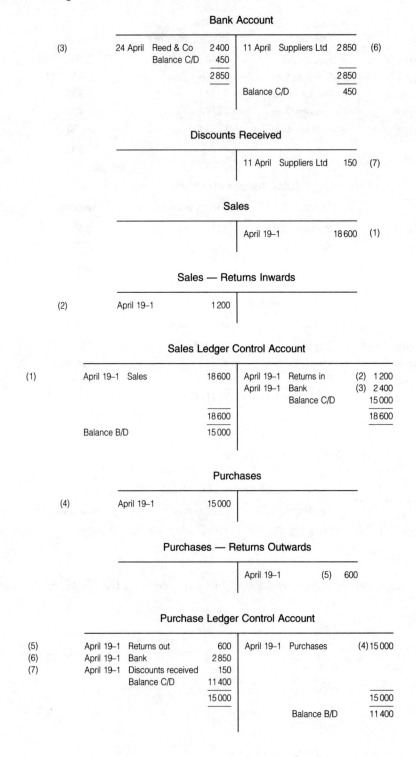

Bank Account

(3)	24 April	Reed & Co	2 400	11 April	Suppliers Ltd	2 850	(6)
		Balance C/D	450				
			2 850			2 850	
					Balance C/D	450	

Discounts Received

			11 April	Suppliers Ltd	150	(7)

Sales

			April 19–1		18 600	(1)

Sales — Returns Inwards

(2)	April 19–1	1 200		

Sales Ledger Control Account

(1)	April 19–1	Sales	18 600	April 19–1	Returns in	(2)	1 200
				April 19–1	Bank	(3)	2 400
					Balance C/D		15 000
			18 600				18 600
	Balance B/D		15 000				

Purchases

(4)	April 19–1	15 000		

Purchases — Returns Outwards

			April 19–1	(5)	600

Purchase Ledger Control Account

(5)	April 19–1	Returns out	600	April 19–1	Purchases	(4) 15 000
(6)	April 19–1	Bank	2 850			
(7)	April 19–1	Discounts received	150			
		Balance C/D	11 400			
			15 000			15 000
					Balance B/D	11 400

Note   Numbers in brackets show cross–reference to other accounts.

From these Nominal Ledger Accounts we can produce a Trial Balance to demonstrate how the Nominal Ledger contains all the accounts required to produce final accounts.

Trial Balance

	Debit	Credit
Bank		450
Discounts received		150
Sales		18 600
Returns inwards	1 200	
Debtors (Sales Ledger control)	15 000	
Purchases	15 000	
Returns outwards		600
Creditors (Purchase Ledger control)		11 400
	31 200	31 200

Now we can go to the Sales and Purchase Ledgers to get the individual details of debtors and creditors.

Sales Ledger

Bood Ltd
Sales	2 800		

Reed & Co
Sales	2 800	Returns in	400
		Bank	2 400
	2 800		2 800

Porters Ltd
Sales	7 300	Returns in	800
		Balance C/D	6 500
	7 300		7 300
Balance B/D	6 500		

Simons Ltd
Sales	2 400		

Vickers Ltd
Sales	3 300		

Sales Ledger Balances

	Debit
Bood Ltd	2 800
Porters Ltd	6 500
Simons Ltd	2 400
Vickers Ltd	3 300
	15 000

We can see that this balances with the debtors total balance on the Sales Ledger Control Account in the Nominal Ledger.

Purchase Ledger

Suppliers Ltd

Bank	2 850	Purchases	3 000
Discounts received	150	Purchases	2 700
Balance C/D	2 700		
	5 700		5 700
		Balance B/D	2 700

Harris & Son

Returns out	600	Purchases	6 200
Balance C/D	5 600		
			6 200
		Balance B/D	5 600

Rowlands & Sons

		Purchases	3 100

Purchase Ledger Balances

	Credit
Suppliers Ltd	2 700
Harris & Son	5 600
Rowlands & Sons	3 100
	11 400

Again, this balances with the creditors total balance on the Purchase Ledger Control Account in the Nominal Ledger.

Credit control

Any business which sells its goods on credit has a most important task to perform: that of controlling the amount of credit extended to customers and ensuring that debtors pay in time. So important is this function that larger companies will employ specialist staff who are trained and experienced in the techniques of *credit control*. Whoever performs this function, the Sales Ledger, containing all the individual debtor accounts is the prime financial record with which the 'credit controller' will work.

There are many aspects to controlling credit which can be broadly summarized as follows:

1. Establishing the creditworthiness of potential customers.
2. Defining the amount of credit to be extended to particular customers.
3. Sanctioning the release of supplies to customers to keep credit within agreed limits.
4. Analysing debtor accounts and identifying overdue accounts.
5. Collecting payment of overdue accounts.
6. Using legal processes to collect long overdue accounts.
7. Writing off bad debts and providing information on doubtful debts.

Establishing the creditworthiness of potential customers

Potential customers could range from the small one-person business to large corporations; from newly formed businesses to long-established firms. It follows that the amount of credit, which may be extended, will vary greatly according to the size and established credit trading record of particular potential customers.

There are a variety of ways in which a business can try to establish creditworthiness, the most common being:

1. *Require the prospective customer to supply a bank and trade references.* However, the fact that, say, two satisfactory trade references are supplied, does not indicate that the prospective customer pays *all* suppliers promptly. It is hardly likely that the name of a supplier with whom a bad trading record exists, will be given as a reference. There are many who will maintain that bank references are so guarded as to render them invalid for this purpose.
2. *Use a credit rating agency.* Such an agency will provide known details about how long a business has been established, its size and financial standing. It may also recommend a credit limit (the maximum amount of credit recommended). The agency will draw its information from a variety of sources, including annual accounts and court judgements for debt. Much of this type of information is somewhat historic, and there is no guarantee that because a business had a good financial standing, say, six months ago, that the same is true today. Agencies obviously charge for this service so there are costs involved in this alternative.

A common problem is that a potential customer first becomes a potential debtor when an initial order is placed. Obviously, whatever method is employed, it does take time to establish the creditworthiness of the client who invariably wants the goods or services quickly. In these circumstances, a device called a *proforma invoice* is used. This is *not* a 'proper' invoice. It is a specimen of what the invoice will look like after the goods have been supplied and requires the prospective customer to pay in full before goods are released. Only after payment has been received will the goods or services be supplied and then a 'proper' invoice will also be rendered, albeit it has been paid in advance.

Defining the amount of credit to be extended to particular customers

This is perhaps the most difficult of all credit control tasks. If creditworthiness has been established by relying on references then it may, for example, be known that the prospective customer trades properly with the referee business on a credit of, say, £10 000. This does not mean, of course, that there is any guarantee that the same will be true with another supplier and, in any event, how reliable is this information if the prospective customer requires £20 000 of credit with 'our' business? If a credit rating agency has been used, it may well recommend a credit limit. However, this is only a recommendation.

One thing is certain, someone within the business is going to have to make a judgement as to the amount of credit that can be 'safely' extended. It will also be important that agreed limits are regularly reviewed in the light of experience and time.

Sanctioning supplies to customers while maintaining agreed credit limits

The prime objective of an organization's sales function is to sell and vigorous pursuit of this objective can sometimes lead to conflict between sales orders and financial control. It is by no means unusual that all orders pass through credit control for approval before orders are fulfilled. This process allows for a check to be made to ensure that goods or services are not supplied to a customer whose account is already overdue or that the order does not take the account over its agreed limit. This is another area where computerized accounting has much to offer. Such systems will often allow the salesperson, or sales order clerk, to access the customer's account and check on availability of credit before the order is taken.

Analysing debtor accounts and identifying overdue accounts

Credit control involves continuously analysing the Sales Ledger so as to identify accounts that have become overdue. Such an analysis will also enable the total of all debtor account balances to be balanced with the Sales Ledger Control Account. It will also involve analysing the debtor account balances into an 'age listing' of which the following illustration could be typical.

Debtors — Age Listing

Debtor	Amount	Overdue		
		30 Days	60 Days	90 Days
Able	1 000.00	600.00		
Baker	3 200.00			
Charlie	2 900.00	2 000.00	900.00	
Drake	860.00		800.00	60.00
Ernie	6 490.00			
Fred	5 230.00	630.00		
Totals	19 680.00	3 230.00	1 700.00	60.00

Yet again, computerized accounting systems can produce such an analysis as part of their operating process.

Collecting payment of overdue accounts

Having produced an age listing of overdue debtor accounts, positive action has to be taken to 'collect' the outstanding debts. Such action can take a variety of forms or a combination of many. The most common processes are:

1. Reminder (chase up) letter(s) being sent to the debtor. The frequency and form of these letters vary widely, but a typical system may be:
   (a) 14 days overdue. A 'gentle' reminder that there is an outstanding sum now overdue for payment
       ... if payment is not then received ...
   (b) 30 days overdue. A 'stronger' demand that payment be made of an account which is now well overdue.
       ... if payment is not then received ...
   (c) 42 days overdue. A 'final' demand that payment be made, failing which, further action will be taken.

   Note It would not be uncommon to put a stop on any further orders after an account is, say, 30 days overdue.
2. Sales personnel may visit or telephone the debtor to remind him or her that the account is overdue. It is arguable that such personal contact is more persuasive and may be the best way of getting 'warning signs' that all is not well with a particular debtor.
3. All, or selected, debtor accounts may be placed with an outside agency. Such agencies will, for a fee, chase up and seek to collect all outstanding accounts.
4. The debts may be factored. That is, the debts will be 'sold' (factored) at a discount to an outside agency. Such a debt factoring agency will, for example, 'buy' the debts for, say, 95 per cent of the face value of invoices. Thereafter, the agency seeks to collect the full value of each debt. The advantage to the client is that it receives, in this case, 95 per cent of all debts paid to a strict timetable and all the problems of collecting debts are transferred to the agency which now 'owns' them.

Note This is, of necessity, only a brief overview of what is a complex and specialized area of operation in which many people and organizations are engaged.

Using legal processes to collect long overdue accounts

After all attempts to collect outstanding debts have failed, the final step is to enforce payment through the process of law. This involves suing the debtor and proving to a court that the debtor does in fact owe the sum claimed. The court, if satisfied, can then order the debtor to pay the debt. If the debtor still does not pay then steps can be taken to enforce the court order.

Writing off bad debts and providing information on doubtful debts

We have already looked at the accounting entries for writing off bad debts and making provision for doubtful debts. It is the credit control process which will determine which debts, in spite of all attempts to collect them, are irrecoverable and need to be written off in the Profit and Loss Account. The statistical data produced by credit control will also provide a reasonably accurate assessment of the proportion of debts which ultimately prove irrecoverable and on which decisions can be made about the level of provision to be made for doubtful debts through the Profit and Loss Account.

Exercises

1. The opening balances in ABC Trading's Ledger at 01 January included the following:

	£
Purchase Ledger Control Account	15 892
Sales Ledger Control Account	34 975

During the year to 31 December, the following transactions (among others) took place:

Cash sales	418 930
Credit sales	86 450
Credit purchases	278 560
Cash purchases	10 398
Amounts received from credit customers	398 764
Amounts paid to credit suppliers	262 318
Returns to credit suppliers	1 456
Returns by credit customers	682

Required:
Write up the Purchase Ledger Control Account and Sales Ledger Control Account for the year. Balance off the two accounts at the end of the year.

2. Wellbuild Co maintains a Purchase Ledger Control Account in its Nominal Ledger. It maintains individual creditor accounts in a subsidiary Purchase Ledger.

   At the end of September 19–7, the balance on the Purchase Ledger Control Account of £25 450 did not agree with a total of balances taken from the Purchase Ledger.

   The following errors were found:

   (a) A cheque paid to a supplier, for £1500, had been entered in the supplier's account as £1550.
   (b) Goods returned to a supplier £800 had not been entered in any ledger.
   (c) The Purchases Day Book from which the Control Account is posted had been totalled to a figure £2200 less than the correct amount.
   (d) Goods purchased for £250 had been entered in the Purchase Day Book at £500.

   Required:
   (i) Write the necessary amendments in the Purchase Ledger Control Account.
   (ii) Calculate the original total of balances drawn from the Purchase Ledger before the errors were discovered.

3.
   (a) Write, briefly, about the advantages of running a Sales and Purchase Ledger Control Account and subsidiary Sales and Purchase Ledgers.

   (b) On trying to balance the Purchase Ledger, the following errors have been discovered:

     (i) A discount of £100, received from a creditor, has been omitted from all accounting records.

     (ii) A credit note for £60 had been treated as an invoice.

     (iii) £600 was owed to A Able. Able also owed the company £400 and this was to be offset against the £600 owed. No entry has been made to record this.

     (iv) £250 has been entered on the wrong side of a supplier's account in the Purchase Ledger.

     (v) An invoice for £654 has been wrongly entered in the Purchase Day Book as £456.

Required:

Prepare a statement showing each correction and a total by which the Purchase Ledger Control Account will need amending.

Unit 11

Miscellaneous matters

Carriage costs

Up to this point in our studies, we have not seen carriage costs included in any accounts. The reason is quite simple. In practice, such charges are rarely accounted for separately, as the cost of transport is usually included in the price quoted for the goods. In other words, this type of charge is largely a relic of the past and even the description 'carriage' seems to have more to do with the 'horse and cart' of years past than with modern transport and delivery systems.

However, examiners, for reasons best known to themselves, do have a habit of including these charges in questions set, so we must be familiar with the accounting treatment of them.

When such items are included, you will see them described as:

- Carriage inwards or Carriage in
- Carriage outwards or Carriage out

Accounting for these charges, should they arise, is very simple.

Carriage inwards is the delivery charge a supplier makes when supplying goods. Therefore, if a business bought goods costing £100 and was also charged £20 delivery (carriage) then the actual cost of acquiring the goods was £120. The accounting entries recognize this by adding the cost of carriage inwards to the cost of purchases in the Trading Account.

The 'Cost of goods sold' section of the Trading Account could therefore appear as (say):

Opening stock	5 000	
Plus: purchases	50 000	
Plus: Carriage inwards	2 000	57 000
Less: Closing stock		6 000
Cost of goods sold		51 000

Carriage outwards is the cost a business might incur in delivering goods it has sold to its customers. Such costs could well appear in the accounts better described as 'distribution costs' whether the delivery is made by a firm's own transport or by an outside haulage contractor, or delivery service. Carriage costs would be just another way of describing these costs. Whether described as Carriage out or distribution costs, the charge is to the Profit and Loss Account as an operating cost.

Helpful hint   Students sometimes become confused by the descriptions Carriage *in* and Carriage *out*. In and out are clearly opposites, so there is often an expectation that account balances in a Trial Balance will also be opposites, one being debit and the other credit. *This is not the case.* Both are expenses and both will have a debit balance. The difference is in how the two accounts are placed in the Trading and Profit and Loss Account.

Summary

Carriage inwards — added to purchases in the Trading Account.

Carriage outwards — listed as an expense in the Profit and Loss Account.

Discounts

There are two categories of discount:

- Trade discounts
- Cash discounts

Each category of discount is then divided into two types:

- Type 1: Received
- Type 2: Allowed

We therefore have:

- Trade discounts
  - Received
  - Allowed
- Cash discounts
  - Received
  - Allowed

Trade discounts

These are discounts given by a supplier to a customer in the course of trading. An example may best explain this. Let us say that a supplier sells goods direct to the public and, on a wholesale basis, to retailers who will then resell the goods. Take, as an example, a supplier who sells a Model X Computer direct to the public via mail order for £1000. The same model of computer is also sold to a number of Computer Shops who, in turn, sell it to their customers for £1000. In these circumstances, the supplier will sell the computer to the Computer Shop for £1000 *less* a trade discount. Let us say the trade discount is 20 per cent. Then the shop will buy the computer for a net price of £800. The £200 difference between the buying and selling price will be the shop's profit on the sale. We can see this clearly in the following invoice comparison:

1. Invoice to the buying public

```
                                    INVOICE

No 147


                              Computer Supplies
                              Unit 18 Any Estate
                                  Anywhere


Joe Public
Any Street
Any Town
_____

To supply of 1 Model X Computer                                  £1000
```

2. Invoice to a Computer Shop (trade customer)

```
                                    INVOICE

No 148


                             Computer Supplies Ltd
                              Unit 18 Any Estate
                                  Anywhere


The Computer Shop
48 The High Street
Anytown
_____

To supply of 5 Model X Computers                             £5000.00
Less Trade Discount – 20%                                    £1000.00
Net Invoice Value                                            £4000.00

Credit Terms:
1        30 days from date of invoice
2        Cash Discount of 1% for payment within 10 days
```

Notes
(i) For simplicity VAT has been excluded.
(ii) Note the trade discount on the Computer Shop invoice. For now, ignore the section on the invoice relating to credit terms.

These examples should help us understand the problems of accounting for trade discount — *there are none*. Trade discounts do not normally appear in the accounts. Using our example, the supplier — Computer Supplies Ltd — will show the sale in its accounts as £4000. The Computer Shop will also show the purchase in its accounts as £4000. Unfortunately, this is not true of cash discounts.

Cash discounts

Cash discounts are a device to persuade a customer to pay an invoice more quickly. If we refer back to the example of an invoice to a Computer Shop, we see at the bottom of the document, Credit Terms. The normal credit terms are payment within 30 days of the date of the invoice. If the customer pays to these terms, the payment is £4000. However, if advantage is taken of the cash discount terms, and payment is made within 10 days, then £40 cash discount can be deducted and the net payment becomes £3960. Now let us look at this transaction firstly from the supplier's and then from the customer's point of view.

Supplier

1. Supply five computers at £4000 to Computer Shop on credit.

Sales

	Computer Shop	4000

Computer Shop

Sales	4000	

2. Receives cheque for £3960 from Computer Shop.

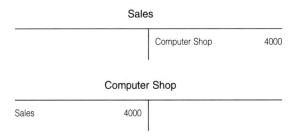

Bank				Computer Shop		
Computer Shop	3960			Sales	4000	Bank	3960

Note At this stage, Computer Shop is still apparently a debtor owing £40. In reality, this is not so as the £40 represents the cash discount deducted by the customer.

3. Adjusting for the discount allowed.
   Debit the discount to a Discounts Allowed Account.

Computer Shop

Sales	4000	Bank	3960
		Discounts Allowed	40
	4000		4000

Discounts Allowed

Computer Shop	40	Transfer to Profit and Loss Account as an expense at end of accounting period

Notes
(i) The Debtor's Account is now clear.
(ii) Discounts Allowed are an expense and are written off to the Profit and Loss Account.

Now let us look at the same transaction from the point of view of the customer, Computer Shop.

Customer

1. Bought five computers at 4000 from Computer Supplies Ltd on credit.

Purchases

Computer Supplies Ltd	4000	

Computer Supplies Ltd

	Purchases	4000

2. Decides to take advantage of cash discount and pays Computer Supplies Ltd £3960, by cheque, within 10 days.

Computer Supplies Ltd				Bank	
Bank	3960	Purchases	4000	Computer Supplies Ltd	3960

Note At this stage, Computer Supplies Ltd is still, apparently, a creditor owed £40.

3. Adjusting for the discount received.
   Credit the discount to a Discounts Received Account.

Computer Supplies Ltd

Bank	3960	Purchases	4000
Discounts Received	40		
	4000		4000

Discounts Received

Transfer to Profit and Loss account as 'income' at end of accounting period	Computer Supplies Ltd	40

Notes
(i) The creditors account is now clear.
(ii) Discounts Received are treated as income and credited to the Profit and Loss Account.

Summary

1. Discounts allowed — listed as an expense in the Profit and Loss Account.
2. Discounts received — credited as 'income' in the Profit and Loss Account.

Profit and Loss Account

Gross profit		xxx
Other income:		
Discounts received		xxx
		xxx
Less: Expenses:		
Expense	xxx	
Expense	xxx	
Discounts allowed	xxx	
Expense	xxx	
Expense	xxx	(xxx)
Net profit		xxx

Sale of fixed assets

Another quite popular examination area is to account for any profit or loss on disposal of fixed assets. It is another topic which appears to cause difficulty for some students, yet it is quite straightforward if we approach the problem in a structured manner. Let us start by looking at a typical situation reflecting the accounts of a particular asset. We will take vehicles as our example. This is how the accounts might look at 01 January 19–5.

Vehicles

01.01.19–1	Bank (purchase of van 1)	6 000			
01.07.19–1	Bank (purchase of car)	8 000	31.12.19–1	Balance	14 000
		14 000			14 000
01.01.19–2	Balance B/D	14 000	31.12.19–2	Balance C/D	14 000
01.01.19–3	Balance B/D	14 000			
01.01.19–3	Creditors (purchase of van 2)	12 000	31.12.19–3	Balance C/D	26 000
		26 000			26 000
01.01.19–4	Balance B/D	26 000			
01.07.19–4	Bank (purchase of van 3)	9 000	31.12.19–4	Balance C/D	35 000
		35 000			35 000
01.01.19–5	Balance B/D	35 000			

Provision for Depreciation on Vehicles (20% per annum)

31.12.19–1	Balance C/D	2 000	31.12.19–1	Profit and Loss	2 000
			01.01.19–2	Balance B/D	2 000
31.12.19–2	Balance C/D	4 800	31.12.19–2	Profit and Loss	2 800
		4 800			4 800
			01.01.19–3	Balance B/D	4 800
31.12.19–3	Balance C/D	10 000	31.12.19–3	Profit and Loss	5 200
		10 000			10 000
			01.01.19–4	Balance C/D	10 000
31.12.19–4	Balance C/D	16 100	31.12.19–4	Profit and Loss	6 100
		16 100			16 100
			01.01.19–5	Balance B/D	16 100

Let us first look at how the provision for depreciation has been built up.

Calculation of depreciation charge — vehicles

		£
Year ending 31.12.19–1	Van 1 £6000 × 20%	1200
	Car £8000 × 20% × 0.5 (6 months)	800
	Charge to Profit and Loss	2000
Year ending 31.12.19–2	Van 1 £6000 × 20%	1200
	Car £8000 × 20%	1600
	Charge to Profit and Loss	2800
Year ending 21.12.19–3	Van 1 £6000 × 20%	1200
	Car £8000 × 20%	1600
	Van 2 £12 000 × 20%	2400
	Charge to Profit and Loss	5200
Year ending 31.12.19–4	Van 1 £6000 × 20%	1200
	Car £8000 × 20%	1600
	Van 2 £12 000 × 20%	2400
	Van 3 £9000 × 20% × 0.5	900
	Charge to Profit and Loss	6100

We will now assume that van 1 has been sold on 01 October 19–5 for £1900 and we will account for any profit or loss made on the sale.

There are two ways in which a disposal can be accounted for. The first method we will look at is usually the method called for in examinations or assignments. It involves using a 'Disposal of Asset' Account and passing all entries concerned with the asset being disposed of through this account. Effectively, the cost of the asset in the Asset Account and the depreciation provided on the asset in the Provision for Depreciation Account are credited to the Disposal Account. The proceeds of the sale are credited into the Disposal Account and then the balance on the account, which represents the profit or loss made on the disposal, is transferred to the Profit and Loss Account.

The second method, which is often used in practical accounting, involves accounting for the disposal within the Asset Account itself.

Disposal of Assets Account method

Accounting steps

1. Enter the provision for depreciation for the year in which the asset is being disposed of in the Provision for Depreciation Account. Include in the provision, a proportion of a year's charge for the asset disposed of, according to the date of sale.

2. Transfer the original cost of the asset to the Disposal of Assets Account by *crediting* the Asset Account with the original cost and *debiting* the Disposal Account.
3. Transfer the depreciation provided on the asset being disposed of from the Provision for Depreciation Account to the Disposal Account. *Debit* the Provision for Depreciation Account, *credit* the Disposal Account.

    Calculate as follows:

Year ending 31.12.19–1	£1200
Year ending 31.12.19–2	£1200
Year ending 31.12.19–3	£1200
Year ending 31.12.19–4	£1200
Year ending 31.12.19–5	£ 900
	£5700

4. *Credit* the Disposal Account with proceeds of sale.
    Debit Bank or Cash, *credit* Disposal Account.
5. Balance on the Disposal Account now represents profit or loss made on the disposal of the asset and is transferred to the Profit and Loss Account.

We can illustrate these steps using our example:

Disposal of Assets Account

01.10.19–5	Vehicles Account (cost of van 1)	6000	01.10.19–5	Provision for depreciation (depreciation provided for van 1)	5700
			01.10.19–5	Bank (proceeds of sale of van 1)	1900

At the end of the year, the balance on this account is transferred to the Profit and Loss Account.

Disposal of Assets Account

01.10.19–5	Vehicles Account (cost of van 1)	6000	01.10.19–5	Provision for depreciation (depreciation provided for van 1)	5700
			01.10.19–5	Bank (proceeds of sale of van 1)	1900
31.12.19–5	Profit and Loss	1600			
		7600			7600

Asset Account method

Accounting steps

1. Enter the provision for depreciation for the year in which the asset is being disposed of in the Provision for Depreciation Account. The provision is a proportion of a year's charge for the asset disposed of, according to the date of sale.
2. Transfer the total depreciation provided on the asset being disposed of to the Asset Account.
3. *Credit* the Asset Account with proceeds of sale.
4. (a) *Credit* the Asset Account with the loss on sale.
   Debit the Profit and Loss Account with the loss on sale
   or
   (b) *Debit* the Asset Account with the profit on sale.
   Credit the Profit and Loss Account with the profit on sale.

Step 1   Enter provision for depreciation for asset disposed of

Provision for Depreciation on Vehicles (20% per annum)

31.12.19–1	Balance C/D	2 000	31.12.19–1	Profit and Loss	2 000
			01.01.19–2	Balance B/D	2 000
31.12.19–2	Balance C/D	4 800	31.12.19–2	Profit and Loss	2 800
		4 800			4 800
			01.01.19–3	Balance B/D	4 800
31.12.19–3	Balance C/D	10 000	31.12.19–3	Profit and Loss	5 200
		10 000			10 000
			01.01.19–4	Balance C/D	10 000
31.12.19–4	Balance C/D	16 100	31.12.19–4	Profit and Loss	6 100
		16 100			16 100
			01.01.19–5	Balance B/D	16 100
			31.12.19–5	Profit and Loss	6 700

Step 2   Transfer depreciation provided on van 1 to Vehicles Account

Provision for Depreciation on Vehicles (20% per annum)

31.12.19–1	Balance C/D	2 000	31.12.19–1	Profit and Loss	2 000
			01.01.19–2	Balance B/D	2 000
31.12.19–2	Balance C/D	4 800	31.12.19–2	Profit and Loss	2 800
		4 800			4 800
			01.01.19–3	Balance B/D	4 800
31.12.19–3	Balance C/D	10 000	31.12.19–3	Profit and Loss	5 200
		10 000			10 000
			01.01.19–4	Balance C/D	10 000
31.12.19–4	Balance C/D	16 100	31.12.19–4	Profit and Loss	6 100
		16 100			16 100
			01.01.19–5	Balance B/D	16 100
			31.12.19–5	Profit and Loss	6 700
01.10.19–5	Vehicle Account depreciation on van 1	5 700			
31.12.19–5		17 100			
		22 800			22 800
			01.01.19–6	Balance B/D	17 100

Vehicles

01.01.19–1	Bank (purchase of van 1)	6 000			
01.07.19–1	Bank (purchase of car)	8 000	31.12.19–1	Balance C/D	14 000
		14 000			14 000
01.01.19–2	Balance B/D	14 000	31.12.19–2	Balance C/D	14 000
01.01.19–3	Balance B/D	14 000			
01.01.19–3	Creditors (purchase of van 2)	12 000	31.12.19–3	Balance C/D	26 000
		26 000			26 000
01.01.19–4	Balance B/D	26 000			
01.07.19–4	Bank (purchase of van 3)	9 000	31.12.19–4	Balance C/D	35 000
		35 000			35 000
01.01.19–5	Balance B/D	35 000	01.10.19–5	Provision for depreciation van 1	5 700

Step 3 Credit *Asset Account with proceeds of sale*

Vehicles

01.01.19–1	Bank (purchase of van 1)	6000			
01.07.19–1	Bank (purchase of car)	8000	31.12.19–1	Balance C/D	14000
		14000			14000
01.01.19–2	Balance B/D	14000	31.12.19–2	Balance C/D	14000
01.01.19–3	Balance B/D	14000			
01.01.19–3	Creditors (purchase of van 2)	12000	31.12.19–3	Balance C/D	26000
		26000			26000
01.01.19–4	Balance B/D	26000			
01.07.19–4	Bank (purchase of van 3)	9000	31.12.19–4	Balance C/D	35000
		35000			35000
01.01.19–5	Balance B/D	35000	01.10.19–5	Provision for depreciation van 1	5700
			01.10.19–5	Bank (van 1)	1900

Step 4 Calculate *profit or loss on sale and transfer the profit or loss on the sale to the Profit and Loss Account*

Calculation:	Sale proceeds		1900
	Cost of van 1	6000	
	Less: Depreciation provided	5700	
	Net book value		300
	Profit on sale		1600

Vehicles

01.01.19–1	Bank (purchase of van 1)	6000			
01.07.19–1	Bank (purchase of car)	8000	31.12.19–1	Balance C/D	14000
		14000			14000
01.01.19–2	Balance B/D	14000	31.12.19–2	Balance C/D	14000
01.01.19–3	Balance B/D	14000			
01.01.19–3	Creditors (purchase of van 2)	12000	31.12.19–3	Balance C/D	26000
		26000			26000
01.01.19–4	Balance B/D	26000			
01.07.19–4	Bank (purchase of van 3)	9000	31.12.19–4	Balance C/D	35000
		35000			35000
01.01.19–5	Balance B/D	35000	01.10.19–5	Provision for depreciation van 1	5700
			01.10.19–5	Bank (van 1)	1900
31.12.19–5	Profit and Loss (profit on sale of van 1)	1600	31.12.19–5	Balance C/D	29000
		36600			36600
01.01.19–6	Balance C/D	29000			

The examination way

In an examination question concerned with the sale of an asset, there would not be time to run through the full practical accounting procedure. Questions are therefore set in such a way as to test understanding without resorting to writing up all the accounts. The following is a typical example:

As at 31 December 19–3, the ledger of ABC Trading included the following accounts:

Vehicles	60 000
Provision for depreciation on vehicles	35 000

Depreciation on vehicles is at the rate of 20 per cent per annum on the straight line method and is calculated on a strict time basis.

During the year 19–4, the following transactions occurred:

July 01 Purchased a van for £11 000.
   01 Sold van for £3500. This van cost £9000 when bought on 01 January 19–1.
Oct 01 Part-exchanged a car which cost £12 000 when bought on 01 January 19–2. A part-exchange allowance of £5000 was made against a new car costing £13 500. The balance of the purchase price of £8500 was paid by cheque.

Open the Vehicles, Provision for Depreciation on Vehicles Account and Disposal of Assets Account and show the entries to reflect these transactions. Close the accounts as at 31.12.19–4.

Answer

1. Calculation of depreciation provided on disposals
   (a) Van sold 01.07.19–4
       £9000 × 20% × 3.5 years   = 6 300
   (b) Car part-exchanged 01.10.19–4
       £12 000 × 20% × 2.75 years   = 6 600
2. Calculation of profit/loss on disposals
   (a) Van sold for   3 500

Van cost	9 000	
Less: Depreciation provided	6 300	
Net book value		2 700
Profit on sale		800

   (b) Car part-exchanged for   5 000

Car cost	12 000	
Less: Depreciation provided	6 600	
Net book value		5 400
Loss on sale		400

3. Calculation of depreciation provision 19–4

01.01.19–4 Cost of vehicles		60 000
Less: Cost of vehicles disposed of		21 000
		39 000

Full year's depreciation £39 000 × 20%	=	7 000
Plus: Part depreciation for van sold:		
£9000 × 20% × 0.5 year	=	900
Plus: Part depreciation for car part-exchanged:		
£12 000 × 20% × 0.75 year	=	1 800
Plus: Part depreciation van bought 01.07.19–4:		
£11 000 × 20% × 0.5 year	=	1 100
Total provision 19–4		10 800

Vehicles

01.01.19–4	Balance B/D	60 000	01.07.19–4	Disposal of assets	9 000
			01.10.19–4	Disposal of assets	12 000
01.07.19–4	Bank (5)	11 000			
01.10.19–4	Purchased car:				
	Part exchange (6)	5 000			
	Bank (7)	8 500			
			31.12.19–4	Balance C/D	63 500
		84 500			84 500
01.01.19–5	Balance B/D	63 500			

Provision for Depreciation on Vehicles

01.07.19–4	Disposal of assets (2)	6 300	01.01.19–4	Balance B/D		35 000
01.10.19–4	Disposal of assets (3)	6 600	31.12.19–4	Profit and Loss A/c (1)		10 800
31.12.19–4	Balance C/D	32 900				
		45 800				45 800
			01.01.19–5	Balance B/D		32 900

Disposal of Assets Account

01.07.19–4	Vehicles	9 000	01.07.19–4	Prov for depreciation	6 300	(2)
01.10.19–4	Vehicles	12 000	01.10.19–4	Prov for depreciation	6 600	(3)
			01.01.19–4	Bank	3 500	(4)
			01.10.19–4	Vehicles:		
				Part-exchange allowance	5 000	(6)
01.07.19–4	P and L Account (8)	800	01.10.19–4	P & L account	400	(9)
	Profit on sale of van			Loss on disposal of car		
		21 800			21 800	

Notes:
(1)   Years' provision for depreciation as calculated.
(2) ⎫ Transferring calculated depreciation provided on the two vehicles disposed of to the
(3) ⎭ Disposal Account.
(4)   Sale proceeds of van.
(5)   Purchase of van.
(6)   Part-exchange is entered in the accounts to reflect the allowance made, *credit* Disposal Account and the equivalent
       cost of purchase represented by the allowance, *debit* Asset Account.
(7)   Payment of balance or purchase price of car after allowance.
(8)   Profit on sale of van as calculated transferred to the Profit and Loss Account.
(9)   Loss on car as calculated transferred to the Profit and Loss Account.

This might appear, after first reading, to be a rather daunting topic. However, once the basic principles are grasped, and the exercises completed, the practice of accounting for disposal of assets is relatively straightforward. Practice, as ever, is the key word.

The Journal

At this stage of our studies, we have become familiar with records which explain, in some detail, entries made in the actual accounts. These records are, of course, the books of *prime entry* such as the Sales Day Book, Purchases Day Book and the Cash Book. Entries in the books of prime entry give a fair amount of detail relating to those transactions entered in them and provide a valuable source of information back-tracking to see why a particular entry has been made in the actual accounts.

For example: let us take an entry in a debtor's account for a customer, P Parker:

P Parker

01.01.19–3	Balance B/D	2000			
			11.01.19–3	Bank	2000
18.02.19–3	Sales	600			

If we wanted to get more detail about the entry on 18 February, we could turn to the Sales Day Book entry on that date. Here we will find greater detail about the transaction including the invoice number. From this we could if we wished turn up the relevant copy of the invoice and see full, comprehensive details relating to the sale — what was sold, how many, at what price, etc.

There are, however, a combination of transactions, sometimes rather complex, which do not pass through any of the above books of prime entry. These pose a problem because at a later date, say on closing the accounts at the end of a year or explaining an entry to an auditor, it may not be readily apparent as to why a particular entry has been made. What we need therefore is a book of prime entry into which such transactions can be noted with an explanation of the reason for the entries. Such a record will not be part of the double-entry system. It will be a 'diary' which can be referred to at some later stage, should the need arise. This is precisely what the *Journal* is.

Before we look at the Journal in detail, let us consider some of the types of transactions which might appropriately be entered in it.

The following list is by no means exhaustive, but will give us a feel for the type of transactions involved:

1. Introduction of capital into the business.
2. Entries made in the accounts to correct previous errors.
3. Details of prepayments and accruals introduced.
4. Details of bad debts written off.
5. Details of provisions for doubtful debts.
6. Details of provisions for depreciation.
7. Detail of year end closing stock being written into the accounts after stocktaking.
8. Goods taken out of the business by the owner(s) for personal use or consumption.
9. Purchase of fixed assets.
10. Sale/disposal of fixed assets.

We will take two such transactions and look at how they might be entered in a Journal.

- 01.07.19–3 It is discovered that P Parker, who owes £600 (see above), has gone into bankruptcy and there is no possibility of recovering the debt.
- A motor vehicle which cost £8000 on 01 January 19–1 is sold on 30 September 19–3 for £3000. The vehicle has been depreciated at the rate of 20 per cent per annum.

Date	Detail	Ledger folio	Debit	Credit
19–3	Bad debts written off	NL 36	600	
	P Parker	SL 18		600
	Being writing off of debt after notification of bankruptcy			
	See letter dated			
	File reference			
30.09	Provision for depreciation on vehicles	NL 14	4400	
	Vehicles	NL 23		4400
	Being transfer to asset account of depreciation provided on vehicle sold 30.09.19–3			
	Bank	CB	3000	
	Vehicles	NL 23		3000
	Being proceeds from above sale			
	Profit and Loss Account	NL 52	600	
	Vehicles	NL 23		600
	Being loss on above sale			

Notes

(i) Note the layout of this Journal, which is a representative sample.

(ii) Note that by convention: the debit entry appears first; the description of the account to be credited is inset.

(iii) Note the use of the word 'Being' at the start of each notation.

(iv) Although they are not mandatory, if you follow this layout and the conventions used in this example, you will please any examiner.

(v) When posting this information in the ledger, the entries will be entered in the accounts as they appear in the Journal, e.g. bad debts account will be debited with £600 and P Parker credited with £600.

Exercises

1. You are to show the Journal entries necessary to record the following:

19–3

May 02 Bought a motor vehicle on credit from Carlton Garage for £6900.00.

  04 A debt of £34.00 owing from J Fears was written off as a bad debt.

  07 Office furniture bought by us for £490.00 was returned to the supplier J A Supplies as being faulty. Full allowance will be given us.

  12 We are owed £150.00 by N Noakes. He is declared bankrupt and we received £30.00 in full settlement of the debt.

  15 We take £20.00 goods out of the business stock without paying for them.

  26 We paid an insurance bill some time ago in the belief it was all in respect of the business. Now we discover that £100.00 of the amount paid was in fact insurance of our private house.

  29 Bought machinery £3400 on credit from Machinery Supplies Ltd.

2. You are to open the books of J Jacks by using the Journal to record the assets and liabilities, and are then to record the daily transactions for the month of March. A Trial Balance is to be extracted as on 31 March 19–3.

19–3

Mar 01	*Assets*: Premises £3900.00, Delivery van £450.00, Stock £1289.00, Fixtures £600.00. Debtors: B Brian £40.00, R Piers £180.00. Cash at bank £1741.00. Cash in hand £60.00. *Liabilities*: Creditors: M Meak £60.00, T Turner £200.00.
01	Paid rent by cheque £15.00.
03	Bought goods on credit from: T Turner £20.00, M Monk £56.00, D Drake £38.00.
04	Sold goods on credit to: R Piers £56.00, N Noon £78.00, B Brian £98.00.
06	Paid for motor expenses in cash £13.00.
08	Cash drawings by proprietor £30.00.
09	Sold goods on credit to: B Brian £220.00, N Noon £67.00.
12	Goods returned to J Jacks by R Piers £16.00, and B Brian £18.00.
14	Bought another delivery van on credit from Able Motors Ltd £900.00.
17	The following paid J Jacks by cheque less 5 per cent cash discount: B Brian, R Piers, K Drain, V Boon.
20	Goods returned by J Jacks to M Monk £9.00.
21	Goods bought on credit from D Drake £89.00; T Turner £72.00.
24	J Jacks settled the following accounts by cheque less 5 per cent cash discount: T Turner, M Monk.
28	Wages paid by cheque £150.00.
30	Paid rates by cheque £66.00.
30	Paid Able Motors Ltd a cheque for £900.00.

Note When dealing with the opening balances remember: capital = assets − liabilities.

3. P Regan is a trader for whom the following balances have been extracted from his books as at 30 September 19–4.

	£
Capital — P Regan, at 01 October 19–4	24 239
Office equipment	1 440
Drawings	4 888
Stock — 01 October 19–4	14 972
Purchases	167 760
Sales	203 845
Rent	1 350
Electricity	475
Insurances	304
Salaries	6 352
Stationery	737
Telephone	517
General expenses	2 044
Commissions paid	9 925
Discounts allowed	517
Discounts received	955
Bad debts written off	331
Debtors	19 100
Creditors	8 162
Balance at bank	6 603
Cash	29
Provision for doubtful debts	143

The following further information is to be taken into account:

(a) Stock at 30 September 19–4 was valued at £12 972.
(b) Provision is to be made for the following liabilities as at 30 September 19–4:
Rent £450; Electricity £136; Commission £806; Accountancy charges £252.
(c) Provision for doubtful debts is to be raised to 3 per cent of closing debtor balances.
(d) Office equipment is to be depreciated by 10 per cent on book value.
(e) Regan had taken stock costing £112 for his own use during the year.

You are to prepare:
A Trading and Profit and Loss Account for the year ended 30 September 19–4 and a Balance Sheet as at that date.

Unit 12

Manufacturing accounts

Direct and overhead costs

In our studies so far we have been accounting only for businesses which sell either a service they provide or goods which they buy in from elsewhere and resell. If we take this last situation as a model, then we can illustrate the position of a firm, let us call it ABC Trading, which trades in bought-in products:

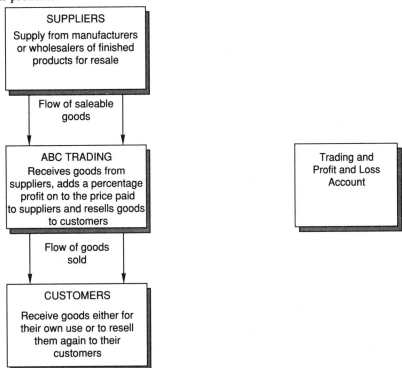

In this situation, ABC Trading will produce a Trading and Profit and Loss Account to show the gross profit from 'buying in' the goods and reselling them. All the stock the firm carries will comprise finished products ready for sale. If, say, ABC Trading trades in household furniture, then its stock might comprise tables, chairs, beds, settees, etc. Now let us suppose that the owners of ABC Trading decide that there is more profit to be made from actually making the furniture they sell. This is an entirely different type of business which will now have a manufacturing as well as a selling function. Let us look at an illustration of this arrangement:

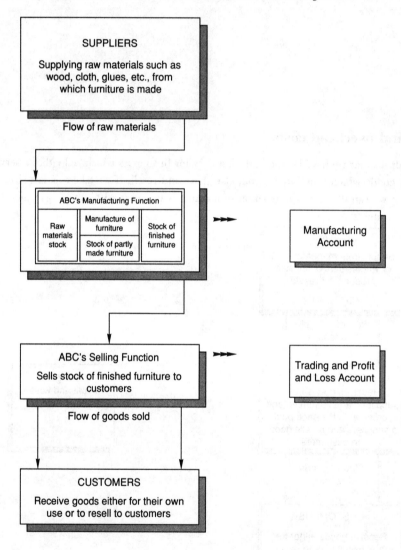

A number of important differences emerge for this firm engaged in manufacturing and selling as opposed to the original trading situation:

1. The management need to know what it is costing to produce the furniture in their own factory, if only to be satisfied that it is indeed a better alternative than 'buying in' finished furniture for resale.

2. Stocks take on a different perspective:

Stocks

Trading only	Manufacturing and selling
Finished products	Raw materials Partly made products (work in progress) Finished products

3. The cost of goods sold will now be the cost of manufacturing the products sold rather than buying them in to resell.

To cater for these new arrangements, we have a different format of final accounts. First, the bad news. We now have to produce a Manufacturing Account as well as a Trading, Profit and Loss Account and Balance Sheet.

Now, the good news. The Trading, Profit and Loss Account and Balance Sheet are substantially unaltered in form from the layout with which we are familiar. The only differences are that Purchases in the Trading Account now becomes 'Cost of manufactured goods' and, in the Balance Sheet, Stock, under Current assets, includes raw materials and work-in-progress.

Let us now look in detail at this 'new' account — the Manufacturing Account.

The Manufacturing Account

If we refer back to our simple illustration of ABC's manufacturing function then the Manufacturing Account is essentially an account of all the costs incurred within this function in making the finished products to be sold by the selling function.

The cost incurred in making a product can broadly be put into one of four categories:

1. Direct materials
2. Direct labour
3. Direct expenses
4. Manufacturing overheads.

Direct materials

These are the raw materials and components that go into making up the finished product. In the case of our furniture manufacturers, they will be able to identify the type, quality and cost of timber used in making a particular frame for a chair, a settee or a table, as they will the cost of cloth used to cover a settee. Conversely, if the manufacturer stopped making a particular product, say a certain type of table, then the materials and components no longer used would have been the direct materials of the particular table now discontinued.

Direct labour

This is the wages of employees *directly* employed in making products. For example, the direct labour cost of making a settee might be the wages cost of the operatives who cut the timber and construct the frame, insert the springs, cut the cloth, and upholster the frame and fit the castors. The wages of the factory supervisors, storekeepers, maintenance staff and cleaners *are not direct costs*. These wages costs cannot be wholly associated with a particular product and, in effect, have to be spread across the whole range of products made. For this reason, they are part of the manufacturing overheads.

Direct expenses

These are costs, other than direct materials and direct labour, which can be directly attributed to a particular product. Another way to identify these costs is to ask 'would this cost disappear if this product was not being made?' Think of the table our furniture manufacturer decided to discontinue. Let us assume that the table was being made in the factory, but was then being sent out to a specialist firm for high quality french polishing. Obviously, when the table is discontinued, the cost of the french polishing will cease. The cost of this service was therefore a direct expense of making that particular table.

Manufacturing overheads

We have seen that costs which can be directly associated with a particular product are direct costs. The opposite of direct is indirect, therefore any cost which cannot be identified as a direct cost is an *indirect cost*. It is helpful to understand and be familiar with this term, as it is often used to describe costs which are not direct costs. However, the more usual description of these types of costs is *overheads*.

Manufacturing overheads might therefore include: wages of storekeepers, supervisors, cleaners, cleaning materials, maintenance and depreciation of plant and equipment and expenses of providing the factory such as rent and rates, heating, electricity, maintenance and repair of the building, etc.

Taking as an example the table we have already examined, the following illustration should help summarize and consolidate the points we have covered:

Simple illustration of a 'cost flow' for a manufacturer making three products

Activity	Tables	Chairs	Settees	Total
1. Wages of storekeeper issuing materials	▼	Spread over	▲	Overhead
2. Materials used in making products	Timber, hinges, screws, etc.	Timber, padding, cloth, etc.	Timber, springs, padding, cloth	Direct materials
3. Wages of production operatives	Engaged in making tables	Engaged in making chairs	Engaged in making settees	Direct labour
4. Contracted out french polishing	French polishing	N/A	N/A	Direct expenses
5. Wages of factory supervisors	▼	Spread over	▲	Overheads
6. Wages of inspectors checking all products	▼	Spread over	▲	Overheads
7. Factory costs:				
Plant maintenance and depreciation				
Electricity				
Rent and rates	▼	Spread over	▲	Overhead
Heating				
Cleaning				
Repairs and maintenance to building				
Consumables				
Total manufacturing costs				xxxxx

165

We can summarize the illustration as:

	Tables	Chairs	Settees	Total costs
Direct materials	xxx	xxx	xxx	xxx
Direct labour	xxx	xxx	xxx	xxx
Direct expenses	xxx			xxx
Total direct/prime costs (1)	xxx	xxx	xxx	xxx
Overheads	————————————————————————→			xxx
Total manufacturing costs				xxx

Note
(1) Total direct costs are more commonly known as prime costs.

In the Manufacturing Account which we will shortly be constructing we will only be concerned with the costs appearing in the Total column. We will not be attempting to identify the total costs of individual product groups.

'Why then have we been looking at cost flows across products?' we might ask. We have done so for three reasons:

1. Doing so leads to a better overall understanding.
2. In practice, the type of Manufacturing Account we are looking at is not used nearly as much as it used to be. In fact some would say it is fast becoming an accounting relic. However, it does still appear in assignments and is a quite popular examination topic.
3. It is a useful lead into further studies.

The last point is most important and warrants further explanation. This section of the book has been concerned with financial accounting and in later sections we will be studying cost and management accounting and the use of financial information in decision making. A good understanding of Manufacturing Accounts forms a useful, if not vital, bridge between those areas of study. Time spent now on grasping the fundamentals will be well rewarded later.

To satisfy ourselves on this point, it is useful to understand that many of our later studies will be concerned with trying to ascertain total costs for products or product groups. We will be concerned with identifying direct costs of particular products and then applying techniques for 'sharing out' overheads to individual products. This 'sharing out' process is technically called apportioning overheads. We can summarize this objective using our previous example as:

Products

	Tables	Chairs	Settees	Total costs
Direct materials	xxx	xxx	xxx	xxx
Direct labour	xxx	xxx	xxx	xxx
Direct expenses	xxx			xxx
Total direct/prime costs	xxx	xxx	xxx	xxx
Overheads	Apportioned	Apportioned	Apportioned	xxx
Total costs	xxx	xxx	xxx	xxx

Whether overheads should be apportioned and the techniques used in apportioning comprise quite an involved area of study. We will be dealing with these issues in later sections of this book but now we will return to our Manufacturing Account which deals only with total costs.

Different stocks

Now we are introducing a Manufacturing Account into our 'final accounts'. We will have to deal with three different types of stock:

1. Direct materials (raw materials and components used in manufacture).
2. Work-in-progress (stock of partly made products).
3. Finished products (products ready to be sold).

The adjustments to be made for opening and closing stocks appear in the accounts and Balance Sheet as follows:

Direct materials

Opening stock	xxx	
Plus: Purchases	xxx	
	xxx	
Less: Closing stock	(xxx)	
	xxx	Manufacturing Account

Work-in-progress

Opening stock	xxx	
Plus: Total manufacturing costs	xxx	
	xxx	
Less: Closing stock	(xxx)	
= Cost of completed production	xxx	Manufacturing Account

Finished goods

Opening stock	xxx	
Plus: Cost of completed production	xxx	
	xxx	
Less: Closing stock	(xxx)	
= Cost of goods sold	xxx	Trading Account

Balance Sheet

All three closing stocks are assets which must appear in the Balance Sheet. Therefore, under Current assets, we might either list the three types of stock with their values or add them together and just put one description — Stocks.

Constructing the Manufacturing Account

Now we have looked at the different categories of costs and stocks we can now look to constructing the Manufacturing Account. The account basically breaks down into three distinct parts:

Part 1	*Direct materials*		
	Opening stock	xxx	
	Plus: Purchases	xxx	
		xxx	
	Less: Closing stock (1)	(xxx)	xxx
	Direct labour		xxx
	Direct expenses		xxx
	PRIME COSTS		xxx
Part 2	*Manufacturing overheads* (say)		
	Supervisors' salaries	xxx	
	Electricity	xxx	
	Premises costs	xxx	
	Depreciation of plant	xxx	xxx
	MANUFACTURING COSTS		xxx
Part 3	*Add*: Work-in-progress (opening):		xxx
			xxx
	Less: Work-in-progress (closing) (1)		(xxx)
	COST OF COMPLETED PRODUCTION (2)		xxx

Notes
(1) These two stocks, together with the stock of finished goods taken from the Trading Account, will appear as Current assets in the Balance Sheet.
(2) The cost of completed production is transferred to the Trading Account. (It becomes the equivalent of purchases of a business which trades in bought-in saleable goods.)

Once we have grasped this structure, then the system of compiling the Manufacturing Account is really no different to the compilation of a Trading and Profit and Loss Account, with which we are familiar.

We will now work through a construction and this time will use the letter M to denote those accounts in the Trial Balance destined for the Manufacturing Account.

Trial Balance 31 December 19–3

	Debit	Credit	Destination
Capital		100 000	B
Plant and equipment	80 000		B
Vehicles	12 000		B
Direct wages	90 000 (4)		M
Purchases of direct materials	30 000 (2)		M
Provision for depreciation:			
Plant and machinery		16 000	B
Vehicles		4 000	B
Factory supervisors' salaries	24 000 (6)		M
Sales staff salaries	28 000		P
Administration staff salaries	19 000		P
Electricity			
Offices	500		P
Factory	3 000 (7)		M
Bank	2 500		B
Debtors	8 000		B
Creditors		11 000	B
Rent			
Factory	20 000 (8)		M
Offices	5 000		P
French polishing of tables	8 000 (5)		M
Stocks 01 January 19–3:			
Raw materials and components	26 000 (1)		M
Work-in-progress	7 000 (10)		M
Finished products	38 000 (12)		T
Sales		270 000	T
	401 000	401 000	

Further information:

1. Stocks 31 December 19–3   £
   Raw materials and components   (3)   24 000
   Work-in-progress   (11)   9 000
   Finished goods   (13)   34 000
2. Depreciation to be provided is:
   Plant and equipment   (9)   8 000
   Vehicles   (14)   2 000

Note The notation numbers in brackets can be traced through in the following accounts.

Manufacturing, Trading and Profit and Loss Account year ended 31 December 19–3

Direct materials			
Opening stock (1)	26 000		
Purchases (2)	30 000	56 000	
Less: Closing stock (3)		24 000	32 000
Direct wages (4)			90 000
French polishing (5)			8 000
PRIME COSTS			130 000
Factory overheads			
Supervisors' salaries (6)		24 000	
Electricity (7)		3 000	
Rent (8)		20 000	
Depreciation, plant and equipment (9)		8 000	55 000
MANUFACTURING COSTS			185 000
Add: Opening work-in-progress (10)			7 000
			192 000
Less: Closing work-in-progress (11)			9 000
COST OF COMPLETED PRODUCTION			183 000*

* (Carried down to Trading Account)

Sales		270 000
Finished goods:		
Opening stock	38 000 (12)	
Cost of completed production	183 000	
	221 000	
Less: Closing stock	34 000 (13)	
Cost of goods sold		187 000
Gross profit		83 000
Sales staff salaries	28 000	
Administration staff salaries	19 000	
Electricity	500	
Office rent	5 000	
Depreciation of vehicles	2 000 (14)	54 500
Net profit		28 500

Balance Sheet as at 31 December 19–3

Fixed assets:	Cost	Depreciation	NBV
Plant and equipment	80 000	24 000	56 000
Vehicles	12 000	6 000	6 000
	92 000	30 000	62 000

Current assets:			
Stocks:			
Raw materials	24 000		
Work-in-progress	9 000		
Finished products	34 000	67 000	
Debtors		8 000	
Bank		2 500	
		77 500	
Less: Current liabilities			
Creditors		11 000	
Working capital			66 500
Net assets			128 500

Financed by:			
Capital 01 January 19–3	100 000		
Profit for year	28 500		128 500

Note For demonstration purposes, the stocks have been listed separately but they could be added
together and shown as one figure for Stocks.

Exercises

1. Prepare Manufacturing, Trading and Profit and Loss Accounts for the following balances of E Hewitt for the year ended 31 December 19–3:

	£
Stocks at 01 January	
Raw materials	18 400
Work-in-progress	23 600
Finished goods	17 470
Purchases	
Raw materials	64 300
Carriage on raw materials	1 605
Direct labour	65 810
Office salaries	16 920
Rent	2 700
Office lighting and heating	5 760
Depreciation	
Works machinery	8 300
Office equipment	1 950
Sales	200 300
Factory fuel and power	5 920

Rent is to be apportioned
   Factory two-thirds
   Office one-third
Stocks at 31 December 19–3 were:
   Raw materials £20 210
   Work-in-progress £17 300
   Finished goods £21 000

2. A Smith is a sole trader who commenced business on 01 September 19–2 manufacturing three types of products. The following balances were extracted from his Trial Balance at 31 August 19–3:

	£	£
Purchases of raw materials	280 000	
Returns	1 000	4 000
Carriage in	2 000	
Selling and distribution costs	20 000	
Rent	15 000	
Royalties	12 000	
Indirect factory labour	24 000	
Direct labour	125 000	
Administrative costs	35 000	
Sales		540 000
General factory expenses	15 000	
Plant and machinery at cost	140 000	
Delivery vans at cost	10 000	

The following information is also available:
(a) Rent was paid until the end of November 19–3 and was to be apportioned between the factory and general administration on the basis of 2 : 1.

(b) Selling and distribution costs of £8000 were accrued on 31 August 19–3.

(c) Plant and machinery are depreciated by 20 per cent per annum on cost and delivery vans are to be depreciated by 30 per cent per annum on cost.

(d) The stock of raw materials at 31 August 19–3 was valued at £40 000.

Required:

(i) Given that finished goods stock at 31 August 19–3 is valued at £145 000, complete Manufacturing, Trading and Profit and Loss Accounts for the year ended 31 August.

(ii) Explain to G Smith the difficulties involved in calculating a separate cost of sales figure for each of the three products produced.

Note You are to assume that royalties are based on production.

Unit 13

Consolidation — accounting 1

Much as we have tried to avoid it, the study of bookkeeping and accountancy tends in places to deal with particular fragments of the subject. Arguably, total understanding is only achieved when all the pieces of the 'jigsaw' are slotted together and the relevance of each fragment within the whole can be properly judged.

In an attempt to do just that, we are now going to embark on two fully worked case studies where we will hope to cover many of the topics we have studied so far. Do try to follow every part of the processes. The degree to which our knowledge will be consolidated will be well worth the effort.

Case Study: Minicabs

In this study, we are dealing with a newly formed business. The proprietor, Mr Jackson, has kept detailed records which provide full, detailed summaries of the first year's trading. From these, we are to carry out the following tasks.

Task	Summary	Requirement
1	Details of 'special' transactions	Journal, Accounts and Cash Book
2	Fares charged	Accounts and Cash Book
3	Cash banked	Accounts and Cash Book
4	Cheque payments	Accounts and Cash Book
5	Year-end adjustments	Journal and Accounts
6		Balancing all Accounts
7		Prepare Trial Balance
8		Destination Notations to Trial Balance
9		Prepare Profit and Loss Account
10		Prepare Balance Sheet

Task 1 Special transactions

Date	Transaction
01.01.19–3	Proprietor Mr J Jackson introduced capital of £46000 in the form of £40000 paid into the Minicab Bank Account and a car valued at £6000.
06.01.19–3	Purchased office equipment and communications system £2800 by cheque.
31.01.19–3	Paid local painters and decorators £1200 by cheque for painting of business premises.
01.02.19–3	Bought two second-hand vehicles for use as cabs £17000 by cheque.
01.02.19–3	Paid a year's insurance premiums in advance by cheque £2400 (premium cover for the period 01.02.19–3 – 31.01.19–4).
01.07.19–3	Traded in the car Mr Jackson brought into the business for £4500 against a new car costing £11500. The balance was paid by cheque.

Task

2	Fares charged	
	Cash customers (cash banked)	48000
	Credit customers	21000
	Total fares charged	69000

3	Cash banked	
	Receipts from debtors	18000
	Insurance claim for damage to vehicle	400

4	Cheque payments	
	J Jackson — drawings	10500
	Wages of drivers	19200
	Garage bills for repairs and maintenance	1800
	Garage bills for petrol and oil	9360
	Heating and lighting of office	1200
	Telephone	600
	Cab licence fees	270
	Road fund licence for cars	400

5 Year-end adjustments
(a) Unpaid bills at end of year

	Garage bill for petrol and oil	460
	Electricity bill (heating and lighting)	180

(b) Payments in advance

	Rent paid on 31.12.19–3 in advance for the period 01.01.19–4 – 31.03.19–4	900

(c) Vehicles to be depreciated at $33\frac{1}{3}$ per cent in a straight line basis
(d) Mr Jackson feels that one debt of £200, owed by A Archer, may prove to be uncollectable

Minicabs
Journal

Date	Detail	Ledger folio	Debit	Credit
01.01.19–3	Bank J Jackson — Capital Account Being introduction of capital by proprietor		40 000	40 000
01.01.19–3	Vehicles J Jackson — Capital Account Being car introduced by proprietor		6 000	6 000
06.01.19–3	Office equipment Bank Being purchase of office and communications equipment		2 800	2 800
31.01.19–3	Building maintenance Bank Being cost of painting premises		1 200	1 200
01.02.19–3	Vehicles Bank Being purchase of two vehicles		17 000	17 000
01.02.19–3	Insurances Bank Being insurance premiums on cars from the start of trading on 01.02.19–3 for a year in advance		2 400	2 400
01.07.19–3	Provision for depreciation on vehicles Vehicles Being depreciation provided on car disposed of (£6000 × 20% × 0.5)		1 000	1 000
	Vehicles Vehicles Being part exchange allowance on above vehicle — contra entry in account to show dual effect of allowance received and use of allowance in purchase		4 500	4 500
	Profit and Loss Account Vehicles Being loss on disposal of car		500	500
	Vehicles Bank Being balance of purchase price of new car		7 000	7 000

Note

'Cost' of vehicle		6 000
Less: Depreciation	1 000	
Allowance	4 500	5 500
Loss		500

J Jackson — Capital Account

		Bank	40 000
		Vehicles	6 000

Office Equipment

Bank	2 800		

Building Maintenance

Bank	1 200		

Vehicles

Capital	6 000	Prov for dep'n	1 000
Bank	17 000	Part ex allce	4 500
Part ex allce	4 500	Loss on disposal	500
Bank	7 000		

Insurances

Bank	2 400		

Provision for Depreciation on Vehicles

Vehicles	1 000		

Profit and Loss

Vehicles			
Loss on sale	500		

Minicabs
Summary Cash Book

19–3	Detail	Cash	Bank	19–3	Detail	Cash	Bank
01.01	Capital		40 000				
				06.01	Office equipment		2 800
				31.01	Building maintenance		1 200
				01.02	Vehicles		17 000
				01.02	Insurances		2 400
				01.07	Vehicles		7 000

Task 2 Fares charged

J Jackson — Capital Account

| | | Bank | 40 000 |
| | | Vehicles | 6 000 |

Office Equipment

Bank	2 800	

Building Maintenance

Bank	1 200	

Vehicles

Capital	6 000	Prov for dep'n	1 000
Bank	17 000	Part ex allce	4 500
Part ex allce	4 500	Loss on disposal	500
Bank	7 000		

Insurances

Bank	2 400	

Provision for Depreciation on Vehicles

Vehicles	1 000	

Fares

| | Cash | 48 000 |
| | Debtors | 21 000 |

Debtors

Fares	21 000	

Profit and Loss

| Vehicles | | |
| Loss on sale | 500 | |

Minicabs
Summary Cash Book

19–3	Detail	Cash	Bank	19–3	Detail	Cash	Bank
01.01	Capital		40 000				
				06.01	Office equipment		2 800
				31.01	Building maintenance		1 200
				01.02	Vehicles		17 000
				01.02	Insurances		2 400
				01.07	Vehicles		7 000
	Fares (cash)		48 000				

Task 3 Cash banked

J Jackson — Capital Account

		Bank	40 000
		Vehicles	6 000

Office Equipment

Bank	2 800		

Building Maintenance

Bank	1 200		

Vehicles

Capital	6 000	Prov for dep'n	1 000
Bank	17 000	Part ex allce	4 500
Part ex allce	4 500	Loss on disposal	500
Bank	7 000		

Insurances

Bank	2 400		

Provision for Depreciation on Vehicles

Vehicles	1 000		

Fares

		Cash	48 000
		Debtors	21 000

Debtors

Fares	21 000	Bank	18 000

Vehicle Running Costs

		Insurance claim	400

Profit and Loss

Vehicles Loss on sale	500		

Minicabs
Summary Cash Book

19–3	Detail	Cash	Bank	19–3	Detail	Cash	Bank
01.01	Capital		40 000				
				06.01	Office equipment		2 800
				31.01	Building maintenance		1 200
				01.02	Vehicles		17 000
				01.02	Insurances		2 400
				01.07	Vehicles		7 000
	Fares (cash)		48 000				
	Debtors		18 000				
	Insurance claim		400				

Task 4 Cheque payments

J Jackson — Capital Account

		Bank	40 000
		Vehicles	6 000

Office Equipment

Bank	2 800	

Building Maintenance

Bank	1 200	

Vehicles

Capital	6 000	Prov for dep'n	1 000
Bank	17 000	Part ex allce	4 500
Part ex allce	4 500	Loss on disposal	500
Bank	7 000		

Insurances

Bank	2 400	

Provision for Depreciation on Vehicles

Vehicles	1 000	

Fares

		Cash	48 000
		Debtors	21 000

Debtors

Fares	21 000	Bank	18 000

Vehicle Running Costs

Bank	1 800	Insurance claim	400
Bank	9 360		
Bank	400		

Drawings

Bank	10 500	

Wages

Bank	19 200	

Heating and Lighting

Bank	1 200	

Telephone

Bank	600	

Cab Licence Fees

Bank	270	

Rent

Bank	4 500	

Profit and Loss

Vehicles		
Loss on sale	500	

Minicabs
Summary Cash Book

19–3	Detail	Cash	Bank	19–3	Detail	Cash	Bank
01.01	Capital		40 000				
				06.01	Office equipment		2 800
				31.01	Building maintenance		1 200
				01.02	Vehicles		17 000
				01.02	Insurances		2 400
				01.07	Vehicles		7 000
	Fares (cash)		48 000				
	Debtors		18 000				
	Insurance claim		400				
					J Jackson — Drawings		10 500
					Wages		19 200
					Vehicle running costs		1 800
					Vehicle running costs		9 360
					Heating and lighting		1 200
					Telephone		600
					Cab licence fees		270
					Vehicle running costs		400
					Road Fund licence		
					Rent		4 500

Task 5 Year-end adjustments

Journal

Date	Detail	Ledger folio	Debit	Credit
31.12.19–3	Vehicle running costs Vehicle running costs Being accrued expense for unpaid garage account at 31.12.19–3		460	460
31.12.19–3	Heating and lighting Heating and lighting Being accrued expenses for unpaid electricity account at 31.12.19–3		180	180
31.12.19–3	Rent Rent Being rent prepaid for the period 01.01.19–4 to 31.03.19–4		900	900
31.12.19–3	Profit and Loss Account Provision for depreciation on vehicles Being depreciation provided on vehicles *Note* Calculated as: Car £6 000 × 33.3% × 6 months = £1 000 Cars £17 000 × 33.3% × 11 months = £5 190 Car £11 500 × 33.3% × 6 months = £1 915 £8 105		8 105	8 105
31.12.19–3	Profit and Loss Account Provision for doubtful debts Being provision for a doubtful debt owed by A Archer		200	200

J Jackson — Capital Account

		Bank	40 000
		Car	6 000

Office Equipment

Bank	2 800	

Building Maintenance

Bank	1 200	

Vehicles

Capital	6 000	Prov for dep'n	1 000
Bank	17 000	Part ex allce	4 500
Part ex allce	4 500	Loss on disposal	500
Bank	7 000		

Insurances

Bank	2 400	

Provision for Depreciation on Vehicles

Vehicles	1 000	Profit and Loss	8 105

Fares

	Cash	48 000
	Debtors	21 000

Debtors

Fares	21 000	Bank	18 000

Vehicle Running Costs

Bank	1 800	Insurance claim	400
Bank	9 360		
Bank	400		
Accrued expense	460	Accrued expense	460

Drawings

Bank	10 500	

Wages

Bank	19 200	

Heating and Lighting

Bank	1 200		
Accrued expense	180	Accrued expense	180

Telephone

Bank	600	

Cab Licence Fees

Bank	270	

Rent

Bank	4 500	Prepayment	900
Prepayment	900		

Provision for Doubtful Debts

	Profit and Loss	200

Profit and Loss Account

Vehicles	
Loss on sale	500
Prov for dep'n on	
vehicles	8 105
Prov for doubtful debts	200

Task 6 Balancing accounts

J Jackson — Capital Account

Balance B/D	46 000	Bank	40 000
		Car	6 000
	46 000		46 000
		Balance B/D	46 000

Office Equipment

Bank	2 800

Building Maintenance

Bank	1 200

Vehicles

Capital	6 000	Prov for dep'n	1 000
Bank	17 000	Part ex allce	4 500
Part ex allce	4 500	Loss on disposal	500
Bank	7 000	Balance C/D	28 500
	34 500		34 500
Balance B/D	28 500		

Insurances

Bank	2 400

Provision for Depreciation on Vehicles

Vehicles	1 000	Profit and Loss	8 105
Balance C/D	7 105		
	8 105		8 105
		Balance B/D	7 105

Fares

Balance C/D	69 000	Cash	48 000
		Debtors	21 000
	69 000		69 000
		Balance B/D	69 000

Debtors

Fares	21 000	Bank	18 000
		Balance C/D	3 000
	21 000		21 000
Balance B/D	3 000		

Vehicle Running Costs

Bank	1 800	Insurance claim	400
Bank	9 360		
Bank	400		
Accrued expense	460	Balance C/D	11 620
	12 020		12 020
Balance B/D	11 620	Accrued expense	460

Drawings

Bank	10 500

Wages

Bank	19 200		

Heating and Lighting

Bank	1 200		
Accrued expense	180	Balance C/D	1 380
	1 380		1 380
Balance B/D	1 380	Accrued expense	180

Telephone

Bank	600		

Cab Licence Fees

Bank	270		

Rent

Bank	4 500	Prepayment	900
		Balance C/D	3 600
	4 500		4 500
Balance B/D	3 600		
Prepayment	900		

Profit and Loss Account

Vehicles:		These items are listed in the	
Loss or sale	500	Trial Balance	
Prov for dep'n on vehicles	8 105		
Prov for doubtful debts	200		

Provision for Doubtful Debts

		Profit and Loss	200

Note   In practice, the Income and Expense Accounts would be balanced by transfers to the Profit and Loss Account. For demonstration purposes, the balances on these accounts are being carried direct to the Trial Balance.

Minicabs
Summary Cash Book

19–3	Detail	Cash	Bank	19–3	Detail	Cash	Bank
01.01	Capital		40 000				
	Fares (cash)		48 000	06.01	Office equipment		2 800
	Debtors		18 000	31.01	Building maintenance		1 200
	Insurance claim		400	01.02	Vehicles		17 000
				01.02	Insurances		2 400
				01.07	Vehicles		7 000
					J Jackson — Drawings		10 500
					Wages		19 200
					Vehicle running costs		1 800
					Vehicle running costs		9 360
					Heating and lighting		1 200
					Telephone		600
					Cab licence fees		270
					Vehicle running costs		400
					Road Fund licences		
					Rent		4 500
				31.12	Balance C/D		28 170
			106 400				106 400
	Balance B/D		28 170				

Task 7 Trial Balance

Minicabs

Trial Balance as at 31 December 19–3

		Debit	Credit
Capital			46 000
Office equipment		2 800	
Building maintenance		1 200	
Vehicles		28 500	
Insurances		2 400	
Provision for depreciation on vehicles			7 105
Fares			69 000
Debtors		3 000	
Vehicle running costs		11 620	
Drawings		10 500	
Wages		19 200	
Heating and lighting		1 380	
Telephone		600	
Cab licence fees		270	
Rent		3 600	
Loss on sale of vehicle		500	
Depreciation on vehicles		8 105	
Provision for doubtful debts		200	
Bank		28 170	
Accrued expenses:			
Vehicle running costs	460		
Heating and lighting	180		640
Prepayment			
Rent		900	
Provision for doubtful debts			200
		122 945	122 945

Task 8 Destination notations to Trial Balance

Minicabs
Trial Balance as at 31 December 19–3

	Debit	Credit	Destination
Capital		46000	B
Office equipment	2800		B
Building maintenance	1200		P
Vehicles	28500		B
Insurances	2400		P
Provision for depreciation on vehicles		7105	B
Fares		69000	P
Debtors	3000		B
Vehicle running costs	11620		P
Drawings	10500		B
Wages	19200		P
Heating and lighting	1380		P
Telephone	600		P
Cab licence fees	270		P
Rent	3600		P
Loss on sale of vehicle	500		P
Depreciation on vehicles	8105		P
Provision for doubtful debts	200		P
Bank	28170		B
Accrued expenses			
Vehicle running costs	460		
Heating and lighting	180	640	B
Prepayment			
Rent	900		B
Provision for doubtful debts		200	B
	122945	122945	

Task 9 Prepare Profit and Loss Account

Minicabs
Profit and Loss Account for the year ended 31 December 19–3

Fares		69 000
Less: Expenses		
Wages	19 200	
Vehicle running costs	11 620	
Depreciation of vehicles	8 105	
Building maintenance	1 200	
Insurances	2 400	
Heating and lighting	1 380	
Telephone	600	
Cab licence fee	270	
Rent	3 600	
Loss on sale of vehicle	500	
Provision for doubtful debts	200	49 075
Net profit		19 925

Task 10 Prepare Balance Sheet

Minicabs
Balance Sheet as at 31 December 19–3

Fixed assets	Cost	Depreciation provided	Net value
Vehicles	28 500	7 105	21 395
Office equipment	2 800	–	2 800
	31 300	7 105	24 195
Current assets			
Debtors	3 000		
Less: Provision for doubtful debt	200	2 800	
Prepayment		900	
Bank		28 170	
		31 870	
Less: Current liabilities			
Accrued expenses		640	
Working capital			31 230
Net assets			55 425
Financed by:			
Capital 01.01.19–3		46 000	
Profit for year		19 925	
		65 925	
Less: Drawings		10 500	
Capital 31.12.19–3			55 425

Case Study: Beta Trading

The following balances have been extracted from the books of Beta Trading as at 01 December 19–4:

	£
Sales on credit	180 000
Purchases on credit	90 000
Returns inwards	4 000
Returns outwards	2 000
Vehicles	20 000
Salaries and wages	30 000
Stock 01.01.19–4	12 000
Heating and lighting	3 000
Vehicle running costs	16 000
Freehold property	100 000
Carriage inwards	2 000
Carriage outwards	4 000
Provisions for depreciation	
Vehicles	8 000
Fixtures and fittings	4 000
Fixtures and fittings	20 000
Long-term bank loan	10 000
Interest on bank loan	1 000
Capital	127 000
Drawings	25 000
Discounts received	2 000
Bank overdraft	6 000
Sales Ledger control	26 000
Purchase Ledger control	14 000

Task 1 Correct errors

The following errors are known about:

- During the month of August 19–4, the Sales Day Book was totalled incorrectly to £15 000. The correct total should have been £14 000.
- Suppliers' accounts for heating oil, totalling £2000, have been charged into Vehicle running costs.

Requirement

1. Write a *brief* account, explaining what corrective action is to be taken for each error and why.
2. Write journal entries to correct the errors.
3. Show (with workings) what the totals of the Sales and Purchase Ledger Control Accounts were *before* the amendments were made.
4. Produce a Trial Balance *after* the corrections have been made.

Task 1 answers

1. The Sales Account and the Sales Ledger Control Account are both posted from the totals of the Sales Day Book and are therefore both overstated by £1000. Reduce Sales by debiting Sales and reduce the Sales Ledger Control Account by crediting £1000.
2. Someone has associated 'oil' with vehicles. The oil in question is, in fact, for heating purposes. Reduce Vehicle running costs by crediting £2000 and increase Heating and lighting by debiting £2000.

Date	Journal Detail	Folio	Debit	Credit
31.12.19–4	Sales		1000	
	Sales Ledger Control			1000
	Being correction of error in totalling the Sales Day Book for August 19–4			
31.12.19–4	Heating and lighting		2000	
	Vehicle running costs			2000
	Being correction of error in posting charge for heating oil			

3. Sales Ledger Control (per list of balances)   26 000
   Less overstatement of August 19–4 total taken from the Sales Day Book   1 000
   Total of Sales Ledger balances   25 000

4.

Beta Trading
Trial Balance as at 31 December 19–4

Sales on credit		179 000
Purchases on credit	90 000	
Returns inwards	4 000	
Returns outwards		2 000
Vehicles	20 000	
Salaries and wages	30 000	
Stock 01.01.19–4	12 000	
Heating and lighting	5 000	
Vehicles running costs	14 000	
Freehold property	100 000	
Carriage inwards	2 000	
Carriage outwards	4 000	
Provision for depreciation		
Vehicles		8 000
Fixtures and fittings		4 000
Fixtures and fittings	20 000	
Long-term bank loan		10 000
Interest on bank loan	1 000	
Capital		127 000
Drawings	25 000	
Discounts received		2 000
Bank overdraft		6 000
Sales Ledger Control Account	25 000	
Purchase Ledger Control Account		14 000
	352 000	352 000

Task 2 Extended Trial Balance

Draw up an extended Trial Balance with adjustment columns to show the effect of the following year and adjustments:

1. Depreciation (straight line) is to be provided as follows:
   (a) Vehicles 20 per cent
   (b) Fixtures and fittings 10 per cent
2. Unpaid bills are:
   (a) Electricity   £1 000
   (b) Garage — fuel and oils   £2 000
3. £2000 worth of the Stock at 01.01.19–4 was deemed to be obsolete and dumped. No entries have been made to reflect this action.
4. A vehicle costing £4000 on 01.01.19–2 was disposed of on 30.06.19–4 for £1000. No entries have been made for this transaction, the proprietor having taken the £1000 cash for his own use.
5. A provision for doubtful debts of £2000 is to be created.
6. Stock at 31.12.19–4 was £9000.

The extended Trial Balance should also have completed columns for the Trading and Profit and Loss Account and Balance Sheet.

Task 2 answer

Workings

1. Depreciation provisions:

(a) Vehicles: cost of all vehicles		20 000
Less: Cost of vehicle sold		4 000
Cost of remaining vehicles		16 000
Depreciation:		
£16 000 × 20%		3 200
£4000 × 20% × 0.5 (6 months)		400
		3 600
(b) Fixtures and fittings:		
£20 000 × 10%		2 000

2. Profit/Loss on sale of vehicle:

Proceeds of sale		1 000
Cost of vehicle sold	4 000	
Less: Depreciation:		
£4000 × 20% × 2.5 years	2 000	
Book value		2 000
Loss on sale		1 000

Beta Trading
Extended Trial Balance

Ledger Balances	Trial Balance		Adjustments		Profit and Loss		Balance Sheet	
	DR	CR	DR	CR	DR	CR	DR	CR
Sales		179 000				179 000		
Purchases	90 000				90 000			
Returns inwards	4 000				4 000			
Returns outwards		2 000				2 000		
Vehicles	20 000			1 000 (4) 2 000 (4) 1 000 (4)			16 000	
Salaries and wages	30 000				30 000			
Stock 01.01.19–4	12 000			2 000 (3)	10 000			
Heating and lighting	5 000		1 000 (2)		6 000			
Vehicle running costs	14 000		2 000 (2)		16 000			
Freehold property	100 000						100 000	
Carriage inwards	2 000				2 000			
Carriage outwards	4 000				4 000			
Provision for depreciation Vehicles Fixtures and fittings		8 000 4 000	2 000 (4)	3 600 (1) 2 000 (1)	3 600 (1) 2 000 (1)			9 600 6 000
Fixtures and fittings	20 000						20 000	
Long-term bank loan		10 000						10 000
Interest on bank loan	1 000				1 000			
Capital		127 000						127 000
Drawings	25 000		1 000 (4)				26 000	
Discounts received		2 000				2 000		
Bank overdraft		6 000						6 000
Debtors	25 000						25 000	
Creditors		14 000						14 000
Accrued expenses				3 000 (2)				3 000
Stock written off					2 000 (3)			
Loss on sale of vehicle					1 000 (4)			
Provision for doubtful debts				2 000 (5)	2 000 (5)			2 000
Stock 31.12.19–4			9 000			9 000	9 000	
Totals	352 000	352 000			173 600	192 000	196 000	177 600
Net profit					18 400			18 400
Grand totals					192 000	192 000	196 000	196 000

Task 3 Trading and Profit and Loss Account and Balance Sheet

Produce a formal Trading and Profit and Loss Account and Balance Sheet.

Task 3 answer

Beta Trading
Trading and Profit and Loss Account year ended 31.12.19–4

Sales			179 000	
Less: Returns inwards			4 000	175 000
Less: Cost of goods sold:				
Opening stock			10 000	
Plus purchases		90 000		
Plus carriage inwards		2 000		
		92 000		
Less: Returns outwards		2 000	90 000	
			100 000	
Less: Closing stock			9 000	
				91 000
Gross profit				84 000
Discounts received				2 000
				86 000
Less: Expenses:				
Salaries and wages		30 000		
Heating and lighting		6 000		
Vehicle running costs		16 000		
Carriage outwards		4 000		
Depreciation provided:				
Vehicles	3 600			
Fixtures and fittings	2 000	5 600		
Interest on bank loan		1 000		
Stock write off		2 000		
Loss on sale of vehicle		1 000		
Provision made for doubtful debts		2 000		67 600
				18 400

Beta Trading
Balance Sheet as at 31 December 19–4

Fixed assets	Cost	Depreciation provided	Net value
Freehold property	100 000		100 000
Fixtures and fittings	20 000	6 000	14 000
Vehicles	16 000	9 600	6 400
	136 000	15 600	120 400
Current assets:			
Stock 31.12.19–4		9 000	
Debtors	25 000		
Less: Provision for doubtful debts	2 000	23 000	
		32 000	
Less: Current liabilities			
Bank overdraft	6 000		
Accrued expenses	3 000		
Creditors	14 000	23 000	
Working capital			9 000
Net assets			129 400
Financed by:			
Long-term bank loan		10 000	
Capital	127 000		
Profit for year	18 400		
	145 400		
Less: Drawings	26 000	119 400	
			129 400

Consolidation exercise

T Thomas started trading under the name of Thomas Trading on 01 October 19–2. You are to work through all of the following tasks and then produce a Trading and Profit and Loss Account and Balance Sheet as at 30 September 19–3. You are then to produce as many relevant ratios as you can to measure the performance and liquidity of the business.

Task 1 Start of business 01.10.19–2

1. Thomas has available private capital of £50 000 to invest in the business.
2. He paid six months' rent in advance on an industrial unit from which the business will operate, £3000.
3. He paid for the following:
   Unit fixtures and equipment, £18 000.
   Office furniture and equipment, £6000.

4. Paid a year's insurance premiums, £1200.
5. Purchased stock for cash, £11 000.
6. Put his privately owned van, valued at £8000, into the business.
7. Having done all of the above, he put the balance of his capital into a business bank account.

You are to complete an opening journal for the transactions and then open up relevant ledger accounts.

Task 2

The following is a summary of Thomas's transactions during the year ended 30 September 19–3.
1. Paid the following expenses   £

	£
Electricity	2 800
Heating oil	1 900
Telephone	1 200
Vehicle running costs	4 700
Carriage inwards	300
Wages	19 000
Repair to premises	800
Advertising	3 400
Rent	3 000
Rates	4 400

2. A summary of Thomas's Sales Ledger as at 30 September 19–3 produced:

Sales on credit	178 000
Goods returned by debtors	2 600
Receipts from debtors	163 000

In addition there were cash sales of £4600.

3. A summary of the Purchase Ledger as at 30 September 19–3 produced:

Purchases on credit	92 000
Goods returned to suppliers	1 700
Payments to creditors	79 000

4. During the year, Thomas had drawn £16 000 for his own personal expenses and had taken goods costing £450 for his own personal use.
5. On 01 April 19–3, Thomas had traded in his van against a new vehicle. The new vehicle cost £12 000 against which Thomas received a £7000 trade-in allowance for his old van. The balance was paid by cheque.
6. At the end of the year all cash had been banked.

You are required to write up all the appropriate ledger accounts including Sales and Purchase Ledger Control Accounts. You are then to produce a Trial Balance in a form which allows year-end adjustments to be made by the Extended Trial Balance method.

Task 3 Year-end adjustments

1. Assets are to be depreciated as follows:
   Fixtures and equipment   20 per cent
   Office furniture and equipment   25 per cent
   Vehicles   25 per cent
   (depreciation is provided pro rata on assets acquired or disposed of)
2. Unpaid expenses are:
   Electricity   £400
   Vehicle running costs   £700
3. A provision is to be made for doubtful debts at 3 per cent of debtors after writing off a bad debt of £520.
4. Bank charges of £1600 have not previously been accounted for, nor has £1100 of bank interest received from the bank.
5. Closing stock at 30 September 19–3 was valued at £13 000.

You are to complete journal entries for all these adjustments and then complete the Extended Trial Balance before producing year-end accounts.

Section 2

Financing

Unit 14

Financing a business

Before a business is set up and starts to operate, it is imperative that financing has been properly assessed and arranged. Many new businesses have failed because the financing structure had not been properly planned. In these units we will be looking at how the financial needs of a business might be assessed; how financing might be obtained; and how we might present a proposal for financial support.

Assessing financing need

Given a perceived business opportunity, the first thing we need to do is make a detailed assessment of the physical resources the business requires in order to operate. Let us assume that we are doing this exercise for a prospective small engineering business. It is useful first to list the broad categories of fixed assets such a business might require. This immediately introduces a methodical approach to the problem, so vital if we are not to omit anything.

Small engineering business

Fixed asset requirement

1. Premises: to house a small engineering workshop and office.
2. Workshop plant and equipment
   (a) Fixed plant and machinery
   (b) Tools
   (c) Storage and shelving facilities
   (d) Lifting and moving gear
   (e) Requirements under Health and Safety Regulations.
3. Administrative requirements
   (a) Office furniture and furnishings
   (b) Office machinery and equipment
   (c) Communications equipment.
4. Staff facilities
   (a) Cloakroom facilities

    (b) Refreshment facilities
    (c) Medical/emergency facilities.
5. Transport
    (a) Vehicles: delivery
    (b) Vehicles: other

Within each category, detailed inventories will need to be drawn up identifying each item to which a purchase cost can then be applied.

The sum total of the whole inventory will then represent the investment to be made in fixed assets.

Let us assume that this has been done and the category costs are:

1. Premises	150 000
2. Workshop plant and equipment	100 000
3. Administration requirements	20 000
4. Staff facilities	5 000
5. Vehicles	25 000
Total	300 000

If the business is to purchase all these assets it therefore requires £300 000 of financing for this purpose. We will shortly be looking at alternative ways of acquiring some of the assets and thereby reducing the level of financing required.

Working capital requirement

So much for the cost of fixed assets. In addition, the business will also need to finance an adequate ongoing level of working capital. Working capital, as we know, is the difference between current assets and current liabilities. Let us assume that the following detail has been calculated:

- Required average stockholding £40 000.
- Forecast monthly credit sales of £30 000 on 30 day terms.
- Forecast monthly credit purchases of £15 000 on 30 day terms.

In utilizing these figures we will be 'conservative' and assume that while the trading terms are approximately four weeks' credit, in reality the debtor repayment period is more likely to be six weeks.

The initial working capital requirement will therefore be:

Current assets		
Stock	40 000	
Debtors $(30\,000 \times \frac{6}{4})$	45 000	85 000
Less: Current liabilities		
Creditors		15 000
Working capital required		70 000

If the business grows and the level of stock increases and number of debtors grows then the financing requirement will also increase. We can also see that *creditors are a form of financing* as they reduce the amount of working capital required.

We can now summarize the financing requirements:

Fixed assets	300 000
Working capital	70 000
Total financing requirement	370 000

We will also see later that additional financing is often required to cover forecast short-term cash deficiencies.

Finding the finances

Before we start to look at alternatives for our small engineering company, let us first consider, briefly, the range of financing alternatives that are normally available.

Sources of long-term finance

Proprietors' capital

In the case of a sole trader or partnership, the owners of the business provide their own private capital to finance the whole, or part, of the capital needed. If they cannot afford to fund the whole requirement, then they have to acquire the shortfall from other, outside, sources. Any private capital they invest in the business is effectively a loan and is at risk. If the business does not make adequate profit then they get little or no return on their investment. If the business fails, they can lose the whole of their investment.

Equity capital

In the case of a *limited* company, shareholder funds are a major part of financing — the company raising finance by selling its shares. We will be looking at the whole question of shares in a later unit. For our purposes, at the moment, we need only appreciate that money invested in ordinary shares of a company is 'risk' capital. A return on the investment is paid, in the form of a 'dividend', according to the level of profits made. As with proprietors' capital, if profits are inadequate then little, or no, dividend might be paid and, if the company fails, then ordinary shareholders may receive only a small proportion or none of their investment back.

Loan capital

Loan capital, that is to say borrowed money, is distinctly different from proprietors' or equity capital in that loans are made on the basis that a rate of interest will be paid on the loan, irrespective of the profitability of the business, and that at the end of the loan period the loan will have been repaid. Whereas the return on proprietors' capital and dividends paid on ordinary shares are effectively a 'sharing out' of any profits made, in contrast, the interest paid on loans (the cost of borrowing) is an expense of the business and is debited to the Profit and Loss Account before the final profits figure is calculated. Lenders, and particularly those lending to new or small businesses, will invariably require some form of guarantee or security against the loan. This could take the form of a legal charge on the assets of the business or even the personal property of the proprietor(s) trying to raise finance for their business. Lenders obviously do this to protect their interests should the business fail. Even when a new business is formed as a limited company (where the liability of the company is limited to the value of its shares), lenders will most likely require the founders of the company to provide personal guarantees and/or a legal charge on their private assets. In these circumstances, should the company fail, the lender can enforce repayment of the loan against the individual(s). We can see, therefore, that raising finances for a new business can indeed be risky, and a business failure can result in the loss of not only the business and personal capital invested in it but also privately owned assets, such as a home which might have been given as security for a loan. There are a number of potential lenders, the main ones being:

1. *Banks.* These are the biggest source of lending to new, small businesses and normally the first port of call for anyone looking to raise finance for such a business. They offer, collectively, an array of finance schemes but the most common forms of business loans are:
   (a) *Fixed repayment loans.* A sum is lent for a fixed term, say, five or ten years during which time the loan and interest is repaid by fixed monthly or quarterly repayments.
   (b) *Variable interest loans.* The rate of interest being charged on a loan can vary as interest rates, generally, change. Repayments can then increase or decrease as the interest being charged varies.
   (c) *Commercial mortgages.* A mortgage may be granted on a business property. The mortgage operates in much the same way as domestic mortgages, except that the period of the loan is normally shorter and the rate of interest higher.
   Note Banks lending to a business will normally require it to keep its current business bank account with them. Not only does this increase the bank's number of customers, it also allows it the opportunity to monitor the progress of the business.
2. *Government initiatives.* From time to time, to encourage the formation of new businesses, governments will introduce and sponsor a variety of schemes aimed at improving the avail-

ability of finance for new and expanding businesses. These schemes can range from regional development grants aimed at encouraging the setting up of businesses in depressed areas of the country, to guaranteeing part of the borrowing made by lenders to new businesses. A good example of this is the 'Small Business Loan Guarantee Scheme' where, as an alternative to the borrower pledging his home or other personal assets, the Government will guarantee a good proportion of the loan. The borrower, of course, pays for the privilege by way of a premium on top of the interest charged.

3. *Building societies*. Like banks, many societies may grant mortgages on commercial properties. Again, the loan period tends to be shorter and the interest charged higher than on private houses.

4. *Others*. There are other methods of raising loan capital but they are, in the main, only available to larger, established companies requiring finance to expand or takeover other companies or when a substantial sum is involved. Briefly, they include:

    (a) *Debentures*. These are simply documents a company issues to the lender acknowledging a debt and agreeing to repay the loan by a given date and to pay interest at a fixed rate.

    (b) *Venture capital organizations*. These organizations may provide risk capital normally for a share of the business. Often, for obvious reasons, they will also require active participation in the management of the business.

Hire purchase

As an alternative to finding the full purchase price of an asset, acquisition through a hire-purchase agreement can reduce initial outlay. This facility can be used for acquiring machinery, vehicles, etc.

Leasing

Equipment and vehicle leasing, as a method of acquiring assets, has grown considerably in recent years. Basically, the business leases the asset from a leasing company over a fixed number of years and makes a fixed monthly, quarterly or yearly lease payment. There can be tax advantages to this and, indeed, to the hire-purchase method.

Factoring debts

Instead of waiting for debtors to pay their accounts, the debts may be 'sold' to a factoring organization. The factor pays quickly and regularly but, of course, deducts a percentage commission. The costs and inconvenience of exercising credit control are now with the factor and can represent a significant saving to a business.

Retained profits

Profits are available for distribution to the owners of a business, be they sole proprietors, partners or shareholders. However, if, instead of paying over all profits to the owner(s), an element of profits is retained in the business, then every £1 retained represents £1 less the business would need if seeking finance for any purpose. It is not at all uncommon to find companies distributing 50 per cent or less of their profits and retaining the balance. Profits retained in this way are a major source of reinvestment.

All the types of potential funding we have looked at so far are long term. However, in addition to long-term funding, there are a number of sources of potential 'short-term' capital.

Sources of short-term finance

Overdrafts

This is a commonly used form of short-term financing. Interest charged by the bank on the overdraft is an expense of the borrower and is debited to the Profit and Loss Account before net profit is calculated. Overdrafts can be a flexible method of financing in that interest is charged only on the balance overdrawn but the rate of interest charged is usually higher than, for example, on long-term loans and the costs can be considerable.

Short-term loans

It is possible to obtain loans on a short-term basis but they are not a very popular method. There are, invariably, legal and administrative costs charged to set up a secured loan facility and these costs can become very expensive when spread over only a short repayment period.

Creditors

For as long as a business owes money to a creditor, that creditor is effectively a source of finance to the business. A simple illustration can demonstrate this point:

	Situation	
	1	2
Current assets	50 000	50 000
Less: Creditors	20 000	None
Working capital requiring finance	30 000	50 000

We can see that in Situation 1, the creditors are a source of £20 000 of financing. (The converse of this is that a business is a source of financing to its own debtors.)

Other alternatives

We have already seen that one of the most expensive assets a business may have to acquire is premises. If premises are rented, rather than bought, this normally has a dramatic effect in reducing the initial amount of capital required to be financed.

Summary — Sources of finance

To fund	Type	Possibilities
Fixed assets	Long-term finance	Proprietors' capital
		Shareholder capital
		Secured loans
		Government grants/schemes
		Debentures
		Venture capital
		Hire purchase
		Leasing
		Factoring debts (1)
		Commercial mortgages (2)
		Retained profits
Working capital	Short-term finance	Overdraft
		Short-term loans
		Creditors
		Factoring debts (1)
		See also Note (3) below

Notes
(1) This can arguably appear under either category.
(2) Renting is an alternative to purchasing a property.
(3) This list is very much a 'textbook approach'. However, we must be careful. In reality, practices are not always so clearly defined. For example, there is always a need for a level of ongoing working capital. In a new business start-up, this is often covered by proprietor(s) or shareholder capital, long-term loans or integral within government grant or loan schemes.

Assembling the package

Assembling the package may indeed be an appropriate description for the work which is now to follow. Having assessed the financial needs of our prospective engineering business and looked at the potential sources of finance, we now need to investigate alternatives and then put together a structured financing plan which will cover the requirements identified.

Let us say that enquiries have revealed the following facts:

1. The prospective owner can provide capital of £80 000 and feels that additional long-term borrowing, from whatever source, should not exceed this sum.
2. Adequate premises can be rented on a seven-year lease at an annual rental of £18 000.
3. Up to £50 000 of the workshop plant and equipment can be leased and the best rate quoted is £23 per £1000 per month over a five-year leasing term.
   Note   In order to compare leasing terms quoted by finance houses it is best to obtain quotes at a monthly repayment rate per £1000 of funding. By doing so, it is then possible to make direct comparisons of alternative quotations.
4. The vehicles can be leased on a full repair and maintenance lease at £700 per month.
5. For a secured loan over a five-year term, the bank is quoting fixed monthly repayments of £24 per £1000 borrowed. Of the £24 monthly repayment, £16.67 is repayment of the loan and £7.33 interest charged on the loan.
6. Proprietor's forecast annual sales and operating expenses:

Sales	360 000
Materials cost	180 000
Staff costs	50 000
Electricity	2 400
Vehicle running costs	4 000
Insurances	1 500
Administration costs	2 500
Other costs	12 000

The proprietor estimates the workshop plant and equipment to have a 10-year life span and a residual value of 10 per cent of the purchase cost. Administration and staff facilities assets are also to be written off over 10 years but with no residual value.

The proprietor, who will manage and work within the business, expects personal 'remuneration' of £30 000 by way of equal monthly drawings plus, at least, a 20 per cent return on his capital investment.

All sales and costs are expected to accrue in equal monthly amounts except:

- Electricity payable quarterly — Jan, Apr, July, Oct.
- Insurances payable annually in advance.

Let us now summarize the situation and our financing possibilities.

Summary — Requirements and sources

Requirements

Fixed assets

Premises	150 000	
Workshop plant and equipment	100 000	
Administration requirements	20 000	
Staff facilities	5 000	
Vehicles	25 000	300 000
Working capital		70 000
Total		370 000

Sourcing possibilities

1. Financing:

Proprietor's capital	80 000	
Bank loan (not to exceed)	80 000	160 000

2. Renting of premises   18 000 p.a.
3. Leasing of £50 000 of workshop plant and equipment

   £50 000 @ £23 per month per £1000

   £23 × 50 (£'000s) × 12 months   =   13 800 p.a.

   Note At £23 per month, this is cheaper finance than a bank loan at £24 per £1000. The bank may also require security of £50 000 for this element of any loan.
4. Lease of vehicles at £700 per month = £8400 per year.

   The monthly rate per £1000 is $£\dfrac{700}{25(£000s)} = £28$

   Note This is £5 per month per £1000 more expensive than the cost of leasing plant and machinery *but* includes all repair and maintenance costs.

Now we can start to structure the financing. A rational allocation to requirement might be:

	Requirement	*Annual cost*
Total	370 000	
Less: Premises (rented)	150 000	18 000
	220 000	
Less: Leasing plant and machinery	50 000	13 800
	170 000	
Less: Leased vehicles	25 000	8 400
	145 000	
Less: Proprietor's capital	80 000	
Bank loan	65 000	18 720 (1)
Total annual cost		58 920

Note

(1) 65 × (£000s borrowed) × £24 × 12 months = £18 720.

We can now do a quick forecast to measure profitability and see if the proprietor's criteria are likely to be met:

Forecast Profit and Loss

Sales		360 000
Less: Material costs	180 000	
Staff costs	48 000	
Rent	18 000	
Leasing of plant and equipment	13 800	
Vehicles:		
Leasing costs	8 400	
Running costs	4 000	
Electricity	2 400	
Insurances	1 500	
Administration costs	2 500	
Other costs	12 000	
Interest — Bank loan (1)	5 720	
Depreciation (2)	7 000	303 320
Net profit		56 680

Notes

(1) The monthly interest on the bank loan is £7.33 per £1000 borrowed. The yearly costs of the loan are:

Interest charged £7.33 × 65 (£000s borrowed)	=	5 720
Capital repayment £16.67 × 65 × 12	=	13 000
Total repayment		18 720

(2) (a) Depreciation: Plant and equipment

Total plant and machinery cost	100 000
Less: Amount leased	50 000
Assets purchased	50 000
Less: Residual value 10%	5 000
	45 000

Depreciation over 10 years = 4500 p.a.

(2) (b) Depreciation: Administrative and staff facilities assets

Total cost: Administration	20 000
Staff facilities	5 000
	25 000

Depreciation over 10 years = 2500 p.a.

Return on capital

Net profit	56 680
Less: Proprietor's remuneration	30 000
Return on capital	26 680

$$\frac{26\,680}{80\,000} \times 100 = 33.35 \text{ per cent}$$

Based on these projected figures, the proprietor could expect his criteria to be met.

Forecasting cash flow and profit

We already know that profitability and liquidity are two different things and both need to be measured. First we need to do a projected cash flow to determine whether there will be a need for any short-term finance to cover any periodic cash deficiencies. If there are deficiencies, then they will need to be financed by an overdraft which, in turn, will bring added interest costs on the business. Remember that the quick profit forecast we have already done only included the costs of long-term loans. If there are to be any overdraft costs then the profit we have forecast will be reduced.

In preparing the cash flow forecast, we need to pick up from the first forecast Profit and Loss Account all those entries which represent a flow of actual cash into, or out of, the business. Entries representing 'non-cash' transactions are ignored. We need to be totally clear about this distinction, and the following should help to avoid any misunderstanding.

1. *Sales on credit.* The supply of goods on credit to debtors does not involve any movement of actual cash and thus *does not* appear in the cash flow forecast.
2. *Receipts from debtors.* When debtors eventually pay for the goods supplied to them on credit, then the receipt of the payment is, of course, a cash receipt.

   It is, therefore, the receipts from debtors which appear in the cash flow forecast *not* monthly sales on credit. Any cash sales would, of course, appear in the forecast. Similarly, it is actual payments made to creditors which appear in the cash flow forecast, *not* the receipt of goods supplied by creditors.

   We know that a Profit and Loss Account can contain a number of accounting adjustments and provisions which do not represent the flow of actual cash. Examples of this type of entry are:
   (a) Depreciation
   (b) Accrued expenses
   (c) Provisions for doubtful debts.
   As these are 'non-cash' transactions, they *do not* appear in a cash flow forecast.

   In addition to entries selected from the initial forecast Profit and Loss Account, we must include in the cash flow forecast: the receipt of a proprietor's capital investment, bank loans, etc.; all payments for the purchase of the assets of the business; any cash drawings the owner(s) may make from the business.

When studying the detail in the following cash flow forecast for our small engineering business, it may be helpful to relate each of the following explanatory notes to each entry.

Notes to cash flow forecast

1. *Debtors* — these are receipts of payments from debtors. Note that we are allowing for an average six weeks' repayment period beyond the first month.
2. *Capital* — receipt of proprietor's capital investment.
3. *Loan* — receipt of bank loan.
4. *Total receipts* — each month's forecast cash inflow.
5. *Assets purchase* — payment for assets as follows:

Plant and equipment	50 000
Administration requirements	20 000
Staff facilities	5 000
	75 000

6. *Creditors* — these are actual payments made to creditors. Note that as the business is new and may not have organized agreed credit limits with suppliers, the forecast for the first month allows for payment with order for the initial stocking up of £40 000 of materials.

7. *Staff costs, rent, leasing* — these are taken from the initial forecast Profit and Loss Account and divided out evenly over the 12 months.

8. *Vehicles* — this is the total of vehicle leasing and running costs. Note that in dividing out the total, the monthly amount included in the cash flow forecast has been 'rounded' to the nearest £10. Remember, this is a forecast and to use figures which suggest any greater degree of accuracy could be misleading.

9. *Electricity* — these are quarterly payments of bills received.

10. *Insurances* — this is a payment in advance for the whole year.

11. *Administration costs; other costs* — taken from the forecast Profit and Loss Account and divided out evenly. Monthly figures rounded to the nearest £10 where appropriate.

12. *Loan repayments* — these are the total monthly repayments of borrowed capital plus interest.

13. *Drawings* — represent the proprietor's intentions to withdraw his 'remuneration' in equal monthly instalments.

14. *Total repayments* — each month's forecast cash outflow.

15. *Excess/deficit* — each month's payments deducted from receipts to give an excess (net inflow of cash) or a deficit (net outflow of cash). Note, figures used to show a deficit are placed in brackets, e.g. (27 960) — February.

16. *Prior month* — the balance from the previous month brought forward.

17. *Running balance* — obtained by adding the excess/(deficit) for the current month to the balance brought forward from the previous month. The forecast balance for each month is effectively a forecast of what the business's bank account is expected to look like at the end of each month. Figures shown in brackets will be overdrawn balances which will need covering by agreed overdraft facilities.

Cash Flow Forecast

DETAIL	January	February	March	April	May	June	July	August	September	October	November	December	TOTAL
Receipts:													
Debtors			15 000	30 000	30 000	30 000	30 000	30 000	30 000	30 000	30 000	30 000	285 000
Capital	80 000												80 000
Loan	65 000												65 000
Total receipts	145 000		15 000	30 000	30 000	30 000	30 000	30 000	30 000	30 000	30 000	30 000	430 000
Payments:													
Assets purchase	75 000												75 000
Creditors	40 000	15 000	15 000	15 000	15 000	15 000	15 000	15 000	15 000	15 000	15 000	15 000	205 000
Staff costs	4 000	4 000	4 000	4 000	4 000	4 000	4 000	4 000	4 000	4 000	4 000	4 000	48 000
Rent	1 500	1 500	1 500	1 500	1 500	1 500	1 500	1 500	1 500	1 500	1 500	1 500	18 000
Leasing	1 150	1 150	1 150	1 150	1 150	1 150	1 150	1 150	1 150	1 150	1 150	1 150	13 800
Vehicles	1 040	1 040	1 040	1 040	1 040	1 040	1 040	1 040	1 040	1 040	1 040	1 040	12 480
Electricity	–	–	–	600	–	–	600	–	–	600	–	–	1 800
Insurances	1 500	–	–	–	–	–	–	–	–	–	–	–	1 500
Administration costs	210	210	210	210	210	210	210	210	210	210	210	210	2 520
Other costs	1 000	1 000	1 000	1 000	1 000	1 000	1 000	1 000	1 000	1 000	1 000	1 000	12 000
Loan repayments	1 560	1 560	1 560	1 560	1 560	1 560	1 560	1 560	1 560	1 560	1 560	1 560	18 720
Drawings	2 500	2 500	2 500	2 500	2 500	2 500	2 500	2 500	2 500	2 500	2 500	2 500	30 000
Total payments	129 460	27 960	27 960	28 560	27 960	27 960	28 560	27 960	27 960	28 560	27 960	27 960	438 820
Excess/(deficit)	15 540	(27 960)	(12 960)	1 440	2 040	2 040	1 440	2 040	2 040	1 440	2 040	2 040	–
Prior month	–	15 540	(12 420)	(25 380)	(23 940)	(21 900)	(19 860)	(18 420)	(16 380)	(14 340)	(12 900)	(10 860)	–
Running balance	15 540	(12 420)	(25 380)	(23 940)	(21 900)	(19 860)	(18 420)	(16 380)	(14 340)	(12 900)	(10 860)	(8 820)	(8 820)

Short-term financing requirement

We can see from the cash flow forecast that there will indeed be a need for short-term financing of the overdrawn balances which peak at £25 380 in March and then decline steadily through to December.

Assuming that the trends continue into the following year we can also calculate that the overdrawn balances should disappear during late May of the second year.

Balance December — Year 1		(8820)
Excess cash income:		
January — Year 2	1440	
February — Year 2	2040	
March — Year 2	2040	
April — Year 2	1440	
May — Year 2	2040	9000
Forecast balance — May Year 2		180

The business will therefore hope to secure overdraft facilities based on the projected cash flow for the 16 months February to May — Year 2.

We will assume the bank has advised that the cost of such facilities will be:

Year 1	£1970
Year 2	£ 190

Given this information, we can now produce a 'final' forecast Profit and Loss Statement and Balance Sheet.

Forecast Profit and Loss — Year 1

Sales			360 000
Less: Expenditure:			
Materials cost		180 000	
Staff cost		48 000	
Rent		18 000	
Leasing plant and equipment		13 800	
Vehicles			
Leasing cost		8 480	
Running costs		4 000	
Electricity		2 400	
Insurances		1 500	
Administration costs		2 520	
Other costs		12 000	
Depreciation		7 000	
Bank interest			
Loan	5 720		
Overdraft (1)	1 970	7 690	305 390
Net Profit			54 610 (2)

Notes

(1) Bank interest charged on overdraft did not appear in the initial Profit and Loss Statement formulated during the testing for viability stage. The figure can only be calculated or ascertained from the bank after the cash flow forecast has been constructed. It is, of course, the cash flow forecast which identifies any need for such financing.

(2) Proprietor's return on capital criteria:

Net profit	54 610
Less: Drawings	30 000
	24 610

$$\frac{24\,610}{80\,000} \times 100 = 30.8 \text{ per cent}$$

Forecast Balance Sheet — Year 1

Fixed assets	Cost	Depreciation		NBV
Plant and equipment	50 000	4 500		45 500
Admin and staff facilities	25 000	2 500		22 500
	75 000	7 000		68 000

Current assets			
Stock	40 000 (1)		
Debtors	75 000 (2)	115 000	

Less: Current liabilities			
Creditors	15 000 (3)		
Accrued expense	600 (4)		
Bank overdraft	10 790 (5)	26 390	
Working capital			88 610
Net worth			156 610

Financed by:		
Capital	80 000	
Plus: Profit	54 610	
	134 610	
Less: Drawings	30 000	104 610
Bank loan		52 000 (6)
		156 610

Notes

(1) It has been assumed, from the information given, that the stockholding will be maintained at £40 000.

(2) Sales	360 000
Receipts from debtors (cash flow)	285 000
Owed	75 000

(3) Original stock	40 000
Purchases 15 000 × 12 months	180 000
	220 000
Paid per cash flow statement	205 000
Owed	15 000

(4) Electricity accrual

Charge for year	2 400
Paid per cash flow statement	1 800
	600

(5) Overdraft per cash flow statement 8 820

    Plus: Overdraft charges

(Profit and Loss Statement)	1 970
	10 790

(6) Total loan repayments per cash flow 18 720

    Interest element charged in Profit and

Loss Statement	5 720
Repayment of loan	13 000

    Therefore:

Original loan	65 000
Less: Loan repaid	13 000
Loan outstanding	52 000

Presenting the proposal

There are two wrong ways to submit a proposal to a prospective lender. The worst is to go along without any supporting documentation and try to present the whole case verbally. The potential lender will merely defer the matter until a detailed cash flow and profit forecast is submitted.

Better, but still far from ideal, is the common practice of presenting the financial statements and then explaining the whole rationale behind the proposal verbally. We have to understand that, invariably, the local bank manager can support an application but the proposal will have to be submitted to head office for final approval. In these circumstances, the problems with a verbal presentation are obvious. Some important points may be missed or the manager's notes may not be an accurate reflection of what has actually been said or meant. The approach is not as 'professional' as it could be.

The right way is to present a full detailed proposal to which the relevant financial statements are appended. It is a 'professional' approach which should impress both the manager and head office.

The proposal should be in the form of a report, laid out in a logical sequence and attempt to give answers to any potential questions. It should be as brief as possible but not compromise on relevant detail.

There are no set rules governing the layout of such a proposal, but the following may be a useful guide.

Section   Contents

1 *The business*

    A brief outline of the business activity being proposed.

2   *The proprietor(s)/manager(s)*
     An outline of background, training and skills relevant to the business.

3   *The market*
     A description of the market place in which the business will compete.

4   *The competition*
     Details of the competitors in the market place. What will give this business 'an edge' over the competition.

5   *Scale of operation and charges/prices*
     Details of operation, pricing criteria, etc.

6   *Asset requirement*
     Details of assets required to operate the business.

7   *Equity and financing*
     Details of:
     (a) Owner's capital input
     (b) Additional financing being sought.

8   *Conclusion*
     Brief summary of the 'virtues' of the proposal and a re-statement of what financing is being requested.

Appendix 'A'   Cash Flow Forecast
Appendix 'B'   Forecast Profit and Loss — Year 1
Appendix 'C'   Forecast Balance Sheet — Year 1
Appendix 'D'   Forecast Profit and Loss — Year 2

Note   Quite often, only a cash flow forecast and forecast Profit and Loss Statement for the first year are submitted. Indeed, this may well be what is required in set assignments.

There is, however, merit in submitting a Balance Sheet and this is certainly the case with a second year forecast of Profit or Loss. Invariably, the first year of operation has a long build-up period before turnover reaches anything like what it is hoped will be 'normal'.

A second year forecast can, in these circumstances, give a better impression of longer-term profitability. We must be clear that in assignment work, we should submit only what is asked for.

Important   Unit 15 contains two full worked case studies on financing proposals. Do persevere and work through the detail and the suggested solutions. Jointly, they cover most of the 'twists and turns' you are likely to encounter if attempting such an exercise. To assist you in tracking through the relevant financial statements, detailed notes have been included.

Investment decisions

From time to time, all successful companies will have to decide whether to invest in new or replacement plant or equipment, information technology, etc. Before it can acquire new assets a company does, of course, have to have the necessary finances or financing arrangements in place.

We will be looking at the whole area of financing in a later section. For the purpose of this study of *investment decisions* we will assume that the finances are available.

In real terms, an investment decision will first have to address one or both of two questions:

- Should we buy or not? In broad terms, the answer to this question is dependent on recognizing that firms exist to make profit. A decision to buy therefore has to be motivated by a belief that the purchase will contribute to profits. Even then, that contribution to profit should be at a rate of return on the investment which exceeds the rate of return that could be obtained by investing the equivalent sum of money elsewhere. All business involves a degree of risk. What is the point of investing in a risk business if a better rate of return can be obtained from a relatively 'safe' investment in, say, deposit accounts, government stocks, etc.?
- What should we buy? Often the company will have a choice of similar products from different potential suppliers. Frequently, the products will perform basically the same but vary in price, life expectancy and, possibly, maintenance costs. Whatever the range of choice, the final decision will inevitably be determined in part, if not wholly, by financial considerations.

We will concentrate on the three main methods used in assessing the financial impact of various choices.

1. Pay-back period method
2. Return on capital method
3. Present-day value method (Discounted Cash Flow)

Pay-back period method

This method determines over what period the asset acquired will pay back the sum invested in its purchase.

Let us assume a company wishes to buy a new piece of production plant. There are two suitable machines on the market. Purchase costs and estimated annual profits generated by each are as follows:

		Machine A	Machine B
Cost		60 000	90 000
Profits	Year 1	6 000	8 000
	2	8 000	10 000
	3	12 000	15 000
	4	17 000	17 000
	5	17 000	20 000
	6	18 000	20 000
	7	—	25 000
	8	—	25 000
	9	—	25 000
	10	—	25 000

Machine A, costing £60 000, has a pay-back period of five years (if we add up the profits generated in years 1–5 we find that they pay back the original cost).

Machine B, costing £90 000, has a pay-back period of six years.

On a purely pay-back basis Machine A would seem to be the best buy. The machine certainly offers the best guarantee of repaying the investment in the shortest period of time.

This method does have obvious flaws. It takes no account of the life expectancy of the machine which will doubtless continue producing profit well beyond its pay-back period. Indeed, if it did not, it is difficult to see why it should be bought. In this context, it is estimated that Machine A will continue for one year beyond break-even, producing another £18 000. Machine B will continue for another four years beyond 'pay back', producing a further £100 000. The pay-back period method can, however, be highly relevant in industries where technology is advancing rapidly. Computers would be a classic example. Such is the rate of development that machines can become obsolete very quickly. In these circumstances, the sooner the investment is repaid the better.

Return on capital method

Here, we are concerned with the annual rate of return the profits generated represent compared to the sum invested in the purchase. We will use our previous example.

Machine A will produce £78 000 over six years which, after deducting the cost of the machine at £60 000, leaves a surplus of £18 000.

If we average the £18 000 out over six years, the average annual return is £3000:

$$\frac{3000 \text{ annual return} \times 100}{60\,000 \text{ cost}} = 5 \text{ per cent return on capital}$$

Machine B will produce £190 000 over 10 years.

Deducting cost of £90 000 leaves a return of £100 000. Averaged out over the 10 years, the average annual return is £10 000:

$$\frac{10\,000 \text{ annual return} \times 100}{90\,000 \text{ cost}} = 11 \text{ per cent return on capital}$$

Using this method, Machine B would seem to be the most sensible buy.

The obvious advantage of this method, over that of 'pay back', is that it does recognize the life span of the machines and all the profits generated. However, it takes no account of the long time period over which the annual returns accumulate and when, as is fact, money depreciates in value year on year, the often dramatic impact of this money depreciation is not recognized.

Present-day value method (discounted cash flow)

This method is broadly similar to the return on capital method but it seeks to address the problem of money depreciating each year. We have to understand clearly what is meant by money depreciation. You will know that every year, the £ in your pocket buys less and less. The reason for this is inflation as prices go on rising. It is reasonable to suppose that the £ we spend today will buy less in a year's time and much less in, say, five years' time. Look at this inevitable fact from another perspective and we can say that if someone promises to give us £1 in five years' time, it will then only be worth maybe 50p at present-day value.

The present-day value method, by applying a technique called *discounted cash flow*, attempts to convert all future receipts into present-day value. In order to apply the method, we first have to decide what annual rate of inflation might be expected. If we could forecast that accurately, maybe we should be government ministers rather than accountants! But, try we must. For the sake of simplicity, let us decide the rate will be 10 per cent. Future cash flows will look something like this:

	Receipt	*Present-day value*
End of Year 1	£1	90.0p
End of Year 2	£1	81.0p
End of Year 3	£1	72.9p
End of Year 4	£1	65.6p
End of Year 5	£1	59.0p

The good news is that to assist you in this endeavour there are pre-printed tables available which give 'discount factors' for every year against different forecast percentages.

We can now apply this method to our Machine A/Machine B investment problem:

Year	Discount factor (10%)	Machine A Receipt	Machine A Discounted	Machine B Receipt	Machine B Discounted
1	0.900	6 000	5 400	8 000	7 200
2	0.810	8 000	6 480	10 000	8 100
3	0.729	12 000	8 748	15 000	10 935
4	0.656	17 000	11 152	17 000	11 152
5	0.590	17 000	10 030	20 000	11 800
6	0.531	18 000	9 558	20 000	10 620
7	0.478	—	—	25 000	11 950
8	0.430	—	—	25 000	10 750
9	0.387	—	—	25 000	9 675
10	0.349	—	—	25 000	8 725
TOTALS		78 000	51 368	190 000	100 907
Purchase price		60 000	60 000	90 000	90 000
Net profit/(loss)		18 000	(8 632)	100 000	10 907

We can now see the dramatic effect discounting has on future cash flows. On this basis, we could really only consider Machine B albeit the profit it produces is only a net £10 907 profit over 10 years. Machine A has produced an £8632 loss over its six-year life span.

Unit 15

Financing proposals

Case Study: Malik Stores

Mr Malik and his wife, for the past eight years, have been employed as managers of a busy convenience foodstore which traded well beyond normal shop opening hours. The Maliks have now decided to run their own store, and that Anytown is an ideal location. While the town is well served by some of the national chain supermarkets, the Maliks are convinced they can attract trade to a store which will not attempt to compete on price but will rely on:

1. Long and late opening hours
2. Personal service
3. A range of speciality foods
4. Quality produce
5. A delivery service.

They have found suitable shop premises which they intend to purchase. Their bank has agreed, in principle, to fund the purchase on a commercial mortgage over 15 years. The offer is subject to:

- The Maliks providing £10 000 of the £49 600 purchase price.
- Sight of a business plan with cash flow and profit forecasts.

The bank has also indicated a willingness to consider other finance for the business depending on its assessment of the proposal it receives.

   The Maliks have assembled all the information they think is needed and have asked us to prepare for them the relevant financial statements, in a form acceptable to the bank. We obtain the following information from the Maliks:

1. *Personal capital.* The Maliks have £24 000 they can invest in the business immediately, and a further £4000 in October when they receive the proceeds of an endowment policy.

2. *Commercial mortgage on shop*
    Monthly repayments of:

Repayment of capital	220
Interest charged	230
Total repayment	450

3. *Cost of shop fixtures and fittings*   £12 000
    (The Maliks expect the equipment to last at least 10 years.)
4. *Cost of initial stock*   £15 000
5. *Sales projections*

July	4 000
August	6 000
September	8 000
October	10 000
November	10 000
December	16 000
January	12 000
February	12 000
March–June	14 000

Sales in the second year are expected to average £16 000 per month.

6. *Margins.* Selling prices will give a gross profit on sales of 25 per cent.
7. *Suppliers.* Fifty per cent of purchases will be on 30-day credit terms and 50 per cent by cash.
8. Mr Malik already owns a suitable van (value £5000) which he intends to use in the business. He thinks the vehicle will last a good three years when he would expect to receive around £500 for it.
9. *Budgeted operating costs*

	£
Electricity (payable Sept, Dec, Mar, June)	1 800
Shop maintenance	2 400
Equipment servicing (annual contract payable in advance)	300
Vehicle running costs	3 600
Other costs	1 200

Part-time assistants — wages:

	£
July	100
August	100
September	150
October	200
November	200
December	300
January	200
February	200
March–June	200

Wages are then expected to stay at this level.

10. All the fitting out of the shop and stocking up will take place in June and the shop will open for business on 1 July.

We can now get to work preparing the required financial statements.

Workings

	Sales	Purchases	Cash	Paid Creditors
	£	£	£	£
July	4 000	3 000 (1)	1 500	–
August	6 000	4 500	2 250	1 500
September	8 000	6 000	3 000	2 250
October	10 000	7 500	3 750	3 000
November	10 000	7 500	3 750	3 750
December	16 000	12 000	6 000	3 750
January	12 000	9 000	4 500	6 000
February	12 000	9 000	4 500	4 500
March	14 000	10 500	5 250	4 500
April	14 000	10 500	5 250	5 250
May	14 000	10 500	5 250	5 250
June	14 000	10 500	5 250	5 250
	134 000	100 500	50 250	45 000

Note

(1) Calculated as:

Gross profit on sales — 25% (of selling price).

Therefore purchases cost = 75% of selling price.

Example July: £4000 × 75% = £3000 purchases.

Cash Flow Forecast

DETAIL	July	August	September	October	November	December	January	February	March	Aprl	May	June	Total
Receipts													
Sales	4 000	6 000	8 000	10 000	10 000	16 000	12 000	12 000	14 000	14 000	14 000	14 000	134 000
Capital	24 000			4 000									28 000
Total receipts	28 000	6 000	8 000	14 000	10 000	16 000	12 000	12 000	14 000	14 000	14 000	14 000	162 000
Payments													
Mortgage	450	450	450	450	450	450	450	450	450	450	450	450	5 400
Cash purchases	1 500	2 250	3 000	3 750	3 750	6 000	4 500	4 500	5 250	5 250	5 250	5 250	50 250
Creditors	—	1 500	2 250	3 000	3 750	3 750	6 000	4 500	4 500	5 250	5 250	5 250	45 000
Electricity	—	—	450	—	—	450	—	—	450	—	—	450	1 800
Shop maintenance	200	200	200	200	200	200	200	200	200	200	200	200	2 400
Equipment maintenance	300	—	—	—	—	—	—	—	—	—	—	—	300
Vehicle costs	300	300	300	300	300	300	300	300	300	300	300	300	3 600
Other costs	100	100	100	100	100	100	100	100	100	100	100	100	1 200
Casual wages	100	150	200	200	200	300	200	200	200	200	200	200	2 250
Property purchase	10 000												10 000
Fixtures and fittings	12 000												12 000
Initial stock	15 000												15 000
Total payments	39 950	4 900	6 900	8 000	8 750	11 550	11 750	10 250	11 450	11 750	11 750	12 200	149 200
Excess/(deficit)	(11 950)	1 100	1 100	6 000	1 250	4 450	250	1 750	2 550	2 250	2 250	1 800	—
Prior month	—	(11 950)	(10 850)	(9 750)	(3 750)	(2 500)	1 950	2 200	3 950	6 500	8 750	11 000	—
Running balance	(11 950)	(10 850)	(9 750)	(3 750)	(2 500)	1 950	2 200	3 950	6 500	8 750	11 000	12 800	12 800

Malik Stores
Forecast Trading and Profit and Loss Account — Year 1

Sales			134 000
Opening stock	15 000		
Purchases	100 500	115 000	
Closing stock		15 000	
Cost of goods sold			100 500
Gross profit			33 500
Less: Expenses			
Mortgage interest		2 760 (1)	
Electricity		1 800	
Shop maintenance		2 400	
Equipment maintenance		300	
Vehicle costs		3 600	
Other costs		1 200	
Wages		2 250	
Bank interest		470 (2)	
Depreciation of fixtures and fittings		1 200 (3)	
Depreciation of van		1 500 (4)	17 480
Net profit			16 020

Notes

(1) Monthly interest charged £230 × 12 = £2760.
(2) Calculated cost of overdraft requirement as per cash flow forecast.
     Note that the bank balance in the Balance Sheet will have to be reduced by this amount.

Bank balance as in cash flow forecast	12 800
Less: Bank interest to be charged	470
Revised bank balance for Balance Sheet	12 330

(3) Depreciation of fixtures and fittings costing £12 000 over 10 years.
(4) Depreciation of van

Initial value	5000
Residual value	500
	4500

£4500 written off over three years = £1500 p.a.

Malik Stores
Forecast Balance Sheet as at end of Year 1

Fixed assets	Cost	Depreciation	NBV
Property	49 600	—	49 600
Fixtures and fittings	12 000	1 200	10 800
Van	5 000	1 500	3 500
	66 600	2 700	63 900
Current assets			
Stock	15 000 (1)		
Bank	12 330	27 330	
Less: Current liabilities			
Creditors		5 250	
Working capital			22 080
Net worth			85 980
Financed by:			
Capital	33 000 (2)		
Profit for year	16 020		49 020
Mortgage			36 960 (3)
			85 980

Notes
(1) Assumed stock level will remain reasonably static.
(2) Capital

Cash introduced	28 000
Value of van	5 000
	33 000

(3) Purchase price of property	49 600
Less: Deposit paid by Maliks	10 000
Mortgage	39 600
Repayments of capital — 1st year £220 p.m. × 12 months	2 640
Mortgage outstanding	36 960

Malik Stores
Forecast Trading and Profit and Loss Account — Year 2

Sales (1)			192 000
Less: Opening stock	15 000		
Purchases	144 000	159 000	
Cost of goods sold			144 000
Gross profit			48 000
Less: Expenses:			
Mortgage interest		2 760	
Electricity		1 800	
Shop maintenance		2 400	
Equipment maintenance		300	
Vehicle costs		3 600	
Other costs		1 200	
Wages (2)		2 400	
Depreciation of fixtures and fittings		1 200	
Depreciation of van		1 500	17 160
Net profit			30 840

Notes
(1) Sales average £16 000 per month
    16 000 × 12 months   =   £192 000
(2) Wages included at £200 per month.

The four financial statements we have produced can be included with the Maliks detailed proposals to be put to the bank.

Case Study: Office Additions

Jane, Paula and Alec are former colleagues who have decided to form a partnership to run an office services bureau.

Jane is an experienced secretary, with good word processing and shorthand skills. She is married with a child in junior school but can make arrangements for him to be looked after during school holidays, etc.

Paula is also an experienced secretary with word processing skills, but no shorthand. She is, however, very proficient with desktop publishing using a PC and with payroll systems. Alec is experienced in payroll systems and the preparation of accounts for small to medium size businesses. Computer literate, he is experienced in setting up hardware systems and conversant with a number of computer accounting and payroll packages and spreadsheets.

Working as a team, the three have spent considerable time during the last three months doing research into their proposed project and have collected the following information.

The market

In this locality, two secretarial bureaux already exist. Sun Secretarial Services is the larger of the two, with a staff of seven. This bureau offers purely secretarial services, producing word processed letters, reports, etc. The main thrust of the business is supplying temporary secretarial staff to local firms. In-house secretarial services are charged at the rate of £12 per hour plus VAT. Clients must call at the town centre premises where car parking is very difficult. Sun Secretarial Services does not offer a collection and delivery service.

The other bureau, Secaid, is also located in the town centre and has a staff of three, two full-time and one part-time. Secaid provides a secretarial service of word processed letters and reports, but this bureau also provides payroll services and a delivery and collection service is offered to clients within a five mile radius. Secaid charges £11.50 per hour for secretarial services and £15 per hour for payroll. Secaid has recently advertised for another member of staff.

The local newspaper regularly carries three advertisements by people providing home-based secretarial services which range from typing letters and reports, to word processed CVs and educational submissions, such as theses, etc. Telephone enquiries have shown that charges range from £8 to £10 per hour.

Accountancy services in the town are provided by professional firms of accountants who charge upwards from £24 per hour. Some also provide payroll services and the minimum charge was found to be £4 per employee payment. The local Chamber of Commerce has advised that there are over 800 businesses of a size and type which make them potential clients of the bureau.

Demand

Demand has been canvassed in two ways:

1. Introductory letters have been sent to 250 small businesses, selected from advertisements in the local press and telephone directory. Follow-up telephone calls have ascertained that 25 have a positive interest in utilizing the service when it starts. It became apparent that three things appealed to these potential clients.
   (a) The fact that the bureau is to provide a full range of secretarial, accounting and payroll services.
   (b) Desktop published mailshots, advertisements, etc., appealed to many.
   (c) Ease of parking and a collection and delivery service were well received.
   Another 40 businesses, although less positive, stated they would be happy to consider the service later, when it actually started operating.
2. Thirty small businesses, not included in (1) above, were selected, and each person visited 10 prospective clients to explain fully the service to be offered. Of six, who said they would definitely use the service, three were already using the existing bureaux.

An analysis of their needs showed a total weekly requirement for:

Secretarial	21 hours
Accounts	6 hours
Payroll	3 hours
Total	30 hours

Time availability

The other bureaux both operate from 9 a.m.–5 p.m., Monday to Friday. It is intended to operate this one from 9 a.m.–6 p.m., Monday to Friday and 9 a.m.–1 p.m. on Saturdays. It is felt that the early evening and Saturday facility will be convenient for many people actively pursuing their business interests during 'normal' working hours.

On this basis, the team calculate their work capacity as:

		Hours	*Hours*
Monday–Friday	9 hours × 5 days × 3 =		135
Saturday	4 hours × 3 =		12
			147
Less:			
Monday–Friday	1 hour × 5 × 3 lunch breaks	15	
	Administration	12	27
Available for chargeable work			120

Charges

Intended charges are:

	Per hour
Secretarial and DTP	£10.00
Accounts and payroll	£12.00

Accounts to be paid the month following.

Projected weekly throughput (hours)

Month	Secretarial	Accounts and payroll	Total
1	21	9	30
2	30	15	45
3	39	21	60
4	48	27	75
5	57	33	90
6	66	39	105
7–12	75	45	120

Equipment and furniture requirements

	£
2 Computers @ £900	1 800
1 Computer @ £1200	1 200
1 Printer @ £400	400
1 Printer @ £2800	2 800
1 Collating photocopier @ £6800	6 800
Telephone equipment @ £450	450
1 Facsimile machine @ £450	450
Office furniture and utilities	2 600
Furnishings	500
Software packages	2 000
Vehicle	7 000
Total	26 000

As an alternative to outright purchase, a suitable vehicle can be leased on a full maintenance basis for £180 per month. The vehicle will cost £300 annually to insure.

Premises

The team have located suitable office premises on a small estate on the periphery of town. The site offers abundant parking facilities and the prospect of business from other firms on the estate. An office, capable of accommodating six staff (to allow for future expansion) costs £250 per month, payable quarterly in advance, heating and electricity inclusive.

Advertising

The team have constructed an advertising budget as follows:

Months	£
1	200
2	200
3	150
4	100

They see, for obvious reasons, the need to spend most initially to get the business established.

Remuneration

The team have agreed their remuneration requirements as £800 each per month. This will be taken at the end of each month by way of drawings. They have agreed that at the year end, after deducting drawings and retaining 20 per cent of the remaining profit in the business, any other profit will be distributed in equal proportions.

Financing

Each partner will contribute £3000 of personal money as start-up capital. They have decided to lease the vehicle. The balance of start-up capital they hope to raise through the bank under the Small Firms Loans Guarantee Scheme. Until they become self-financing, they intend to seek a bank overdraft facility to finance working capital requirements.

They calculate their requirements as:

Loan requirement:	£
Equipment and furniture	26 000
Less: Vehicle	7 000
	19 000
Less: Personal capital 3 × £3000	9 000
	10 000

We have been asked to prepare the relevant financial statements and the completed full proposal for submission to the bank.

Office Additions
Business Proposal

Anytown
February 19– –

1 THE BUSINESS

1.1 It is intended to launch, on or about 01 April 19– –, a new business called Office Additions. The business will be based in Anytown and will be run by three working partners.

1.2 The business will be an office services bureau providing a comprehensive range of secretarial, accountancy and payroll services to small businesses in the town and surrounding area.

2 THE PARTNERS

The business will be run by three working partners.

2.1 Jane Jones: Jane is an experienced secretary, with good word processing and shorthand skills. She is married with a child in junior school but can make arrangements for him to be looked after during school holidays, etc.

2.2 Paula Morrison: Paula is also an experienced secretary with word processing skills, but no shorthand. She is, however, very proficient with desktop publishing using a PC and with payroll systems.

2.3 Alec Morrow: Is experienced in payroll systems and the preparation of accounts for small to medium size businesses. Computer literate, he is experienced in setting up hardware systems and conversant with a number of computer accounting and payroll packages and spreadsheets.

3 THE MARKET

3.1 According to the Local Chamber of Commerce, there are over 800 businesses of type and size, which could make them potential clients for the bureau.

3.2 During the past three months, extensive market research has been carried out and the following information is based on its findings.

3.3 Demand has been canvassed in two ways:

(a) Introductory letters have been sent to 250 small businesses, selected from advertisements in the local press and telephone directory. Follow-up telephone calls have ascertained that 25 have a positive interest in utilizing the service when it starts. It became apparent that three things appealed to these potential clients.

(i) The fact that the bureau is to provide a full range of secretarial, accounting and payroll services.

(ii) Desktop published mailshots, advertisements, etc., appealed to many.

(iii) Ease of parking and a collection and delivery service were well received.

Another 40 businesses, although less positive, said that they would be happy to consider the service later, when it actually started operating.

(b) Thirty small businesses, not included in (a) above, were selected, and each person visited 10 prospective clients to explain fully the service to be offered. Of six, who said they would definitely use the service, three were already using the existing bureaux.

An analysis of their needs showed a total weekly requirement for:

Secretarial	21 hours
Accounts	6 hours
Payroll	3 hours
Total	30 hours

The Local Chamber of Commerce has indicated that there are over 800 firms of a type and size that meet the partners' criteria of potential clients.

4   THE COMPETITION

4.1 In the intended area of operation, two secretarial bureaux already exist.

4.2 Sun Secretarial Services is the larger of the two, with a staff of seven. This bureau offers purely secretarial services, producing word processed letters, reports, etc. The main thrust of the business is supplying temporary secretarial staff to local firms. In-house secretarial services are charged at the rate of £12 per hour plus VAT. Clients must call at the town centre premises where car parking is very difficult. Sun Secretarial Services does not offer a collection and delivery service.

4.3 The other bureau, Secaid, is also located in the town centre and has a staff of three, two full-time and one part-time. Secaid provides a secretarial service of word processed letters and reports, but also provides payroll services and a delivery and collection service is offered to clients within a five mile radius. Secaid charges £11.50 per hour for secretarial services and £15 per hour for payroll. Secaid has recently advertised for another member of staff.

4.4 The local newspaper regularly carries three advertisements by people providing home-based secretarial services which range from typing letters and reports, to word processed CVs and educational submissions, such as theses, etc. Telephone enquiries have shown that charges range from £8 to £10 per hour.

4.5 Accountancy services in the town are provided by professional firms of accountants who charge upwards from £24 per hour. Some also provide payroll services and the minimum charge was found to be £4 per employee payment.

5   SCALE OF OPERATION AND CHARGES

5.1 The other bureaux both operate from 9 a.m.–5 p.m., Monday to Friday. It is intended to operate this one from 9 a.m.–6 p.m., Monday to Friday and 9–1 p.m. on Saturdays. It is felt that the early evening and Saturday facility will be convenient for many people actively pursuing their business interests during 'normal' working hours. On this basis, the team calculate their work capacity as:

			Hours	Hours
Monday–Friday	9 hours × 5 days × 3	=		135
Saturday	4 hours × 3	=	12	
				147

Less:				
Monday–Friday	1 hour × 5 × 3 lunch breaks	15		
	Administration	12	27	
Available for chargeable work			120	

5.2 Charges

Intended charges are: *Per hour*
  Secretarial and DTP   £10.00
  Accounts and payroll   £12.00
Accounts to be paid the month following

5.3 Projected hours and charges

Month	Secretarial			Accounts and Payroll				
	Weekly hours	× £	= Total	Weekly hours	× £	= Total	Weekly total	Monthly total
01	21	10	210	9	12	108	318	1272
02	30	10	300	15	12	180	480	1920
03	39	10	390	21	12	252	642	2568
04	48	10	480	27	12	324	804	3216
05	57	10	570	33	12	396	966	3864
06	66	10	660	39	12	468	1128	4512
07–12	75	10	750	45	12	540	1290	5160

Note Each month is taken as four weeks. This will allow for four weeks closedown for holidays.

6   ASSET REQUIREMENTS
6.1 Suitable office accommodation has been found on the High Tech Estate on the periphery of town. The site offers abundant parking facilities and the prospect of business from other firms on the estate. An office, capable of accommodating six staff (to allow for future expansion) costs £250 per month, payable quarterly in advance, heating and electricity inclusive.

6.2 Equipment and furniture will be required as follows:

	£
2 Computers @ £900	1 800
1 Computer @ £1200	1 200
1 Printer @ £400	400
1 Printer @ £2800	2 800
1 Collating photocopier @ £6800	6 800
Telephone equipment @ £450	450
1 Facsimile machine @ £450	450
Office furniture and utilities	2 000
Furnishings	500
Software packages	2 000
	18 400
Start-up stationery and consumables	600
Grand Total	19 000

6.3 A vehicle suitable for the collection and delivery service can be acquired, under a full maintaining lease, for £180 per month.

7   EQUITY AND FINANCING
7.1 Each partner can contribute £3000 of personal capital to the business.
7.2 Beyond the partners' capital, there is a requirement for £10 000 of additional, long-term financing. The partners are looking to raise this sum by way of a loan under the Small Firms Loan Guarantee Scheme, repayable over a 10-year term.
7.3 The Cash Flow Forecast contained in Appendix 'A', illustrates the need for short-term financing during the first year of operation. This requires an overdraft facility of up to £10 000 during the first 13 months of operation.

8   CONCLUSION
This is an exciting proposition and one to which the partners will be devoting their energies with great commitment. It is hoped that the bank, too, wish to be part of this enterprise and that it will feel it appropriate to extend all the facilities outlined in 7.2 and 7.3 above. The partners will, of course, be pleased to supply any further information that may be required.

Appendix 'A'

Cash Flow Forecast

DETAIL	Apr	May	Jun	Jul	Aug	Sept	Oct	Nov	Dec	Jan	Feb	Mar	Total
Income: Fees	—	1 272	1 920	2 568	3 216	3 864	4 512	5 160	5 160	5 160	5 160	5 160	43 152
Partners capital	9 000												9 000
Bank loan	10 000												10 000
Total income	19 000	1 272	1 920	2 568	3 216	3 864	4 512	5 160	5 160	5 160	5 160	5 160	62 152
Expenditure													
Capital expenditure	19 000												19 000
Operations costs:													
Drawings	2 400	2 400	2 400	2 400	2 400	2 400	2 400	2 400	2 400	2 400	2 400	2 400	28 800
Vehicle lease	180	180	180	180	180	180	180	180	180	180	180	180	2 160
Rent	750			750			750			750			3 000
Vehicle running costs	200	200	200	200	200	200	200	200	200	200	200	200	2 400
Advertising	200	200	150	100	100	100	100	100	100	100	100	100	1 450
Consumables	64	96	128	160	193	226	258	258	258	258	258	258	2 415
Insurances:													
Vehicle	300												300
Other	400												400
Loan repayment		215	215	215	215	215	215	215	215	215	215	215	2 365
Total expenditure	23 494	3 291	3 273	4 005	3 288	3 321	4 103	3 353	3 353	4 103	3 353	3 353	62 290
Excess (deficit)	(4 494)	(2 019)	(1 353)	(1 437)	(72)	543	409	1 807	1 807	1 057	1 807	1 807	—
Prior month	—	(4 494)	(6 513)	(7 866)	(9 303)	(9 375)	(8 832)	(8 423)	(6 616)	(4 809)	(3 752)	(1 945)	—
Running total	(4 494)	(6 513)	(7 866)	(9 303)	(9 375)	(8 832)	(8 423)	(6 616)	(4 809)	(3 752)	(1 945)	(138)	(138)

243

Appendix 'B'

Forecast Profit and Loss Account — Year 1

Income		
Fees		48 312
Less: Expenses:		
Vehicle costs (1)	4 860	
Rent	3 000	
Advertising	1 450	
Consumables	2 415	
Insurances	400	
Interest and charges on overdraft (2)	587	
Interest on bank loan (3)	1 365	
Depreciation	3 800	17 877
Forecast net profit		30 435

Notes

(1) Vehicle costs: (from Cash Flow Forecast)

Vehicle lease	2 160
Vehicle running costs	2 400
Insurances — vehicle	300
	4 860

(2) Bank interest and charges are based on figures provided by the bank and calculated on the periodic overdraft as shown on the Cash Flow Forecast. These will be added to the overdraft, as per the Cash Flow Forecast, to produce the Balance Sheet overdraft of £725.

(3) The loan repayment of £2365 is:

Repayment of loan	1 000	(Deducted from loan in Balance Sheet)
Interest on loan	1 365	
	2 365	

Appendix 'C'

Forecast Balance Sheet — end of Year 1

	Cost	Depreciation	Book value
Fixed assets			
Equipment and furniture	19 000	3 800 (1)	15 200
Current assets			
Debtors		5 160 (2)	
Less: Current liabilities:			
Bank overdraft		725 (3)	4 435
			19 635
Financed by:			
Proprietor capital	9 000		
Plus: Profit	30 435	39 435	
Less: Drawings		28 800	10 635
Long-term bank loan			9 000
			19 635

Notes
(1) Depreciation has been calculated at the rate of 20% on the straight line basis.
(2) March fees — receivable April.
(3) Overdraft at ... as per Cash Flow Statement   138
       Interest and charges on overdraft   587
       Overdraft as at 31 March 19– –   725

Appendix 'D'

Forecast Profit and Loss Account — Year 2

Income		
Fees		61 920
Less: Expenses:		
Vehicle costs	4 860	
Rent	3 000	
Advertising	1 200	
Consumables	3 096	
Insurances	400	
Interest on overdraft	20	
Interest on bank loan	1 365	
Depreciation	3 800	17 741
Forecast net profit		44 179

Note This forecast is based on current prices and takes no account of any possible expansion in the level of business activity.

Exercises

1. Carlton Manufacturing is considering buying a new machine which will considerably speed up part of the manufacturing process. Three machines have been identified as being suitable for the process and all have differing costs, life spans and profit potential as follows:

| | Machine | | |
	X	X	X
Cost	30 000	40 000	60 000
Estimated profit generation:			
Year 1	10 000	8 000	15 000
Year 2	10 000	8 000	15 000
Year 3	10 000	12 000	15 000
Year 4	12 000	12 000	15 000
Year 5	12 000	15 000	15 000
Year 6		15 000	18 000
Year 7		15 000	18 000
Year 8			18 000
Year 9			18 000
Year 10			18 000
Estimated life span (years)	5	7	10

Compare the merits of each machine using the following investment appraisal methods:
   (a) Pay-back period
   (b) Return on capital
   (c) Present-day value (using the following discount factors)

Year 1	0.9620	Year 6	0.6546
Year 2	0.8902	Year 7	0.6061
Year 3	0.8245	Year 8	0.5612
Year 4	0.7635	Year 9	0.5197
Year 5	0.7070	Year 10	0.4813

2. For the past 12 years, Alec Jones has worked as a vehicle mechanic in three different main car dealerships where he has gained valuable experience of servicing and repairing a variety of vehicles. In the town where he lives, there is one main car dealership whose average labour charge for servicing and repair is £28 per hour. A local petrol station also has a small repair shop where labour charges are £19 per hour. All oils and parts are, of course, charged as extras to the labour charge.

   Alec has found suitable workshop premises at an annual rent of £6000 per annum on a five-year lease, payable monthly in advance, and is contemplating starting his own business and repair garage. He has personal capital of £20 000 to invest in the business but he realizes that equipment will cost around £30 000. Alec believes he can secure an adequate amount of work at an hourly charge of £15 per hour.

For the first 12 months of operating, Alec has estimated the following:

Month	Hours charged	Cost	Materials/parts charged
1	200	800	1000
2	200	800	1000
3	200	800	1000
4	200	800	1000
5	200	800	1000
6	200	800	1000
7	360	1400	1800
8	360	1400	1800
9	360	1400	1800
10	360	1400	1800
11	360	1400	1800
12	360	1400	1800

He estimates his operating expenses as:

Wages:	Months 1–6	400 per month
	Months 7–12	1400 per month
Insurances	£800 annual premium paid at commencement	
Heat and light	£150 per quarter paid April, July, October, January	
Telephone	£90 per quarter paid April, July, October, January	
Misc expenses	£250 per month	
Tool replacements	£30 per month	
Advertising	£100 per month	

Alec has enquired about a bank loan of £20 000 over 10 years and has been advised that monthly repayments will be interest £80 and repayment of loan capital £170. Overdraft facilities will be charged at 10 per cent on month-end balances.

Alec estimates that work promised by a local taxi firm and local business contacts will account for 50 per cent of his turnover. Payment for this work will be by the end of the month following. Private motorists will account for the other 50 per cent and all work will be paid for on completion.

He intends to draw £1500 per month out of the business to cover his personal expenses.
From the information provided, prepare a Business Proposal for submission to the bank. This should include a Cash Flow Forecast; first year projected Profit and Loss Account and Balance Sheet.
Note Materials/parts are paid for on monthly credit terms, all other expenses are paid in the month incurred unless stated otherwise.

Section 3

Costs and Budgets

Unit 16

Costs are critical

Cost behaviour

Costs are of critical importance to any organization. By costs, we mean every item of expense incurred by a firm in order to manufacture its products and run its business. Examples of such costs will range from the cost of materials used in manufacturing a product and the cost of the labour making the product, to the rent paid for the firm's premises and the interest charged by its bank on a business loan.

However, all costs can be broadly identified as belonging to one of two types. Let us first consider those costs which are most readily identified as being *directly* associated with producing a firm's products. In this context, think of this type of cost as being those costs incurred in establishing prime cost in the manufacturing account. Expenses such as materials used in manufacture, labour (wages) employed to make products and the cost of packaging materials.

Let us now examine how these costs might 'behave' at varying volumes of sales and production. Imagine a computer manufacturing company where costs for each computer manufactured are:

Materials	250.00
Labour — assembling computer	65.00
Labour — inspecting and testing	20.00
Packaging materials	5.00
	340.00

Now let us look at the firm's total production costs at different volumes of production:

Units produced	100	200	300
Production cost (units × £340)	34 000	68 000	102 000

We can plot these costs on a graph:

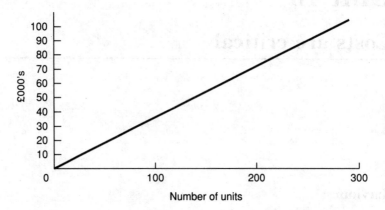

We can see that the total production cost is rising in a totally uniform manner as volume of production increases. *In other words these costs are increasing in proportion to the increase in production.* Such costs are identified as *variable costs* because they vary in relation to production levels.

If all costs behaved this way, most managers would sleep more soundly! Imagine their joy at a situation where costs are incurred only in proportion to their level of sales and production. Even in the worst possible situation where they neither made nor sold anything they would not incur a loss. (They would not make any profit either, of course.) If they were not producing anything then they would have no costs. They would not be using materials, employing production workers or using packaging.

However, as any manager who has had a restless night will testify, reality is far removed from this idyllic situation. And the cause of the problem is *fixed costs*. These indirect costs are, for example, the types of cost we have seen lurking about in the Profit and Loss Account. Costs such as rent on premises, interest payable on business loans, etc. The problem with these types of cost is that they are incurred *irrespective of the volume of sales or production*. If the firm sold nothing and made nothing it would make a loss equal to the total of all these costs.

To understand fully the significance of the impact of these costs let us return to our Computer Manufacturing Company which sells computers for £500 and whose 'fixed costs' total £20 000 per year.

Now let us do a profit statement at sales of 100, 200 and 300 units:

Units sold	100	200	300
Sales revenue	50 000	100 000	150 000
Variable (production) costs	34 000	68 000	102 000
	16 000	32 000	48 000
Less: Fixed costs	20 000	20 000	20 000
Net profit/(loss)	(4 000)	12 000	28 000

Now we can see the dramatic impact of fixed costs, we have a situation where the firm must manufacture and sell a large number of computers just to cover its fixed costs. Only after doing this will it then start to move into profit.

So, we may ask, what is the number of computers it must sell to reach a situation where it is not making a loss nor is it making any profit? This critical point is called the *break-even point*.

We can see from the previous table that the point must be somewhere between 100 computers sold at a total loss of £4000 and 200 sold at a total profit of £12 000. But, where is it precisely?

In the next section we will see how this point is determined and start to understand its significance in making business decisions.

Before we leave this section it is right to point out that our examination of costs and their behaviour has only been superficial. It is an area which can be subjected to advanced theory and techniques and one on which whole volumes are now written. However, this basic understanding will help us considerably as we progress to a more in-depth study of cost accounting in the next unit.

Break-even analysis

How then do we find this point called break-even — the point at which a firm's income and costs will be in balance? In other words, at which point will the firm be making neither profit nor loss?

This technique, which seems to cause difficulty for many students, is in fact quite straightforward provided that the basics have been understood. In practice the break-even point is calculated, and we will be looking at this shortly. However, many students appear to grasp the concept more easily if first the technique is illustrated graphically. Let us take the computer manufacturing company we looked at in the previous section. First we must draw the skeleton of a graph. In the example shown in the following graph the units sold/produced range from 0 to 300 and total costs (variable + fixed costs) from £0 to £122 000 while sales income ranges from £0 to £150 000. To fit these parameters into a graph we need a line 0–300 to represent the number of units sold and a line 0–£150 000 to represent sales income and costs:

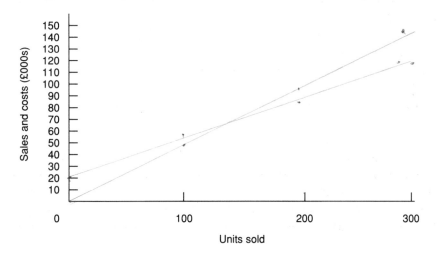

We are now going to insert three lines on the graph:

(1) A line to represent the fixed costs.
(2) A line to represent total costs (fixed + variable costs).
(3) A line to represent sales revenue.

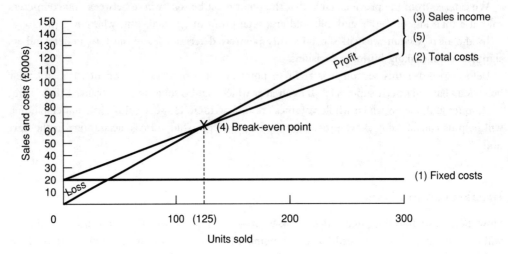

Notes

(1) *Fixed costs line.* Fixed costs are £20 000 so we draw a horizontal line across the graph from the £20 000 point. We do this because at any level of sales the fixed costs are the same.

(2) *Total cost line.* The first question to ask is 'What is the total cost at nil units of sales/ production?' The answer is £20 000 — being the fixed costs the firm will incur whether it produces or not. Therefore our total cost line will start for nil units sold from the £20 000 point, i.e. from the fixed cost line. Our furthest point will be at 300 units sold where total costs are £122 000 (£20 000 fixed costs + £102 000 variable costs).

(3) *Sales income line.* At zero sales, sales revenue will be zero. The line therefore starts from zero. At 300 units sold, sales income is £150 000.

(4) *Break-even point.* This is where the total of income and costs is the same (in this case at 125 units).

(5) *Total profit.* For any level of units sold the total profit can be read from the graph.

We can now see that the break-even point is where the sales income and the total cost lines intersect (marked with an X on the graph). If we read down from this point to the units sold (the graph abscissa) we will see that break-even has occurred at 125 units sold. We can also see that below 125 units sold the firm is making a loss and that above this point it is making a profit. We can also read from the graph the profit or loss the firm will make at any particular number of units sold.

We will be returning to the graph later because there is more interesting information it can reveal. However, before we do, let us now look at how we might calculate the break-even point without drawing a graph.

Calculation of break-even

In the case of the Computer Manufacturing Company, we have seen that every unit sold produces an 'excess' of sales revenue over variable cost of £160, i.e. selling price £500 − variable cost £340 = excess £160.

The term 'excess' is a rather loose description in this context. In practice it is therefore properly called *contribution*. This latter term leads us very nicely towards the solution we seek. Contribution to what? we may ask. What it means is that every single unit sold is contributing to the firm's fixed costs and, when they have been covered, to the firm's net profit. In the case of the Computer Manufacturing Company, the first unit sold 'contributes' £160 towards the firm's fixed costs of £20 000 as does the second unit sold, the third, fourth, fifth, and so on, until the whole of the fixed costs, in this case £20 000, have been covered. At the point where the number of contributions made have a total value equal to the fixed costs, we have break-even. In the case of the Computer Manufacturing Company, we know from the graph that this point is at 125 units sold, i.e. 125 units sold × £160 contribution = £20 000 fixed costs. Beyond this point the contribution of the 126th, 127th, 128th, and so on, units sold will be to the firm's net profit.

In practice, therefore, we could have calculated the break-even point for the Computer Manufacturing Company quite easily, without resorting to a graph. All we needed to know was the selling price per unit (£500), the variable cost per unit (£340) and the total of fixed costs (£20 000):

SP (selling price)	500
Less: VC (variable cost)	340
Equals contribution per unit	160

If we now divide the contribution of one unit into the total fixed costs, we arrive at a number of units whose total contributions will just cover fixed costs. This point is the number of units sold to break even:

$$\frac{£20\,000 \text{ (fixed costs)}}{£160 \text{ (contribution per unit)}} = 125 \text{ units}$$

Let us take another situation where a firm has a selling price of £150, a variable cost of £100 per unit and fixed costs totalling £50 000:

SP	=	150
VC	=	100
Contribution	=	50

Break-even is therefore:
$$\frac{£50\,000}{£50} = 1000 \text{ units sold}$$

We will see later in our study how this technique, and variations of it, can be an extremely valuable tool in making business decisions.

Before leaving this section, let us return to the graph to learn how it can give us another piece of useful information. If the Computer Manufacturing Company was actually selling 126 units, its management would be far from happy. Firstly, the firm would only make a net profit of £160 — being the contribution of the one unit sold above break-even. Perhaps more importantly, the managers would feel very vulnerable. If the level of sales dropped by only two units, the firm will be in a loss-making situation. In other words, the trading *margin of safety* would be so small as to be almost non-existent.

On the other hand, if the firm were selling 300 units, its margin of safety would be 175 units (300 – 125). This means that sales could fall by 175 units or 58 per cent before it started to become unprofitable. At 250 units sold, its margin of safety would be 125 units or 50 per cent and at 200 units sold its margin of safety would be 75 units or 37.5 per cent.

If you think carefully about this topic, you will see how critical cost behaviour is to any business. You will also appreciate how, if sales fall, it is firms whose fixed costs represent a high proportion of their total costs who will probably get into difficulty first. For this reason, it is vital that any business must try to restrict its fixed costs to the lowest possible level commensurate with being able to run its business efficiently.

Cost accounting in focus

The first two sections of this unit have, hopefully, stimulated interest in how financial information can be used objectively and become a management tool — a means of controlling events in an informed way to try and ensure that the objectives of a business are met.

We may well be forgiven for thinking that we have been following that strand since we started reading this book and became immersed in the intricacies of financial accounting. Indeed we were, but only to a limited extent. Financial accounts suffer from major drawbacks as far as day-to-day management is concerned. Quite simply, they are historic and they are a global representation of the business as a whole.

The financial accounts report what has actually happened in a period now past. Nothing can be done to change the events which the figures represent. Sure, some lessons may be learnt and different tactics deployed, but it is fact that financial accounts are not a user-friendly tool for management charged with the task of making things happen on a day-to-day basis. In any event, the financial accounts are global sums for the business and could hide a multitude of sins, as well as successes. To illustrate this point crudely, consider a diverse business making a range of products. Overall, it may be producing acceptable profits but, underlying this apparent success, may be all manner of worrying trends. It may be that, say, while 70 per cent of its product range is producing handsome profits, the other 30 per cent is trading at a loss. The point is that management needs to know. Cost accounting is designed to fill this role.

A broad comparison between financial accounting and cost accounting may help us understand the essential differences.

Cost accounting and financial accounting compared

1. *Mandatory or optional*
   (a) Cost accounting is optional and can be organized and used in a way that best suits local management.
   (b) Financial accounting is mandatory and governed by external rules.
2. *Purpose*
   (a) Cost accounting is for internal management.
   (b) Financial accounts provide global information to the owners of a business and external agencies.
3. *Accounting conventions*
   (a) Cost accounting only needs to follow one rule — *is the information produced useful to local management?*
   (b) Financial accounts follow accounting conventions and externally imposed rules.
4. *Focus*
   (a) Cost accounting focuses on every part of a business, on individual products and activities.
   (b) Financial accounts take a 'bird's high' view of the business.
5. *Historical versus current*
   (a) Cost accounting is applied to the future, present and past.
   (b) Financial accounts record and represent events that have happened in the past.
6. *Information*
   (a) Cost accounting can be tailored to the needs and understanding of the user.
   (b) Financial accounts are targeted at a wide and varied external audience, while they convey general information they are not tailored to specific individual requirements.

The result of these comparisons may lead us to the conclusion that cost accounting has it by 6 to nil. That is not the answer. Both play a vital role in the financial control and manipulation of a business. The purpose of the exercise was to be persuasive that cost accounting *does* play a vital role and deserves the kind of thought and attention we have been giving to our previous studies of financial accounting.

The next four units are a brief introduction to what is a wide subject area of ever increasing complexity.

Unit 17
Direct costs

Understanding the basics

Cost accounting deals with expenditure under three separate headings:

1. Labour
2. Materials
3. Other expenses.

If we think about this carefully, it does seem to be a totally rational approach. Think of any business and we will find that some, or all, of these costs are present. We must also conclude that in total they cover the range of costs a business can incur.

However, for reasons we started to understand in the previous unit, and which we will explore further, to make information meaningful and to be able to manipulate figures to reflect our knowledge of the way in which certain costs behave, we need a more detailed analysis of costs.

To achieve this more detailed analysis, we divide each cost heading into direct and indirect costs:

Direct costs	Indirect costs (overheads)
Labour	Labour
Materials	Materials
Expenses	Expenses

Note that we have dropped the word 'other' before expenses. This is purely for convenience. Labour and materials are, of course, expenses but we will interpret expenses as meaning any costs other than labour or materials.

The analysis may seem extremely simple and indeed it is. However, it is surprising that many students do not appear to grasp this simple concept at an early stage. Think about it now and life will be much easier as we progress.

Knowing the way in which costs are analysed is one thing. Let us think of the manufacture of, say, a bicycle. The business will consist of a production facility where the bikes are actually made;

an administration function dealing with the finances and general administration of the business; a sales function selling the bikes; and a distribution function getting the bikes to dealers.

Cost accounting is concerned with producing information which aids management in its task of ensuring that each function operates efficiently towards meeting the objectives of the business.

A prime responsibility of the management of the production facility will be to ensure that the costs of actually producing a bike are within a target cost (we will be looking at this in detail later).

The direct costs of a bike will be:

1. The cost of labour directly involved in making the bike — be it welding the frame together; painting the frame; fitting the components to the frame such as wheels, brakes, pedals, handlebars and seat.
2. The cost of the materials which go into making the bike and form part of the finished product — tubing from which to make the frame; paint applied to the frame; tyres fitted to the wheels, etc.
3. Expenses directly attributable to a bike. Direct expenses are not as prevalent as labour or materials but can occur where an expense can be totally identified as relating to a particular unit of production. If, say, our bicycle manufacturer sent some frames out to a specialist firm for stove enamelling, then the cost of this service would be a direct expense of producing the particular bikes by having this finish applied to their frames.

We can see that this information, presented in this way, is a powerful tool in the hands of management responsible for the manufacturing function. It is powerful for a number of reasons:

1. These important costs are, in total, the prime costs incurred in producing a bike. The costs can be continually monitored and controlled against some form of accepted target cost.
2. In theory, if not always in practice, these costs are variable. If the direct (or prime) cost of producing a particular bike is £50 then the total direct cost of producing 10 bikes should be £500 and 100 bikes £5000.

   In other words, the direct costs will vary directly in proportion to the number of bikes produced.
3. Knowing the direct cost of a product enables management to invoke analytical techniques which can aid decision making in areas such as pricing. These techniques rely heavily on the behaviour of costs in so far as they vary with the level of production. In Unit 16, we had a taste of how the variability of costs can be used to construct useful information.

In the remainder of this unit, we will be looking more closely at direct costs, at how they can be identified and the relevant data collected.

Before moving on, however, what of indirect costs? Quite simply, indirect costs are those costs which cannot be identified as being direct costs. A common description of these costs is *overheads*. The overheads of a business are, therefore, the sum total of the indirect costs. As we saw earlier, like direct costs, indirect costs can comprise labour, materials and expenses.

To illustrate this point, we will return to our bicycle manufacturer. We will assume that the business makes a variety of different types of bike — mountain bikes, racing bikes, folding bikes, shopping and children's bikes. Because of the different styles, complexity of construction and material quality used, each type of bike has its own direct cost parameters.

Indirect costs (overheads) for this manufacturer will be found in the following:

1. *Production*
   (a) *Labour*. Cost of production management, supervisors, cleaners, storekeepers, etc. Their work ranges across the whole spectrum of production and their salaries and wages cannot be identified with a particular bike.
   (b) *Materials*. These could include lubricants for machinery, replacement parts and components for machinery, gases for welding, welding rods, cleaning materials, etc. They might also include materials which go into the finished product but are too insignificant to warrant the time and trouble of trying to identify the direct cost. One example might be the low cost of grease used in assembling wheel and pedal bearings.
   (c) *Expenses*. These are expenses which can be associated with the production facility. They could include rent and insurance of a factory; repair and maintenance of plant and equipment; power; light; heat, etc.
2. *Administration*. The total cost of the function which may include:
   (a) Salaries of administrative staff.
   (b) Printing and stationery.
   (c) Office rent; insurances; legal expenses; repair and maintenance of office equipment, etc.
3. *Sales*. The total cost of the sales function may include:
   (a) Sales staff salaries and commissions.
   (b) Advertising and promotional costs, etc.
4. *Distribution*. The total cost of distribution may include:
   (a) Rent and insurances of warehouse(s).
   (b) Salaries and wages of distribution staff; management; packers; drivers.
   (c) Depreciation and running costs of delivery vehicles.

The following illustration should help put the cost structure into perspective:

	Costs		
Function	Direct	Indirect	Total
Production:			
Labour	XX		
Materials	XX		
Expenses	XX		
Prime cost (total direct costs)			XX
Labour		XX	
Materials		XX	
Expenses		XX	
Production overheads (total indirect production cost)			XX
Total production cost			XX
Administration		XX	
Selling		XX	
Distribution		XX	
Administration, selling and distribution overheads			XX
Total cost			XX

Unit 18 is concerned with how we take the whole wedge of costs appearing in the Indirect costs column and seek to spread those costs equitably over units of production to arrive at a reasonable cost per unit of production based on this simple formula:

Prime cost of production	XX
Apportioned overheads	XX
Cost of unit of production	XX

Direct labour

In order to determine the cost of direct labour we need to know three things:

- Details of employees engaged in direct labour activities.
- Costs of employing these workers.
- Time spent by these workers on various direct labour activities.

Time spent

This can be recorded in a variety of ways, for example:

1. *Clock cards.* The employee has a personal time card which is inserted into the recording mechanism of a special clock. The time of arrival at, or departure from, work is recorded

on the card, hence the term 'clocking on' and 'clocking off'. This system is normally used just to record total attendance and provide details for working out total wage entitlement. Used in this way, the information recorded is not sufficient to enable an analysis of total wages over individual jobs to be made.

2. *Time sheets*. These are designed to enable an analysis to be made of time spent on jobs. The type of system used will depend mainly on the nature of the business, for example:

Weekly time sheet: when workers tend to be engaged on repetitive work on the same product.

Daily time sheet: when workers may move between different jobs, sometimes often during a day.

Job cards: these often move along with the job to which they relate. As a worker completes a task on the job, the time spent will be entered on the card.

To illustrate how this might work, let us take a simple example of one worker's weekly wages and time analysis.

The clock card of Bill Brown shows that he has attendance hours for a particular week of 35 hours. Assuming his pay is £6 per hour, the payroll will show a gross wage of 35 hours × £6 = £210.

This information is sufficient for making the appropriate entries in the financial accounting records. However, it is not detailed enough for cost accounting purposes. Bill's time sheet provides the additional information required:

Name: Bill Brown	Employee No 123					Week Ending . . . .
	PRODUCT					DOWN TIME
DAY	A	B	C	D	E	
Monday	3		4			
Tuesday	1	2	3.5			0.5
Wednesday	1		1	5		
Thursday	2	2		2		1
Friday	2	1	2	2		
TOTAL	9	5	10.5	9		1.5

The payroll facility can now be extended to produce an analysis of the cost of Bill Brown. (By inputting the detail of the time sheet, a modern computer system can allocate the costs of direct labour efficiently for large numbers of employees.) For example:

Employee	Hours	Rate	A	B	C	D	PO/6	Gross Wage
B Brown	35	£6	54.00	30.00	63.00	54.00	9.00	210.00

Note PO/6 is an imaginary cost account code for down time (idle time) which is part of production overheads.

Complexities in allocation of direct labour costs

In order that we can keep a proper perspective on the allocation of direct labour costs, we need to appreciate that, in reality, the task can involve a number of complexities:

1. *Wage rates*. In our illustration, we saw a straightforward, hourly rate. In practice, a business may have an incentive system of payment where pay is related in some way to the productive output of workers. Premium rates, overtime and bonuses may be paid. All these permutations make the determination of an hourly rate more complex. Annual bonuses, holiday pay, employers' contributions to National Insurance and pension schemes, also further complicate matters.
2. *Idle time*. In our illustration, idle time was charged to a specific production overhead account. As an alternative, another business may decide to build an element into the hourly rate to cover idle time which is accepted as an inevitable consequence of the business's particular production process.

The important point we must recognize is that there are a variety of ways in which these issues can be dealt with. The solution is to construct a system which meets the needs of a particular business and gives local management the information that it feels best meets its requirements. Beyond this, consistency is the important criterion.

If comparisons are to be made of cost performance from one period to another and with targets, then those comparisons will only be valid provided a consistent, period-to-period approach has been used.

Direct materials

Direct materials are those materials which form part of the finished product. The cost of these materials constitutes the direct material cost. Therein lies the problem associated with allocating material costs. Simply stated, '*what cost?*'

As we know, from our previous study, there are adjustments which can be made to the basic purchase cost shown on an invoice — to the extent that the sum actually paid is a different sum. Let us look at a skeleton invoice to clarify this point:

Invoice				
Quantity	Unit price	Commodity	£	p
10	£28.00 (1)	XXXXXXXXX	280	00
		Less: Trade discount 20%	56	00
			224	00 (2)
		Cash discount 5%	11	20
		NET INVOICE	212	80

Notes
(1) VAT has been omitted. VAT paid does not affect the cost as it is charged to a VAT input account and offset against VAT collected on outputs.
(2) The price used in the cost accounts is normally the net price after deduction of any trade or quantity discounts.

Cash discount is normally seen as a benefit accruing from the financial policy of the business and is treated as income under the heading of Discounts received.

Having resolved this problem area, we have still not answered the question '*what cost*'? Let us identify the next problem by way of an illustration:

The stock of a particular component numbers 27 but the components in stock have been bought at three different prices. We can represent this as:

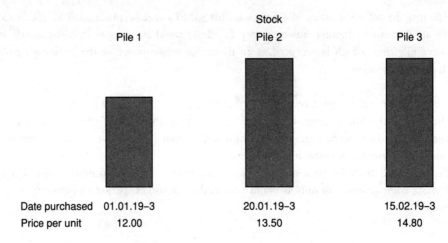

	Stock	
Pile 1	Pile 2	Pile 3

Date purchased	01.01.19–3	20.01.19–3	15.02.19–3
Price per unit	12.00	13.50	14.80

Assume that 12 components are taken from stock on 16.02.19–3. Should they be priced at £12.00, £13.50 or £14.50?

The answer is by no means clear-cut. It depends on the method used by the business for pricing issues from stock. There are, in fact, a variety of methods in use. This is a sample:

1. First in, first out — FIFO
2. Last in, first out — LIFO
3. Simple average cost
4. Weighted average cost
5. Periodic simple average cost
6. Periodic weighted average cost
7. Replacement cost
8. Standard cost

We will examine the four which are perhaps most commonly used in exercises and examinations, if not in practice.

First in, first out — FIFO

This method of pricing assumes that the materials that have been in stock longest will be issued first. Using our example, the pricing would be:

(Stock 1)	7 units @ 12.00	84.00
(Stock 2)	5 units @ 13.50	67.50
	12	151.50

Advantages

1. Materials are priced at actual cost.
2. Closing stock valued on this basis represents latest prices paid.
3. It is easily understood.

Disadvantages

1. Can be misleading as a cost on which selling prices are set.
2. In a period of rising prices, cost charged to production is low compared to current prices.
3. It is relatively complex to operate.

Last in first out — LIFO

This method assumes that the most recently acquired stock is the first to be issued. Again, using our example, the pricing would be:

(Stock 3)	10 units @ 14.80	148.00
(Stock 2)	2 units @ 13.50	27.00
	12	175.00

Advantages

1. Issues are priced at latest prices paid.
2. It is relatively simple to understand.

Disadvantages

1. Closing stock is valued at early prices and if prices are rising could be well below current replacement cost.
2. It is complex to operate.
3. The theory of this method is in conflict with the practical sense of rotating stock.

Weighted average cost

The average cost is recalculated every time new stock is bought. The calculation is the total cost of stock divided by the quantity in stock. Using our example:

(Stock 1)	7 units @ 12.00	84.00
(Stock 2)	10 units @ 13.50	135.00
(Stock 3)	10 units @ 14.80	148.00
	27	367.00

£367.00 ÷ 27 = £13.59 average cost
Issue price is 12 units @ £13.59 = £163.08

Advantages

1. It is only necessary to recalculate the average price after each purchase, not necessary after issues.
2. Issue prices are representative of the cost of stock as averaged.
3. Closing stock valuation is based on average of actual price paid.

Disadvantages

1. Can be complex to operate.

Standard cost

A standard cost is a result of a previous planning exercise where future costs are anticipated. Under such a system material issues are priced at a 'standard' or predetermined cost. Issues are priced at the standard cost, irrespective of the actual cost of purchase.

Again, using our example and assuming a standard cost of £14.
Issue price   12 units @ £14.00 = £168.00.

Advantages

1. Ease of calculating issue costs.
2. Production is charged with a known anticipated cost. The production management are not held responsible for buying prices which may be outside of their control.
3. The efficiency of the buying functions, as measured by the actual price variances from the standard (anticipated) price, can be monitored.
4. Standard prices designed to anticipate average price over a future period can be useful as a cost on which selling prices are set.

Disadvantages

1. If average actual prices fluctuate significantly from the standard, then prime production cost becomes unrealistic.
2. If actual prices and standard prices get too out of step, revision of standards may be necessary.

These systems may appear complex to operate and we have seen this as a disadvantage of some systems. However, in practice, this is less true than in the past. Modern computer-based systems can handle these complexities quickly and efficiently.

Issue documentation

The most usual method of recording material issues to provide a basis for pricing mateials into production is a Materials Requisition Note. This is an authorization to the stores personnel to issue the materials required and records, among other things:

1. Description of materials
2. Material code number
3. Quantity
4. Job number (to which issue is to be charged).

In a manual system, there would also be provision for adding the cost for pricing purposes. Again, computer-based systems have revolutionized this process. At the point of issue, the storekeeper can key in the material code, quantity and job number and, without any further action, the system will price the issue, charge it to the appropriate job and update the stock records. Very similar to our visit to the supermarket. Every time the checkout operator passes goods over the optical bar code reader the sale is registered, the cost of the goods sold is ascertained, the stock record is updated and purchase orders raised when stock reaches its re-order level.

Unit 18

Overheads

The nature of overheads

We have already learnt that any costs which are not direct costs are, by definition, indirect costs. The total of indirect costs represents the overheads of a business. Having established the direct costs of a unit of production, many businesses then seek to establish a system whereby overheads can be shared out between units of production to arrive at a total cost. Apportionment is the term used whereby overheads are 'shared' out. This system is referred to as *absorption costing* as the overheads apportioned are 'absorbed' into the product cost.

We have seen that identification of direct costs to production can be achieved with a high degree of accuracy, by means of time booking and materials requisitions. However, this is not the case when apportioning overheads.

Overhead (indirect) costs are categorized as such for the very reason that they cannot be wholly identified with a particular unit of production. It follows that any system of apportioning overheads has to be a subjective exercise based on assumptions and judgements. To state this simply, given the problem of apportioning a particular overhead, two accountants could produce different answers because they used a different basis on which the apportionment was made. To the extent that each believed that he or she was right and could show that his or her basis of apportionment came from sound reasoning then, indeed, either answer could be acceptable.

What then is an acceptable system of apportioning overheads? The criteria could broadly be defined as follows:

1. The method chosen to apportion overheads should result in the fairest and most accurate application possible of overheads to units of production.
2. As most overhead costs relate more to time than to level of activity, the basis of apportionment should have some relation to time.

Apportioning production overheads

Let us return to the model we saw earlier in this study.

	Costs		
Function	Direct	Indirect	Total
Production			
Labour	XX		
Materials	XX		
Expenses	XX		
Prime cost (total direct costs)	—		XX
Labour		XX	
Materials		XX	
Expenses		XX	
Production overheads (total indirect production cost)		—	XX
Total production cost			XX
Administration		XX	
Selling		XX	
Distribution		XX	
Administration, selling and distribution overheads		—	XX
Total cost			XX

Generally speaking, we will find that the more divorced from actual production a function is, the more arbitrary a system of apportionment will become. If this is true then, using our model, if we first look at how the overheads of the production facility might be apportioned we should obtain the best idea of how overheads might be apportioned to achieve a reasonable degree of fairness and accuracy.

Production overheads

Let us say that production overheads for our model consist of:

Management and supervisory salaries	105 000
Rent and rates	30 000
Storekeeping costs	26 000
Depreciation of plant and equipment	18 000
Power	12 000
Heating and lighting	9 000
	200 000

We also have the following information:

	Products			
	A	B	C	Total
Units produced	8 000	5 000	7 000	20 000
Direct costs per unit:				
Labour	25.00	40.00	35.00	
Materials	15.00	30.00	25.00	
Prime cost	40.00	70.00	60.00	
Direct labour hours per unit	5	7	5	
Machine hours per unit	4	6	5	
Floorspace occupied	40%	30%	30%	

A reasonable apportionment may be:

Overhead	Basis	A	B	C	Total
1 Management salaries	Direct labour hours	38 182	33 409	33 409	105 000
2 Rent and rates	Floorspace	12 000	9 000	9 000	30 000
3 Storekeeping costs	Direct material cost	7 011	8 764	10 225	26 000
4 Depreciation	Machine hours	5 938	5 567	6 495	18 000
5 Power	Machine hours	3 959	3 711	4 330	12 000
6 Heat and light	Floorspace	3 600	2 700	2 700	9 000
		70 690	63 151	66 159	200 000

Workings:
1. Direct labour hours

Units	8 000	5 000	7 000	
Hours per unit	5	7	5	
Total hours	40 000	35 000	35 000	110 000

Rate per direct labour hour = £105 000 ÷ 110 000 = £0.954 55

Apportionment A	40 000 × 0.954 55	=	38 182
Apportionment B	35 000 × 0.954 55	=	33 409
Apportionment C	35 000 × 0.954 55	=	33 409
			105 000

2. Rent and rates based on floorspace

Apportionment A	30 000 × 40%	=	12 000
Apportionment B	30 000 × 30%	=	9 000
Apportionment C	30 000 × 30%	=	9 000
			30 000

3. Direct material cost

	A	B	C	
Units	8 000	5 000	7 000	
Material cost per unit	15.00	30.00	25.00	
Total material cost	120 000	150 000	175 000	445 000

Percentage on materials = £26 000 ÷ 445 000 × 100 = 5.84269%

Apportionment A	120 000 × 5.842 69%	=	7 011	
Apportionment B	150 000 × 5.842 69%	=	8 764	
Apportionment C	175 000 × 5.842 69%	=	10 225	
			26 000	

4. Machine hours

	A	B	C	
Units	8 000	5 000	7 000	
Machine hours per unit	4	6	5	
Total machine hours	32 000	30 000	35 000	97 000

Rates per machine hour = £18 000 ÷ 97 000   =   £0.185 57

Apportionment A	32 000 × 0.185 57	=	5 938
Apportionment B	30 000 × 0.185 57	=	5 567
Apportionment C	35 000 × 0.185 57	=	6 495
			18 000

5. Machine hours
   Rate per machine hour = £12 000 ÷ 97 000 = £0.123 71

Apportionment A	32 000 × 0.123 71	=	3 959
Apportionment B	30 000 × 0.123 71	=	3 711
Apportionment C	35 000 × 0.123 71	=	4 330
			12 000

6. Heat and light based on floorspace

Apportionment A	9 000 × 40%	=	3 600
Apportionment B	9 000 × 30%	=	2 700
Apportionment C	9 000 × 30%	=	2 700
			9 000

We can now construct a statement to show total production costs:

	A	B	C	Total
Direct costs				
Labour	200 000	200 000	245 000	645 000
Materials	120 000	150 000	175 000	445 000
Prime cost	320 000	350 000	420 000	1 090 000
Production overheads	70 690	63 151	66 159	200 000
Total production cost	390 690	413 151	486 159	1 290 000
Units produced	8 000	5 000	7 000	
Production cost per unit	£48.84	£82.63	£69.45	

We can probably agree that this looks to be a reasonable method of having apportioned the production overheads.

Let us now have another look at the basis of apportionment. Instead of allocating management salaries on the basis of *direct labour hours*, we could have apportioned them on the basis of *direct labour cost*. Had we done so, the apportionment of management salaries would have been:

	A	B	C	
Direct labour costs	200 000	200 000	245 000	645 000

$$\text{Percentage on labour costs} = \frac{\pounds105\,000}{645\,000} \times 100 = 16.2791\%$$

Apportionment A	200 000 × 16.2791%	=	32 558
Apportionment B	200 000 × 16.2791%	=	32 558
Apportionment C	245 000 × 16.2791%	=	39 884
			105 000

If we compare the two alternatives, we have:

Apportionment basis	A	B	C
Direct labour hours	38 182	33 409	33 409
Direct labour costs	32 558	32 558	39 884

We can also see the extent to which production cost per unit would change:

	A	B	C
Total production cost would become	385 066	412 300	492 634
Units produced	8 000	5 000	7 000
Production cost per unit	£48.13	£82.46	£70.38
Differences	−£0.71	−£0.17	−£0.93

We can see that using a different basis of apportionment for just one overhead cost can produce a difference. How significant that difference is must be a matter of judgement. We can summarize the possible bases of apportionment we have looked at:

- Rate per direct labour hour.
- Percentage on direct labour costs.
- Rate per machine hour.
- Percentage on direct material costs.
- Space used.

The methods on this list are in common use. However, this list is by no means exhaustive. In fact, the ability to invent a reasonable basis to apportion a particular cost is constrained only by the limit of human ingenuity.

Before we move on, it is only fair to point out that some organizations will use one basis on which to apportion the total overheads rather than apply a reasoned basis to each type of cost. This is certainly a much easier option but whether it meets our criteria of what constitutes a fair and reasonable basis is doubtful. However, as this method can be used and, perhaps surprisingly, is the only method covered in some textbooks, we will have a quick look at what is involved.

We will use two bases of apportionment that we have not so far considered but which may be used by those adopting this total apportionment approach:

1. Rate per unit.
2. Percentage of prime cost.

Using our previous example

1. Rate per unit

$$\frac{\text{Total production costs}}{\text{Total units produced}} \quad \frac{200\,000}{20\,000} = \text{£10 per unit}$$

2. Percentage of prime cost

$$\frac{\text{Total production overheads}}{\text{Total prime costs}} \quad \frac{200\,000 \times 100}{1\,090\,000} = 18.348\%$$

The total production costs using these methods would be:

1. Rate per unit

	A	B	C
Units produced	8 000	5 000	7 000
Rate per unit	£10	£10	£10
Production overheads apportionment	80 000	50 000	70 000
Prime costs	320 000	350 000	420 000
Total production costs	400 000	400 000	490 000
Production cost per unit	£50	£80	£70

2. Percentage of prime cost

	A	B	C
Prime cost	320 000	350 000	420 000
Production overheads apportioned (18.3486% of prime cost)	58 716	64 220	77 064
Total production costs	378 716	414 220	497 064
Units produced	8 000	5 000	7 000
Production cost per unit	£47.34	£82.84	£71.01

Finally, we will compare the global results of the three methods we have now seen:

Production cost per unit

	A	B	C
	£	£	£
1. Detailed apportionment using appropriate basis for each overhead cost	48.84	82.63	69.45
2. Apportionment of total production overhead using one basis			
(a) Rate per unit method	50.00	80.00	70.00
(b) Percentage of prime cost method	47.34	82.84	71.01

Without commenting on the significance of the variations, we can safely say that different methods produce different unit costs. It follows that if each cost is deducted from selling price per unit, then the 'gross profit' per unit will also vary in the same proportion. Now we can better understand the comment in Unit 16 that any system of absorption costing (where overheads are apportioned to units of production and are hence 'absorbed' into the unit cost) is, at least, somewhat arbitrary. This will help us understand why management might have reservations about using total costs as a basis for pricing decisions as will be suggested in Unit 19.

Administration, sales and distribution

Just as we have sought to find an equitable basis on which to apportion production overheads to units of production, so too can we try to apportion the cost of other non-production functions.

We saw the comment earlier, that the further removed a function is from the production process, the harder it is to find an equitable basis of apportionment. However, if these departmental costs are to be apportioned, then as sensible as possible a basis must be found.

Administration overheads

Administration services are provided not only for the production facility but also for sales and distribution. It is not unusual to find that the overhead cost of administration was first apportioned out over production sales and distribution so that a proportion of administration costs becomes part of the sales and distribution function. The basis of apportionment might, for example, be numbers of staff employed in each department.

Sales and distribution overheads

It may be possible to apportion some sales costs on a specific basis because they can be more readily identified with a particular product. Examples of where this might happen are:

1. Commissions paid to sales personnel for selling particular products.

2. Significant advertising or promotional costs incurred in promoting a particular product.

Any other sales costs could be apportioned on the basis of a sales overhead rate calculated as:

$$\text{Sales overhead rate} = \frac{\text{Sales and distribution overheads} \times 100}{\text{Total production cost of all sales}}$$

Note that it is the production cost of units sold, not units produced, which is used.

Having looked at some of the intricacies of absorption costing, we should be aware that to many accountants overhead absorption has become a discredited technique. They would argue that the practice of sharing out overheads such as administration among cost units is so arbitrary as to make the information produced for management dubious. It is a matter to which we can all apply our minds. The fact that the topic continues to appear in exercises and examinations is clear evidence that not everyone subscribes to that view.

The main lesson we can learn is that overhead absorption is not, and cannot be, a precise 'science'. The reality is that, constrained only by common sense and an informed, rational approach, businesses can design or tailor systems to meet their own particular needs. We have given a taste, and only a taste, of what is a continually developing, complex and often controversial area of accounting.

Unit 19

Costs as an aid to decision making

Full cost pricing

In this section we are concerned with looking at some of the factors that may influence the price at which a firm sells a product. We will also see how our knowledge can help in arriving at these pricing decisions.

The first thing we have to understand is that costs and finances are only one factor, albeit an important one, to be considered when setting prices. Let us just quickly look at a few of these 'other' factors.

A company may, for instance, deliberately set a selling price for a product at a level where it only breaks even on that particular product or even makes a loss. This ploy is commonly referred to as 'loss leaders'. Supermarkets are perhaps a good example of this selling technique. They will vigorously promote loss leaders, not as an act of charity but to entice us into their stores. They hope, of course, that we will buy not only their loss leaders but also other products on which they are making profit, often substantial profit. Perhaps the main factor which will determine selling price is the price being charged by competitors selling a similar product. Unless they are in the happy position of being a monopoly, and this is rare, most firms have to sell in competition with others.

We need not concern ourselves with the range of 'other factors', a study of which is a specialist area. All we need to be aware of is that there are many apparently non-financial factors that will influence pricing decisions.

However, pricing does have to recognize one simple truth. Firms exist to make profit and if they fail in meeting this objective they eventually go out of business. Profit in its simplest form is the difference between sales income and costs. Pricing, therefore, which is a major determinant in shaping sales income, is of paramount importance.

One technique of pricing is based on a pricing system called *full cost pricing*. Perhaps because it is simple to apply, the technique is widely used. It relies on costing a product using *absorption costing*, a system with which we became acquainted in Unit 18. Absorption costing, as we know, implies that in costing products we will allocate to each product a share of the firm's fixed costs. Essentially, the fixed costs are going to be 'absorbed' into the cost of individual products. Let us look at this in the context of a computer manufacturing company with the following direct production costs and fixed overheads.

276

Materials	250.00
Labour — assembling computer	65.00
Labour — inspecting and testing	20.00
Packaging materials	5.00
	340.00
Fixed costs	20 000

Let us say that the management is predicting sales of 200 computers over the year and aiming at net profit being 20 per cent of sales income.

A pricing calculation representing this would be:

Variable costs		340
Allocation of fixed costs	$\dfrac{20\,000}{200}$	= 100
Total cost		440
Plus percentage for profit 440* × 25%	=	110
Selling price		550

*You may be puzzled as to why we have added 25 per cent for profit when the management target was 20 per cent of sales income. The answer is very simple. Management wants a return of 20 per cent on the selling price of £550. Now 20 per cent of £550 is £110 which is the figure we have included. But to achieve the 20 per cent return on selling price we had to *mark up* the cost price by 25 per cent. In other words, a percentage *mark up* on cost and a percentage *return* on sales *are not* the same thing.

Let us take another example:

Say we have a product costing		£10
Selling price is to be a 50% mark up on cost then £10 × 50%	=	£5
Therefore selling price is		£15

But as a percentage return on selling price, the profit of £5 represents a $33\frac{1}{3}$ per cent return, i.e. £5 is $33\frac{1}{3}$ per cent of £15.

Going back to our first example, where the cost was £440 and the selling price had to be a figure which would give a 20 per cent return on selling price, how can we calculate the selling price?

Answer: We know that, of the selling price, 20 per cent is to be profit. Therefore 80 per cent must be cost. We know that the cost is £440 so, if we divide £440 by 80 and multiply the answer by 100, we arrive at £550.

As we know, the real problem with using absorption costing comes when the firm makes more than one product, and some firms of course make hundreds. In this situation, the problem is knowing how to allocate the fixed costs between the different products. What basis should we use for allocating the fixed costs? Should it be in proportion to the variable costs of products? Should it be in proportion to the time it takes to make each product? The answer, as we have already seen, is that either or indeed any of the many other possible bases would be acceptable. There is no positively right way, only possible ways and the choice would depend on the views of the individual accountant. In other words, it is an *arbitrary* system of allocating fixed costs and can quite easily lead to management making wrong decisions.

Let us look at how this could happen: say we have two firms — Firm A and Firm B. Firm A makes product X with a variable cost of £20. The firm's accountant uses a basis of allocating fixed costs which results in an allocation of £4 to product X. The firm marks up cost price by 50 per cent to arrive at a selling price.

Firm B also makes a product Y which competes with Firm A's product X. Its variable costs are also £20 but its accountant's basis of allocating fixed costs results in an allocation of £8. The firm, like Firm A, marks up 50 per cent on cost to arrive at a selling price.

Now compare the results:

	Firm A	Firm B
Variable cost	20	20
Fixed cost	4	8
Total cost	24	28
Mark up 50%	12	14
Selling price	36	42

Assuming that the products are equally good, then it is likely that Firm A will capture the market with such a wide price difference. Firm B's product sale might fall dramatically and management may well decide to discontinue the product on the basis that the firm cannot compete.

Now, assuming that Firm B did not in fact use absorption costing for setting prices, it may well look at the product this way. Firm B knows that it is in competition with Firm A's product which sells for £36. Firm B may then decide to undercut Firm A and put its product out at £35, based on the following reasoning:

Selling price	£35
Variable cost	£20
Contribution (to fixed costs and profit costs and profit)	£15

If management thinks that at this price it can capture, say, 70 per cent of the market worth 100 000 units of sales per year, then the total contribution made by this product at £1 500 000 may seem very attractive indeed and management may make a totally different decision than if they had used absorption cost pricing.

Marginal cost pricing

We are already familiar with marginal costs because it was the cost structure and rationale used when we studied break-even analysis. A costing system based on this rationale is called *marginal costing*. Pricing decisions based on such a system are referred to as marginal cost pricing. The concept behind this system of pricing is that it does not have to rely on an arbitrary system of allocating fixed costs. It is easier to make decisions about what products to manufacture and sell because the judgement is made on which products make the largest total contribution to fixed costs and profit. Let us look at a simple illustration of how this might work.

Suppose a company makes two products, A and B, and details are:

	Product	
	A	B
Unit sales	5 000	5 000
Selling price	30	25
Variable cost	20	18
Contribution per unit	10	7
Total contribution	50 000	35 000

Now let us suppose that the company has developed another product — product C — which it can sell competitively for £23. The variable cost is £14 with projected sales of 5000 units per year. If the company (for reasons which need not concern us) has decided not to expand the size of its operation in order to make the additional product, the choice comes down to which two, of three possible products, should it produce (it cannot make all three because maximum production capacity is 10 000 units).

Making a decision based on marginal costs would rely on the following:

	Product		
	A	B	C
Unit sales	5 000	5 000	5 000
Selling price	30	25	23
Variable cost	20	18	14
Contribution per unit	10	7	9
Total contribution	50 000	35 000	45 000

Leaving other considerations aside, the sensible course of action would be to produce and sell product C rather than product B in the expectation of a £10 000 increase in profits.

We will be returning to the concept of marginal costs in the next section. However, all the aspects of costs, break-even and pricing we have looked at so far will give you a good working knowledge of how financial understanding can assist in making management decisions. Of necessity, our overview has been simplistic in terms of what is a vast and complex area.

However, this basic, and very necessary, understanding provides a firm foundation on which to build.

Case Study: Beyond the margin

In this unit we have looked at costs generally: the concept of break-even and what might influence pricing decisions. In the last section, we looked at the relevance of marginal costs to pricing decisions. We will now try to pull these ideas and concepts together and apply them, in the form of a case study, to a more complex management problem.

We are the accountants of our old friend the Computer Manufacturing Company. The management has convened a meeting to consider what action should be taken on a a quickly deteriorating level of sales. A rival firm is marketing an imported computer with a similar specification to the one produced by the Computer Manufacturing Company but at a selling price of £420, which is well below CMC's selling price of £500. The Sales Director, in the face of this competition, predicts that sales will fall to around 150 computers from the present level of 300. Research has shown that for an increase in production cost of £60 per computer, the firm could produce an enhanced, more powerful model for which the Sales Director predicts sales of 250 units at a selling price of £600. The company has of course the capacity to produce 300 units. An overseas agent has said it will take 50 of the new, improved computers under contract, but at a price of £520 each. We have been asked to assess the financial implications of various options.

Let us start by looking at the marginal costs of each type of computer:

	Marginal Cost	
Existing machine		340
Enhanced machine: Existing	340	
Plus	60	
		400

(*Remember* fixed costs are £20 000)

1. If the company continues to produce the existing machine and nothing else:

Selling price	500
Variable cost	340
Contribution per unit	160
Total contribution (150 × £160)	24 000
Less: Fixed costs	20 000
Net profit	4 000

$$\text{Break-even is } \frac{£20\,000}{£160} = 125 \text{ units}$$

The margin of safety is low at 25 units (150−125) or 16 per cent of sales.

2. If the company discontinues the existing machine and produces only the enhanced version:

Selling price	600	
Variable cost	400	
Contribution per unit	200	
Total contribution (250 × £200)		50 000
Less: Fixed costs		20 000
Net profit		30 000

$$\text{Break-even is } \frac{£20\,000}{£200} = 100 \text{ units}$$

The margin of safety is a respectable 150 units (250−100) or 60 per cent of sales.

So far, so good, but what about the spare production capacity to make another 50 units? Should the company continue to make 50 of the existing units or supply the potential export order?

	Existing	Export
Selling price	500	520
Variable cost	340	400
Contribution per unit	160	120
Total contribution (50 units)	8000	6000

Leaving aside all other considerations (and they are many), from a purely financial point of view, it seems sensible to sell 250 of the new, enhanced computers and 50 of the existing model.

Let us now do a comparison of the firm's profitability under the existing and proposed arrangements:

	Existing	Proposed
Contribution from existing product	48 000 (300 × £160)	8 000 (50 × £160)
Contribution from revised product		50 000 (250 × £200)
Total contribution	48 000	58 000
Less: Fixed costs	20 000	20 000
Net profit	28 000	38 000

On this basis, the company will improve its profitability by £10 000.

Remember, there are many other factors that will influence a decision of this type and we have looked only at the financial implications based on the information given. The importance of this exercise is two-fold. Firstly, we have practised using a variety of the concepts we have learnt but we have also looked at a frequent event, that of trading beyond the margin. This latter statement obviously warrants more explanation.

It is a fact that a large proportion of companies, in normal trading conditions, do have surplus production capacity. In times of recession most will have this problem. Marginal costing and marginal cost pricing can be very effective in these circumstances. Let us take a situation where a company has a production capacity of 10 000 units of product. In buoyant trading conditions, the company is normally trading at 9000 units sold, which is obviously 90 per cent of its capacity, on the following basis:

Selling price per unit	20.00
Variable cost per unit	13.00
Total fixed costs	30 000

In a time of adverse trading conditions, sales fall by 20 per cent to 7200 units. The Managing Director asks for advice on a number of points:

1. Will we still be profitable at the lower sales level?
2. If the company can still maintain total sales at 9000 units by doing 'special deals' on the 1800 units required to maintain normal sales levels, at what price can 1800 units be sold and achieve an overall 15 per cent return on capital employed (invested) in the business?

Capital employed in the business is £180 000.

First we will look at the previous position when trading at 9000 units, and at the new situation in a depressed market where sales have fallen to 7200 units.

	Previous	Now
Unit sales	9 000	7 200
Sales revenue	180 000	144 000
Variable cost	117 000	93 600
Contribution	63 000	50 400
Less: Fixed costs	30 000	30 000
Net profit	33 000	20 400
Return on capital	18.3%	11.3%

$$\text{Note} \quad \text{Return on capital} = \frac{\text{Net profit}}{\text{Capital employed}} \times 100$$

To achieve a 15 per cent return on capital employed, we need net profits of:

$$£180\,000 \times 15\% = £27\,000$$

Of the £27 000 net profit we require, the lower level of sales of 7200 units will produce £20 400:

Profit target	27 000
Profit on 7200 units	20 400
Required from 'extra' units	6 600

Therefore, the contributions from 1800 units must total £6600.

$$\frac{£6600}{1800} = £3.67 \text{ contribution required per unit}$$

The selling price of the 1800 units can now be calculated as:

Variable cost	13.00
Contribution	3.67
Selling price	16.67

A profit statement would now be:

Sales revenue:		
7200 units @ 20.00	144 000	
1800 units @ 16.67	30 006	174 006
Less: Variable costs (9000 × £13.00)		117 000
Contribution		57 006
Less: Fixed costs		30 000
Net profit		27 006

$$\text{Return on capital} = \frac{27\,006 \times 100}{180\,000} = 15\%$$

The answers to the Marketing Director's questions would therefore be:

1. Yes. Profits will be £20 000 representing a return on capital of 11.3 per cent.
2. Selling the 'extra' 1800 units @ £16.67 will produce profits of £27 006 representing a 15 per cent return on capital.

The Managing Director is pleasantly surprised with the answers. He now feels that at such a low price he may well be able to sell all the factory can produce. He now asks what the profit and return on capital will be if he can use all the capacity by selling a further 1000 units at the lower price.

$$\text{Contribution on 1000 units @ 3.67 per unit} = 3\,670$$
$$\text{Profit on 'existing' 9000 units} \qquad \underline{27\,006}$$
$$\underline{30\,676}$$

$$\text{Return on capital} = \frac{30\,676 \times 100}{180\,000} = 17\%$$

This practical exercise should have demonstrated the relevance of marginal cost pricing and its usefulness where decisions have to be made about taking 'marginal' business. We can see that when a business is trading above break-even (beyond the margin) the contribution made by every extra unit sold is a total contribution to profit.

Before we leave this section, we should perhaps briefly consider some other factors which make it imperative that management can respond to this type of changing situation.

The Managing Director in our example would be concerned not only about the financial effect of falling sales but also for his staff. In looking at the concept of variable costs, we have necessarily taken a very sympathetic approach. In reality many costs, although variable in nature, are not variable in the short term. This would be true as far as many of the production staff are concerned in this company. Leaving moral judgements aside, employment legislation prevents staff being 'hired and fired' on the whim of management. If a firm does have to shed staff through redundancies, it can face considerable costs and time delay while redundancies are being negotiated, and statutory periods of notice operate.

In our example, the benefit to the company of seeing a way to surmount what it hopes is a short-term problem, goes well beyond the profit motive we have covered. It takes time and money to train and retain a reliable, experienced workforce, so the prospect of maintaining its workers in full employment has social and 'hidden' financial benefits for the company as well.

When dealing with any scenarios involving management decisions, do try to look beyond the strictly obvious financial implications. By doing so, you will doubtless discover many social and 'hidden' benefit factors which warrant serious consideration.

Unit 20

Budgetary control

Nature and purposes

Intentionally or not we have all indulged in budgeting at various stages of our lives. A simple statement, such as 'Yes, I can afford that', or 'No, I cannot afford it' is the result of a budgetary process — elementary though it may be.

A more comprehensive example would be an attempt to control household finances. We will pursue this example. Let us say a family plans its income and expenditure for the coming year as:

Salaries (net)		16 500
Interest from savings		300
Total income		16 800
Expenses		
Mortgage repayments	3 600	
Electricity	350	
Heating	400	
Telephone	320	
House maintenance	400	
Car loan repayments	1 300	
Car running costs	1 800	
Food	3 000	
Clothes	1 000	
Holiday	2 500	
Insurances	700	15 730
Savings		1 430

This plan is a budget of what the family anticipates will be its income, expenditure and savings. If we now assume that the family keeps an adequate record of income and expenditure throughout the year, then it can compare its actual income with what it thought would happen. It can do this for each category of expense to see where any under- or over-spending has occurred.

	Budget	Actual	Variance	
			Positive	Adverse
Salaries (net)	16 500	17 300	800	
Interest from savings	300	250		50
	16 800	17 550	800	50
Mortgage repayments	3 600	3 600		
Electricity	350	360		10
Heating	400	380	20	
Telephone	320	420		100
House maintenance	400	360	40	
Car loan repayments	1 300	1 300		
Food	3 000	2 700	300	
Clothes	1 000	1 150		150
Holiday	2 500	2 350	150	
Insurances	700	740		40
Car running costs	1 800	2 300		500
	15 370	15 660	510	800
Savings	1 430	1 890	1 130	850

If the family had not kept records of income and expenditure for each type of income and expense, then all it would know at the end of the year is that anticipated savings are £460 more than planned. While this result may well please the family, it may not realize that if it had not 'overspent' by £100 on the telephone and £500 on running the car, its savings could have been £2490 (£1890 + £600).

Indeed, we could do a useful summary to explain in detail how the increase in savings came about.

Budgeted savings			1 430
Plus: Salaries increase		800	
Underspending on:			
Heating	20		
House maintenance	40		
Food	300		
Holidays	150	510	1 310
Possible savings			2 740
Less: Reduction in interest on savings		50	
Overspending on:			
Electricity	10		
Telephone	100		
Car running costs	500		
Clothes	150		
Insurances	40	800	850
Actual savings			1 890

Now, if the family has not died of malnutrition or talked too much on the telephone, it may find this information useful. It would certainly be most useful in helping to plan an even more accurate budget for the following year. However, the most immediate problem is that Dad is blaming his teenage son and daughter for the overspend on the telephone (sounds familiar). Now, let us assume that the telephone budget of £320 was based on 3200 dialled units, at a cost of 10p per unit. Let us also assume that the actual charge per unit made by the telephone company for the year was 12p for each of the 3500 actual dialled units.

Try to follow these calculations:

Telephone usage variances:

(Actual usage − Budgeted usage) × Budgeted cost per unit

$$3500 - 3200 \times 10p \quad = \quad 30$$

Telephone price variance:

(Actual price − Budgeted price) × Actual usage

$$12p - 10p \times 3500 \quad = \quad \underline{70}$$

$$\underline{100}$$

Now we can see that increased usage accounted for only £30 of the £100 overspend. Price increases imposed by the telephone company accounted for the other £70. Hopefully, Dad will now remonstrate twice as hard with the telephone company as he does with the teenagers.

If you have followed, and understood, this family example, then you understand the basis of budgeting and budgetary control. We have even had a brief exposure to variance analysis — a technique that needlessly worries many students.

Budgets for business

In our study of bookkeeping and accountancy, we were concerned with recording transactions that had taken place and producing Profit and Loss Accounts at the end of a year's trading. This information is useful to the owner(s) of the business and fulfils statutory requirements to provide year-end accounts to outside bodies such as the Inland Revenue. However, we have seen that this information has limited value to the management of the business who have the responsibility of ensuring that the business is run efficiently and profitably. The reason, of course, is that the information is historic and nothing can be done retrospectively to change what has happened.

Bearing in mind our family example, if a company also planned what should happen in the next year then it could compare the actual results produced by the accounting process with the budget to see where things have gone according to plan, or differed from what was planned. This would certainly be an improvement from not having a budget at all but, as a technique to foster effective management control, it would still be far from ideal. Comparing actual results against a plan (budget) at the end of a year will identify those areas where things have not gone according to plan but, again, it is historic information and nothing can be done to change it.

If, however, the budget is broken down into periods of, say, a month then the actual monthly results produced by the accounting function can be compared with the budget and immediate corrective action taken if things are not going as planned. In other words, if a business takes action each month to rectify variations from its master plan, then it has an infinitely better chance of achieving its profit target than if it just waits, with bated breath, for the year-end accounts. This is essentially what budgetary control is all about.

A budget represents the *corporate plan* for the coming year and it is a management responsibility to strive to achieve the targets set and to control costs to the levels allowed for in the budget. In this way, individual managers can be held responsible, and accountable, for that part of the budgeted activity under their control. The vehicle for exercising this control is therefore periodic comparison of actual performance against budget. This system also facilitates a management technique called *management by exception*.

Let us think about this carefully. If we were part of management responsible for performance against budget, would we really need, or indeed want, to receive each month a very detailed financial statement, telling us that everything was going according to plan? Probably not. We need only to be told about those activities where a significant variance from the plan has developed or is developing. This might be a more positive way of highlighting problem areas to which we should give maximum attention. If a manager is, say, responsible for five areas of activity and all is going well with the exception of one particular activity, then it will further the cause of management efficiency and speed of reaction, if only that activity is reported on. How effectively many companies follow this principle is debatable and a common management complaint is about the volume of statistical and financial reports they have to wade through. It is arguable that if a company cannot produce a viable management information system which reports only exceptions, then the system is not as effective as it should be.

So far, we have discovered that budgetary control is designed to achieve three things:

1. Ongoing control of costs and activities to achieve a corporate target.
2. Facilitating management responsibility and accountability for certain costs and activities.
3. Facilitating management by exception so that corrective action can be taken.

We must appreciate that the degree of sophistication necessary in a management reporting system will in large measure be dictated by the size and structure of a business. Let us try to illustrate this point:

A business is budgeted to produce 100 units of a product in a particular month. The budgeted material content of one unit is 2 tonnes of steel at £200 per tonne, making a total material cost of one unit £400 (2 tonnes × £200). The material budget for this particular month is therefore 100 units to be produced at £400 each = £40 000.

Net let us say that the monthly report shows the following information for 100 units actually produced, based on a usage of 220 tonnes at £210 per tonne = £46 200

	Budget	Actual cost	Variance
Material	40 000	46 200	(6200)

If the company is relatively small, and the Production Manager not only manages the production activity but also performs the buying function for production materials, then he is responsible and accountable for the £6200 variance.

However, now let us consider a situation where a company has a Production Manager responsible for the production activity and a Purchasing Officer responsible for buying in the material. In this situation, who do we hold responsible for the variance? We could report the whole variance to both managers but we can all guess as to what the outcome would be.

Let us try, instead, to analyse the variance to highlight its causes so as to see if more meaningful information can be supplied to the Production Manager and the Purchasing Officer individually.

Material usage variance
    (Actual usage   − Budgeted usage) × Budgeted cost
    220 tonnes   − 200 tonnes   × £200 per tonne = £4000

Material price variance
    (Actual price   − Budgeted price) × Actual usage
    £210 per tonne   − £200 per tonne   × 220 tonnes   = £2200

    Total variance   £6200

(You can see that the mechanics of doing this is no different to our Family analysis.)

Now, the Production Manager is accountable for the usage variance of £4000 and the Purchasing Officer is responsible for the £2200 price variance. Altogether a more satisfactory approach.

Note Do not worry too much about the mechanics of analysing variances at this stage. We will be covering this subject matter later.

Preparing a budget

In this example we will use a small manufacturing company which has the following functional structure:

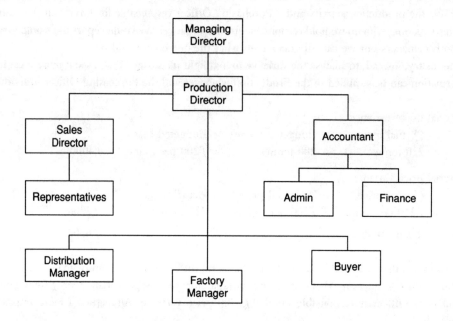

It would be quite logical to prepare the following individual sectional budgets:

Budget	Prepared by
1. Capital expenditure budget	Managing Director
2. Sales budget	Sales Director
Based partly on information from	Representatives
3. Production budget	Production Director
Based on	
Factory budget	Factory Manager
Purchasing budget	Buyer
Distribution budget	Distribution Manager
4. Administration budget	Accountant
5. Cash budget	Accountant

We can see immediately that proper budgeting involves a spectrum of people within the organization and the fact that it does so is most important. Regrettably, in some organizations, budgets have been set by a few of the top management, often with the connivance or influence of interested parties who are not part of the day-to-day management structure. Such budgets are viewed by managers who are accountable for performance against a particular budget heading as being unobtainable edicts imposed from above. Understandably, this fuels resentment and does little to aid staff development or commitment to corporate objectives. We may feel that there has been much evidence of this in recent years, in particular in public sector organizations such as health, education, etc.

It could be said that budgeting has as much to do with people and human nature as with business objectives. If we subscribe to this view, then we too will believe that managers involved in setting realistic targets are more likely to be motivated towards achieving them.

Informed budgeting involves producing a corporate plan to attempt to control the direction of an organization. If, through lack of adherence to good practice, the budgets are regarded as shackles on management initiatives then many undesirable consequences will result. Anyone with experience in this area of business can quote the classic examples:

- Unnecessary spending towards the end of a budget period on the basis of 'if I don't spend the budget allowance, it will be cut next year.'
- An able and enthusiastic member of the sales team, wishing to follow up a firm lead for a substantial overseas order, being denied the trip because the particular budget provision has been spent.

So much for the basics and theory. In the next section we will turn to the mechanics of budget preparation.

Mechanism of budget preparation

Sales budget

As anyone with experience of budgeting will likely confirm, the sales budget is probably the most critical and certainly the most difficult budget to prepare. Estimating sales revenue successfully can depend as much on a knowledge of economic trends, activity among competitors and shifts in consumer demand as making projections from past statistics and turnover. Even then, who can forecast the extent to which the direction of the national or indeed world economy will change? If governments cannot do this, what chance has the Sales Manager?

Whatever the problems, the fact remains that the sales budget is critical. Profit, as we know, is the difference between income and expenses and if the sales budget proves to have little relationship to actual events, profit forecasts will be severely affected. There is perhaps another way in which human nature can have an effect on this critical area of budgeting. Sales personnel are in the main an enthusiastic bunch, often accustomed to the rigours of appraisal against sales targets and commission-based payments. It could be felt that often enthusiastic optimism can easily overtake reality. The old adage 'if you divide a sales budget by 2 you will be nearer the truth' may overstate this point, but should alert us to the possibility of a degree of over-ambition.

There is always a tendency, when we think of sales budgets, to think only of sales income. However, in many ways, sales expenditure of organizations can be very significant and planned promotional campaigns can involve considerable costs.

The production budget

The production budget has to be carefully coordinated with the sales budget and the means of doing this is to determine what levels of finished stock must be held to meet sales requirements. The degree of complexity in achieving this coordination will depend in large measure on how evenly spread sales are throughout the year. We can illustrate this important point quite easily:

Imagine a situation where a firm has produced the following six months' sales forecast:

Month	1	2	3	4	5	6
Forecast sales (units)	100	100	100	100	110	110

It has been decided that the minimum finished stock level should be 50 per cent of the estimated sales for the following month:

Month	1	2	3	4	5	6
Sales (units)	100	100	100	100	110	110
Closing stock	50	50	50	52	52	52
Requirement	150	150	150	152	162	162
Less: Opening stock	50	50	50	50	52	52 (say)
Production required	100	100	100	102	110	110

Now let us take the same situation but with the following sales forecast:

Month	1	2	3	4	5	6
Sales units	100	60	50	90	170	130

This different sales forecast produces the following results:

Month	1	2	3	4	5	6
Sales	100	60	50	90	170	130
Closing stock	30	25	45	85	65	65 (say)
Requirement	130	85	95	175	235	195
Less: Opening stock	50	30	25	45	85	65
Production required	80	55	70	130	150	130

We can immediately see that the second situation, where there is a very uneven sales pattern, presents a far more difficult situation for the production manager. It is not usually practical, economic or indeed possible to vary continually the production pattern over short time spans, not least because staff, and particularly skilled staff, cannot be 'hired and fired' at will over short periods.

What then could be done in the situation outlined? There are many possibilities but we can only cover a few which, hopefully, will serve to demonstrate the kind of action that might be taken.

1. With the problem identified, the Sales Manager suggests that sales during months 2 and 3 can be increased by 50 per cent if a vigorous 'special offer' promotion is undertaken, during which selling price per unit is cut from £600 to £450. Sales cannot be increased beyond this level during these months.
2. It is decided that stock levels can rise but never fall below a 'new' minimum stock of 40 per cent of forecast sales for the following month.
3. The Production Manager points out that the maximum production that can be achieved is 130 units per month, without significant expansion of the production facilities (130 units is the absolute maximum and, allowing for breakdowns, etc., 120 units is a more realistic, sustainable output).

Let us first take a look at a projection allowing only for the revised sales forecast and 'new' minimum stock levels:

Month	1	2	3	4	5	6	
Sales	110	90	75	90	170	130	
Closing stock	36	30	36	68	52	52	(say)
Requirement	146	120	111	158	222	182	
Less: Opening stock	50	36	30	36	68	52	
Production required	96	84	81	122	154	130	

We can see in month 5 that the production requirement has gone over the production capacity limit of 130 units. Let us try now to resolve this problem and, at the same time, even out the production flow.

We could now re-cast the projection this way:

Month	1	2	3	4	5	6
Opening stock	50	51	72	108	129	70
Production (1)	111	111	111	111	111	111
	161	162	183	219	240	181
Less: Sales	110	90	75	90	170	130
Closing stock (2)	51	72	108	129	70	51

(1) This suggestion is arrived at as follows:

Stock start of month 1	50	
Stock end of month 6 (say)	52	
Stock increase		2
Sales months 1–6		665
Production required months 1–6		667

Average monthly production requirement 667 ÷ 6 = 111 approx.

(2) Found by calculation

Notes

(i)   There are of course other ways of working this out which would meet the laid down criteria. The main point is to grasp the general idea of how different managers can each contribute to resolving such situations.

(ii)   A most important point to recognize is that without detailed budgeting, the problem may well not have been anticipated.

(iii)   This has been a simplistic approach ignoring the many other factors which, in practice, would need to be considered such as:

– the effect on profitability of the 'special offer'
– the cost of financing increased stocks
– storage space for increased stocks
– whether it would be more financially viable to 'lay off' staff and whether the firm would keep staff on, even at the expense of reduced profits as a matter of social responsibility.

Yet again, we get a measure of the complexity of many business decisions and even some of the non-financial considerations which can influence those decisions.

We will move on and look at the other budgets that can now be prepared using the following information to build on the sales, production and stock forecasts we have just seen.

1. Unit costs

Direct labour	130.00
Direct materials	100.00
Prime cost	230.00

2. Forecast overheads: months 1–6

Production	72 600
Sales and distribution	40 200 + 10% of monthly sales
Administration	28 800

All expenses accrue evenly and are paid in the following month.

3. All purchases and sales are on credit terms, payable the following month.

4. Selling price per unit £600, except months 2 and 3 sales at £450.

5. Assets and liabilities — start of month 1

Fixed assets	300 000	
Current assets		
Stock: Raw materials	40 000	
Finished goods	11 500	
Debtors	72 000	
Bank	18 000	
Current liabilities		
Creditors (purchases)		11 000
Other creditors		20 000
Capital		250 000
Bank loan		160 500
	441 500	441 500

Loan repayments are £3000 per month.

Finished goods are valued at prime cost.

Raw materials stock is to be reduced to £20 000 as soon as possible.

Sales Budget

Month	1	2	3	4	5	6
Sales income
Unit sales	110	90	75	90	170	130
Selling price	600	450	450	600	600	600
Sales revenue	66 000	40 500	33 750	54 000	102 000	78 000
Sales expenses (£40 200)	6 700	6 700	6 700	6 700	6 700	6 700
+ 10% Sales	6 600	4 050	3 375	5 400	10 200	7 800
Total	13 300	10 750	10 075	12 100	16 900	14 500

Production Budget

Month	1	2	3	4	5	6
Units produced	111	111	111	111	111	111
Direct labour (@ 130.00)	14 430	14 430	14 430	14 430	14 430	14 430
Direct materials (@ 100.00)	11 100	11 100	11 100	11 100	11 100	11 100
Prime cost	25 530	25 530	25 530	25 530	25 530	25 530
Production overhead	12 100	12 100	12 100	12 100	12 100	12 100
Production cost	37 630	37 630	37 630	37 630	37 630	37 630

Material purchases budget

	1	2	3	4	5	6
Opening stock	40 000	28 900	20 000	20 000	20 000	20 000
Less: Production	11 100	11 100	11 100	11 100	11 100	11 100
	28 900	17 800	8 900	8 900	8 900	8 900
Purchases	—	2 200	11 100	11 100	11 100	11 100
Closing stock	28 900	20 000	20 000	20 000	20 000	20 000

Creditors' Budget (purchases)

	1	2	3	4	5	6
Opening balance	11 000	—	2 200	11 100	11 100	11 100
Purchases	—	2 200	11 100	11 100	11 100	11 100
	11 000	2 200	13 300	22 200	22 200	22 200
Less: Payments	11 000	—	2 200	11 100	11 100	11 100
Closing balance	—	2 200	11 100	11 100	11 100	11 100

Debtors' Budget

	1	2	3	4	5	6
Opening balance	72 000	66 000	40 500	33 750	54 000	102 000
Sales	66 000	40 500	33 750	54 000	102 000	78 000
	138 000	106 500	74 250	87 750	156 000	180 000
Receipts	72 000	66 000	40 500	33 750	54 000	102 000
Closing balance	66 000	40 500	33 750	54 000	102 000	78 000

We can now construct a most important budget, the cash budget. We need to be sure, at this stage, that the business has the cash resources to operate as planned.

Cash Budget

Opening balance	18 000	41 570	59 940	53 160	31 405	27 875
Receipts (debtors)	72 000	66 000	40 500	33 750	54 000	102 000
	90 000	107 570	100 440	86 910	85 405	129 875
Payments:						
Creditors (purchases)	11 000	—	2 200	11 100	11 100	11 100
Labour	14 430	14 430	14 430	14 430	14 430	14 430
Loan repayments	3 000	3 000	3 000	3 000	3 000	3 000
Overheads						
Production		12 100	12 100	12 100	12 100	12 100
Sales and distribution	20 000	13 300	10 750	10 075	12 100	16 900
Administration		4 800	4 800	4 800	4 800	4 800
Closing balance	41 570	59 940	53 160	31 405	27 875	67 545

Although our example has been relatively rudimentary, it gives some idea of the complexity and fragmentation of a 'real life' budget build-up. Having got the individual forecasts and being satisfied that cash does not present a problem, we can now proceed to producing the *master budget*.

Master Budget
Projected Trading and Profit and Loss Account for the 6 months ended ...

(1)	Sales		374 250
	Less: Cost of goods sold		
(2)	Opening stock – Finished goods	11 500	
(3)	*Add*: Cost of completed goods	153 180	
		164 680	
(4)	*Less*: Closing stock – Finished goods	11 730	152 950
			221 300
(5)	*Less*: Production overheads		72 600
	Gross profit		148 700
	Less:		
(6)	Sales and distribution costs	77 625	
(7)	Administration costs	28 800	106 275
	Net profit		42 275

Notes
(1) Sales budget.
(2) Opening statement of assets and liabilities.
(3) Production budget – prime costs.
(4) 51 units @ £230 prime cost.
(5) Production budget.
(6) Sales and distribution budget.
(7) Administration budget (not actually produced) taken from information.

Balance Sheet as at ...

Fixed assets			300 000
Current assets			
(1) Stocks: Finished goods	11 730		
(2) Materials	20 000		
(3) Debtors	78 000		
(4) Bank	67 545	177 275	
Less: Current liabilities:			
(5) Creditors (purchases)	11 100		
(6) Creditors (other costs)	31 400	42 500	
Working capital			134 775
			434 775
Financed by:			
Opening capital	250 000		
Profit for period	42 275	292 275	
Long-term liability:			
(7) Loan		142 500	434 775

Notes
(1) As per Trading Account.
(2) Materials purchases budget.
(3) Debtors' budget.
(4) Cash budget.
(5) Creditors' budget (purchases).
(6) Month 6 overheads:

       Sales and distribution   14 500 (Sales budget)
       Administration   4 800
       Production   12 100 (Production budget).
(7) Loan at start *less* six repayments of £3000.

Alternative budgets

Assuming the budget we have just seen is held to be an attainable target, then it should represent what management thinks is the most likely outcome over the six months. However, some firms would also prepare budgets for what could perceivably be the worst and best situations that might arise.

Using our model, let us imagine that the sales manager had been asked to prepare a sales budget at two levels:

- The most optimistic estimate of sales over the six months.
- The most pessimistic estimate of sales over the six months.

The master budget could then logically be prepared on a mid-point between the two forecasts. The likely outcome could reasonably be expected to be the mid-point between these two extremes. In addition, budgets could be prepared at the optimistic and pessimistic forecast levels of sales. These alternatives could be useful to gauge what profit or cash flow problems might ensue should the worst scenario become reality. Also the best scenario could set a 'high' target to aim for, to which staff could be motivated.

Flexible budgets

It is also possible to produce a series of flexible budgets where income and costs are assessed at varying levels of sales activity. The benefit of these budgets is that at varying levels of actual sales activity achieved, it is possible to see the budget allowance for every budget factor at the level of activity reached.

Limiting factors

Before moving on, let us cast our minds back to the situation where the Sales Manager increased the sales forecast to help smooth out a very uneven production flow. It was also stated that the revised forecast was the limit to which sales could be increased. The Production Manager meanwhile put a limit on production capacity of 130 units per month. In this instance, we saw two limiting factors being identified. In any budgeting process, there has to be a 'limiting factor(s)'. Such factor(s) need to be identified otherwise a plan might be produced which, if followed, will come to a grinding halt as soon as the limiting factor is reached.

Limiting factors could stem from many causes, for example:

- Production capacity limit
- Limit of sales, regardless of prices
- Insufficient cash resources
- Availability of suitable staff
- Constraint of physical space
- Statutory prohibition
- Firm's 'social' policy taking precedence.

Actuals versus budget

A budget is a statement of corporate objectives and also a means of control, hence the term *budgetary control* — control, in the sense that actual income and expenditure can be compared with budget and corrective action taken when variances occur. If management is to be accountable then it needs this information on a regular basis so that deviations (variances) can be addressed at an early stage.

Just a fragment of what could be a monthly report is adequate to illustrate the technique:

Production report summary		Month 1	
	Budgets	Actual	Variances
Units produced	111	109	(2)
Direct labour	14 430	13 625	805
Direct materials	11 100	11 336	(236)

Analysis of variances

Beyond the summary reports we have just seen, there may be more detailed reports which explain the variances in more detail to assist management in locating problem areas requiring corrective action. Using the production report as an example:

Production report		Month 1	
	Variance	Volume	Price
	£	£	£
Units produced	(2)	(2)	—
Direct labour	805.00	260.00	545.00
Direct materials	(236.00)	200.00	(436.00)

Notes

Labour variances:

Volume: (Budgeted units − Actual units) × Budget cost
= (111 − 109) × £130 = £260

Cost: (Budgeted cost − Actual cost) × Actual units
= (£130 − £125) × 109 = £545

Material variances:

Volume: (Budgeted units − Actual units) × Budget cost
= (111 − 109) × £100 = £200

Price: (Budgeted cost − Actual cost) × Actual units
= (£100 − £104) × 109 = (£436)

From this we can see that the formulae for calculating activity/volume/usage variances or price/cost variances are:

Activity/volume/usage variance:
   (Budgeted volume − Actual volume) × Budgeted price/cost
Price variance:
   (Budgeted price − Actual price) × Actual volume

To judge how useful this type of analysis is, let us look at the direct materials variance. Overall there was an overspend of £236. This was brought about as follows:

1. The fact that two units fewer than budget were actually produced. At a budget cost of £100 per unit this resulted in an underspend of £200 as we would expect.
2. The material cost has increased by an average of £4 per unit, causing a 'price' overspend of £436. This would need investigation as it could be caused by a variety of factors such as: a price increase imposed by supplier(s) not anticipated; undue wastage of materials in production, resulting in a higher material cost or even 'loss' of materials after issue into the production facility. Whatever the cause, this would have a significant effect on profit were it to continue.

Every budget heading can have actual income, or expenditure, compared to budget provision. *The net total of all the variances will equal the difference between budgeted profit and actual profit.*
    Variances can arise from a host of causes. Here is a sample:

Variance	Cause
Volume	When actual activity varies from budget
Labour	Change in wage rates not budgeted
	Labour inefficiency or efficiency
Materials	Price increases not budgeted
	Abnormal wastage
	Unforeseen changes in the exchange rate for imported materials
Expenses	Excessive usage
	Increased charges not anticipated, e.g. electricity, telephone, etc.
	Increase or decrease in interest rates charge on overdrafts and other borrowing not anticipated
Sales	Increase or decrease in volume of sales from budget
	Variation in selling prices from budget
	Bad debts not provided for
	Changes in exchange rates for goods exported and not anticipated

Finally, *we must realize that variances can arise for reasons outside the control of management. Changes in the economic policy of government would be a classic example of this.* A good example would be an increase in the duty on diesel fuel, on which a firm's vehicle fleet might run.

Section 4

Accounting 2

Unit 21

Limited companies

Ownership, shares and debentures

In Section 1, Accounting 1, we covered the basics of accountancy in the context of a business owned by a sole trader. We now need to widen the scope of our study to take in other forms of organization. We shall be looking at the different accounting aspects of limited companies, partnerships, clubs and societies.

We will start by considering the accounting implications of a limited company but, before we do so, let us be clear that all the basic accounting techniques we have learnt in Accounting 1 still apply. Limited companies impose some extra requirements and it is to these that most of this unit will be devoted.

Ownership and mechanics of a limited company

Unlike a sole trader, a limited company has a 'separate legal identity' from the owner(s) of the company. This statement can best be understood by comparing the legal status of a sole trader with that of a limited company.

Although, in practice, a sole trader keeps business accounts separate from personal finances with a Capital Account representing his or her investment in the business, in legal terms the business and the owner (sole trader) are the same person. This means, for example, that if the business fails, creditors can claim any moneys owed to them from the proprietor personally.

Limited companies are very different. Ownership of such a company is shared among a number of individuals who are known as shareholders. In large companies, the number of shareholders can run into thousands, as is the case with many of the recently privatized companies. These organizations were previously nationalized industries (owned by the state) and were sold off as private enterprises with members of the public being invited to buy shares in the newly privatized companies.

What precisely do these shares represent? In simple terms, a share is a share in the company, not in the business run by the company. The company owns the assets of its business and can enter into legal contracts in its own name. In this way, there is a separation of the owners of a company (shareholders) from the business which the company operates. This has many implications, the most important being that creditors can only enforce their debts against the company,

305

not against its shareholders, and shareholders are not entitled to run the day-to-day business operated by the company. Day-to-day management of the business of a company is the responsibility of its directors, who are individuals appointed by the shareholders to manage the company and its business.

The vital differences in the accounting requirements for a limited company stem from this separation of the company from its shareholders. These differences can be summarized as follows:

1. The funds of a company, initially, come from the selling of shares.
2. Shareholders can sell their shares to other people.
3. Whereas sole traders can, through drawings, withdraw profit from their business as they see fit, shareholders have no direct access to the profits of a company. How much of any profit made should be given (distributed) to the shareholders, is decided by the company directors.
4. Sole traders pay tax on income from their business and any other income they may have. Because a company has a separate legal identity, it is treated as a taxable person in its own right. As such, it pays corporation tax on its profits.
5. Sole traders can take out, from their business, any capital they have invested in it. A company can only pay shareholders a share of the profits (called dividends) from the profits of the company. In most circumstances, if a shareholder wants to 'cash in' his or her investment made in a company's shares, he or she has to sell shares to another party.

In order to focus on all these points, the accounts of a limited company differ from a sole trader in two prime ways:

●   The structure of Capital Accounts
●   Companies produce an extra account called an 'Appropriation Account' which shows how the profit of the company has to be divided out (appropriated).

A company is required to maintain a register of shareholdings. This register, called the *share register*, lists the names, addresses and number of shares owned by all shareholders. When a shareholder's details have been entered in the share register, he (or she) is provided with a *share certificate* which confirms the number of shares held in the company. If a shareholder sells shares to another person then the share certificate has to be returned to the company and a new one issued to the new shareholder.

When a company is first formed, a number of legal documents have to be submitted to the Registrar of Companies. Only when the Registrar issues a certificate of incorporation does the company come into existence as a separate legal entity. We can liken this to the birth of a child. A child is born and a birth certificate is issued. Likewise, a company comes into being and a certificate of incorporation is issued. Much of the documentation submitted to the Registrar is concerned with setting out how the company will be organized, where the Head Office will be, what kind of business it will be involved in, etc. From an accounting point of view, a most important document is the *memorandum of association*. Among other things, this document states what share capital the company is authorized to issue. While on the matter of the memorandum of association, it is worth clearing up an uncertainty which many students have over the difference between a public and a private company. We have all seen the terms Ltd and Plc behind a company name. ABC Ltd would be a private company whereas XYZ Plc would be a public company. If a company is to be a public company, then this *must be stated* in its memorandum of association. The essential differences are:

1. In the case of a public company, the memorandum of association must contain a clause stating that it is a public company.
2. A public company must have an authorized share capital of at least £50 000. A private company can have an authorized share capital less than this amount.
3. A public company must end its name with the term 'Public Limited Company' or Plc.
4. A public company can offer its shares to the general public, whereas a private company cannot. We have all recently seen how the shares in newly privatized industries such as British Telecom, electricity, water, etc., have been widely advertised in the press and on television. These are prime examples of public limited companies offering their shares to the general public. The Stock Exchange is merely a market where shares in public limited companies are traded (bought and sold).

Because of their size and advertising, etc., many of the larger companies are household names. However, it is worth noting that there are far more private than public limited companies.

Authorized and issued share capital

We now need to look more closely at the subject of shares and what they mean in accounting terms. We have seen that the memorandum of association states the authorized share capital of a company. The first thing we must understand is that this does *not* mean that the company has issued that amount of shares. It simply means that the company is allowed to issue *up to* that amount of share capital. What a company might have actually issued is a different matter altogether. The situation could, for example, be:

Share capital:
Authorized 50 000 ordinary shares of £1.00 each.
Issued 20 000 ordinary shares of £1.00 each, fully paid.

We will see later what 'fully paid' means in this context. For now, we need to understand the difference between authorized and issued share capital.

Using our example, this company is allowed to issue 50 000 ordinary shares of £1.00 each. It has actually issued 20 000 and can, therefore, at some future stage, issue (sell) a further 30 000 shares. It might do so if it wanted to raise more finance to, say, expand its business.

Types of shares

There are two main types of shares which a company might issue:

1. Ordinary shares
2. Preference shares.

Ordinary shares

These are by far the most common form of shares and represent the real 'risk capital' invested in a company. The value of an 'ordinary share' held by a shareholder is basically whatever anyone else is prepared to pay for the share. This will be determined by a host of factors, not least by the strength of the company and the profits it is making. Let us suppose we bought 1000 £1.00 ordinary shares in a newly formed company. Two things can happen:

1. Assuming the company trades profitably, we will receive an annual dividend (share of profits) at a rate decided by the company directors. If, say, the dividend declared is 5 per cent then the company will send us a cheque for £50.00 (£1000 × 5 per cent). Meanwhile, because the company is doing well, others anxious to buy its shares may be prepared to pay us, say, £1.80 per share. If we sold all our shares, we would receive £1800 and make a profit of £800.00
2. Assuming the company is not profitable and its prospects are worsening, it is likely that any dividend will be reduced or no dividend will be declared. Others, clearly, will not be anxious to buy the shares and consequently their prices will fall. If the company should become insolvent, the shares will become worthless.

This range of possibilities adequately demonstrates why ordinary shares are properly regarded as the risk capital of a company.

Preference shares

The very title 'preference' indicates that this type of share has preference over ordinary shares to certain rights. These rights can broadly be summarized as follows:

1. The right to be paid a dividend (normally at a fixed percentage of the nominal value of the shares) before dividends are paid on ordinary shares. This *does not mean* that the dividend on preference shares must be paid, only that if dividends are declared, then preference shares have priority over ordinary shares. For this reason, the dividend payable on preference shares is deducted before determining how much is available for distribution to ordinary shares.
2. In the event of a company being 'wound up', the preference shareholders are normally entitled to be repaid the nominal value of their shares before ordinary shareholders receive any repayment.

There are basically two types of preference shares.

Non-cumulative preference shares

If the dividend paid on these shares in any year is less than the maximum agreed dividend percentage, then the underpayment *cannot* be carried forward to be made good in the next year(s).

Cumulative preference shares

If the dividend paid on these shares in any year is less than the maximum agreed dividend percentage, then the underpayment is carried forward for payment in the next year(s) and before payment of dividend on ordinary shares.

Share capital and debentures

Share capital

The term 'share capital' is a common term used when referring to the company accounts. However, we must be most careful when using this description as it can mean different things. A brief summary may help us to understand better the different criteria to which this 'umbrella description' is often applied.

1. *Authorized share capital* — the total of share capital which a company is allowed to issue. This is laid down in the memorandum of association.
2. *Issued share capital* — the total of share capital that has actually been issued at any moment in time.
3. *Called-up share capital* — often, when a company issues new shares, it will make payment for the shares available in instalments. This has certainly been the case with many of the privatized company shares sold by government. The total amount paid and due at any moment in time is known as the called-up share capital.
4. *Uncalled share capital* — the total amount of share capital which has not yet become payable. In other words, it has not yet been asked for (called for).
5. *Paid-up share capital* — the total amount of share capital which has actually been paid for.
6. *Calls in arrears* — the total amount of share capital not yet paid by shareholders after an instalment was due (called for).

Debentures

Debentures are a means of raising loan capital, so are a completely different means of financing than shares. They are often referred to as loan stock or loan capital. Companies can raise capital by issuing debenture certificates to lenders. A debenture can be redeemable (repayable) on a specified date or irredeemable in that it is only repayable when a company is liquidated.

Debentures can be secured against specific assets or the whole assets of a company. These secured debentures are sometimes known as 'mortgage' debentures. Debentures not secured on any of the assets of a company are commonly known as simple or naked debentures.

Whatever the possibilities for variation, in the form of debentures, they all have four things in common:

1. The interest payable on debentures has to be paid whether the company makes a profit or not.
2. Directors have no choice over the payment of debenture interest. Failure to pay could result in the company being placed into liquidation by the debenture holders, who are creditors of a company.
3. Debentures can be issued (sold) at a discount from their face (nominal) value.
4. If a company goes into liquidation, the debenture holders are entitled to repayment before preference or ordinary shareholders.

Because debentures are loans, the interest payable on them is charged against profit in the Profit and Loss Account and is deductible for tax purposes. This contrasts sharply with dividends paid on preference shares which is *not deductible* for tax purposes and helps to explain why preference shares are now a much less popular means of raising finance.

Unit 22

Accounts and records of limited companies

Outline requirements and records

By law, companies are required to maintain proper accounts and to prepare, each year, a set of 'published' accounts which include a Profit and Loss Account and Balance Sheet. The accounts are subject to an audit by an independent auditor appointed by the shareholders and a copy of the annual final accounts must be forwarded to every ordinary shareholder and to the Registrar of Companies.

Before we look in detail at the accounts of companies, it is useful to consider briefly the other statutory books which, by law, a company must maintain.

1. *Register of Members* — recording the name, address and number of shares held by each shareholder.
2. *Register of Directors and Company Secretary* — recording the name, address and occupation(s) of every director.
3. *Register of Directors' Shareholdings* — recording the number of shares held by each director.
4. *Minute Book of Directors' Meetings* — recording details of every resolution passed.
5. *Minute Book of General Meetings* — recording details of proceedings and resolutions passed at these meetings of the company's ordinary shareholders.
6. *Register of Debenture Holders* — recording the name, address and number of debentures held by each debenture holder.
7. *Register of Mortgages and Secured Loans* — recording the name, address of each lender and the amount of each loan.

Limited company accounts explained

The first thing to understand is that the basics of accounting we covered in Accounting 1 as applied to sole traders applies equally to companies. What we do find with company accounts is that there are additional items which only appear in such accounts. We must now look at these additional items in some detail. To do this, we will look at the Trading Account and Profit and Loss Account and then turn to an account that is new to our studies — an Appropriation Account. Finally, we will look at the Balance Sheet.

1. *Trading Account.* This account is no different to the Trading Account of a sole trader or, as we will see later, a partnership.

2. *Profit and Loss Account.* In this account we can expect a number of additional items of expense beyond those we found in the account of a sole trader. The principal examples are:

   (a) *Directors' remuneration.* Directors are, legally, employees of a company and as such their remuneration (fees, salaries, etc.) are charged to the Profit and Loss Account.

   (b) *Auditors' fees.* The auditors are appointed annually by the shareholders at an annual general meeting. Their agreed remuneration (fees and expenses) are charged to the Profit and Loss Account.

   (c) *Debenture interest.* The interest payable on debentures must be paid whether or not profits are made. This expense is charged to the Profit and Loss Account.

   (d) *Preliminary, formation and promotion expenses.* These are the expenses associated with forming a company and might include registration fees and costs of preparing the company's memorandum and articles of association, etc. Again, these expenses are charged to the Profit and Loss Account.

   Any of the expenses listed above appear in the expenses part of the Profit and Loss Account along with other expense items with which we are familiar, such as salaries, insurances, provisions for depreciation, etc.

3. *The Appropriation Account.* This account breaks new ground in our study but it is effectively only an extension of the Profit and Loss Account. It merely shows how the net profit is to be distributed, or used, i.e. appropriated.

   Before we look at the structure of the account, we need to consider the items we might expect to find within the account. We will consider the items in the order that they normally appear in the account.

   (a) *Corporation tax.* As a legal entity, in its own right, a company is subject to corporation tax. The tax is the first deduction from net profit (which is described as profit for the year before taxation). The resulting figure is described as 'Profit for the year after taxation'.

   (b) *Profit retained from last year.* As we will see later, it is often the case that not all profit will be distributed, or put into reserves. It is quite usual to find a balance left on the Profit and Loss Account at the end of a year and this balance is brought forward into the Appropriation Account the following year. It is usually shown as '*add*: Retained profits from last year'.

   (c) *Transfers to reserves.* The directors may consider it prudent to set aside some profit for future expansion or to purchase additional assets for the business. This is sometimes done by transferring profit to a 'General reserve' or a specific reserve such as a 'Fixed assets replacement reserve'.

   (d) *Dividends.* Distribution of profit to shareholders by way of dividend may be divided between interim dividends paid and a final proposed dividend. Dividends payable on preference shares are shown before ordinary shares as follows:

6% Preference shares:

Interim dividend paid	3 000	
Final dividend proposed	3 000	6 000

Ordinary shares:

Interim dividend paid	8 000	
Final dividend proposed	14 000	22 000

(e) *Retained profit*. Any profit remaining after deducting tax, transfer to reserves and dividends, is described as 'Retained profits carried forward'.

Constructing limited company accounts

The following illustration should help us to understand what additional items we might expect to find in a limited company Profit and Loss Account when compared with that of a sole trader, and to see how the items are actually displayed.

Trading and Profit and Loss Account

	Sole Trader			Limited Company
Sales	XX			XX
Less: Cost of goods sold	XX			XX
Gross profit	XX			XX
Less expenses				
....	XX			XX
....	XX			XX
....	XX			XX
Net profit	XX			
Directors' remuneration				XX
Auditors' fees				XX
Formation expenses				XX
Debenture interest				XX
Profit for the year before taxation				XX
Less: Corporation Tax				XX
Profit for the year after taxation				XX
Add: Retained profit from last year				XX
				XX
Less: Appropriations:				
Transfer to general reserve	XX			
Transfer to replacement of assets reserve	XX	XX		
6% Preference shares				
Interim dividend paid	XX			
Final dividend proposed	XX	XX		
Ordinary shares				
Interim dividend paid	XX			
Final dividend proposed	XX	XX	XX	XX
Retained profits carried forward to next year				XX

Note   The items shown are a guide only. They may not necessarily apply in an individual company's accounts nor is the list exhaustive.

Balance Sheet

The Balance Sheet of a limited company is essentially the same as for a sole trader except for some additional items we might expect to find.

The following illustration highlights some of these items and demonstrates the layout of a company Balance Sheet.

Company Balance Sheet

Fixed assets			
(as for sole trader)			XX
Current assets			
(as for sole trader)		XX	
Less: Current liabilities			
(as for sole trader) *plus*			
	XX		
Proposed dividends	XX		
Corporation tax	XX		
Debenture interest	XX	XX	
Net current assets			XX
Total assets *less*: Current liabilities			XX
Less: Long-term liabilities			
Debentures			XX
			XX
Authorized share capital: (1)			
x ordinary shares of £X each			XX
x preference shares of £X each			XX
Issued share capital: (2)			
x ordinary shares of £X each		XX	
x preference shares of £X each		XX	XX
Reserves:			
Share Premium Account (3)		XX	
General reserve		XX	
Profit and Loss Account		XX	XX
			XX

Notes
(1) The authorized share capital (the amount of share capital the company is permitted to issue) is shown as a note (memorandum) item. It is *not* added into the Balance Sheet figures.
(2) If shares have been sold on an instalment basis then only the called-up share capital would be shown.
(3) Companies can sell their shares for more than the nominal (face) value. The excess received above nominal value is credited to a Share Premium Account. This is classified as a reserve although there

are limits as to how this reserve can be used. Although it is a reserve it is described as Share Premium Account.

Ledger Accounts

To try to consolidate what we have learnt by our first, quick excursion through company accounts, we will now look at the ledger entries for some of these 'new' transactions. We will then look at what might be a typical company Trial Balance drawn from the ledger accounts and then track the 'new' company-related items and proposed appropriations of profit through to the final accounts.

Transactions

1. The company has authorized share capital of:
   150 000 ordinary shares of £1.00 each.
   50 000 5 per cent preference shares of £1.00 each.
   The company has actually issued, and been paid for:
   100 000 ordinary shares @ £1.40 each.
   50 000 preference shares @ £1.00 each.
2. The company has issued, and been paid for:
   £80 000 of 7 per cent debentures.
3. The company's directors have decided to transfer £30 000 of profit to a general reserve.
4. The company's liability to corporation tax has been assessed at £35 000.
5. The company's directors have declared dividends of:
   6 per cent on ordinary shares.
   5 per cent on preference shares.
6. The company has a retained profit brought forward from the previous year of £17 000.

Ledger accounts

Transaction 1

Bank				Ordinary £1 shares		
100 000 Ordinary shares @ £1.40	140 000				Bank	100 000
50 000 5% Preference @ £1.00	50 000					

5% Preference shares				Share premium account		
	Bank	50 000			Bank	40 000

Note The share premium of 40p × 100 000 shares = £40 000 credited to a Share Premium Account.

Transaction 2

Bank		
100 000		
Ordinary shares		
@ £1.40	140 000	
50 000		
5% Preference		
@ £1.00	50 000	
7% Debentures	80 000	

7% Debentures		
	Bank	80 000

Transaction 3

Profit and Loss Account		
General reserve	30 000	Balance B/D	17 000

General Reserve		
	Profit and Loss A/c	30 000

Transaction 4

Profit and Loss Account		
General reserve	30 000	Balance B/d	17 000
Corporation tax	35 000		

Corporation Account		
	Profit and Loss A/c	35 000

Transaction 5

Profit and Loss Account		
General reserve	30 000	Balance B/d	17 000
Corporation tax	35 000		
Dividend		
Ordinary shares	6 000	
Preference shares	2 500	

Ordinary Share Dividend		
	Profit and Loss A/c	6 000

Preference Share Dividend		
	Profit and Loss A/c	2 500

Note Dividend on ordinary shares is calculated on the nominal (face) value of the shares, *not* on the premium price they were actually sold for, i.e. 100 000 sold @ £1.00 (nominal value) = £100 000 × 6% = £6000

Final Accounts

The following Trial Balance has been extracted from the books of AT Trading Ltd as at 31 December 19–3.

	DR	CR
Ordinary share capital		80 000
8% Preference share capital		30 000
Buildings	120 000	
Equipment	15 000	
Vehicles	18 000	
10% Debentures		40 000
Provision for depreciation:		
Equipment		5 000
Vehicles		6 000
Stock 01.01.19–3	23 000	
Share Premium Account		18 000
Vehicle expenses	9 000	
Rent and rates	14 000	
Debenture interest	2 000	
Debtors	16 000	
Creditors		13 000
Administration expenses	18 000	
Directors' remuneration	32 000	
General expenses	4 000	
General reserve		8 000
Bank	24 000	
Sales		130 000
Purchases	61 000	
Profit and Loss Account 31.12.19–2		28 000
Interim dividend paid on ordinary shares	2 000	
	358 000	358 000

Complete the following adjustments by way of an Extended Trial Balance.

1. Provide depreciation:
   - Equipment £1500
   - Vehicles £6000
2. Accrue debenture interest £2000
3. Proposed dividends are:
   - 8% Preference shares £2400
   - Final ordinary shares £2800
4. Provide £2000 for corporation tax
5. Transfer £3000 to general reserve
6. Stock at 31.12.19–3 valued at £24 500

From the Extended Trial Balance, prepare a Trading and Profit and Loss Account and Balance Sheet.

The company has authorized share capital of:

100 000 ordinary shares of £1.00		£100 000
50 000 preference shares of £1.00		£50.00

AT Trading Ltd
Extended Trial Balance as at 31 December 19-3

	Trial Balance		Adjustments		Profit and Loss Account		Balance Sheet	
	DR	CR	DR	CR	DR	CR	DR	CR
Ordinary share capital		80 000						80 000
8% Preference shares		30 000						30 000
Buildings	136 000						136 000	
Equipment	15 000						15 000	
Vehicles	18 000						18 000	
10% Debentures		40 000						40 000
Provision for depreciation:								
Equipment		5 000		1 500	1 500			6 500
Vehicles		6 000		6 000	6 000			12 000
Stock 01.01.19–2	23 000				23 000			
Share Premium Account		18 000						18 000
Vehicle expenses	9 000				9 000			
Rent and rates	14 000				14 000			
Debenture interest	2 000		2 000	2 000	4 000			2 000
Debtors	16 000						16 000	
Creditors		13 000						13 000
Administration expenses	18 000				18 000			
Directors' remuneration	26 000				26 000			
General expenses	4 000				4 000			
General reserve		8 000		3 000	3 000			11 000
Bank	24 000						24 000	
Sales		130 000				130 000		
Purchases	51 000				51 000			
Profit and Loss 31.12.19–2		28 000				28 000		
Dividend paid — ordinary	2 000				2 000			
Final dividends proposed:								
Ordinary shares				2 800	2 800			2 800
Preference shares				2 400	2 400			2 400
Corporation tax accrued				2 000	2 000			2 000
Stock 31.12.19–3			24 500			24 500	24 500	
	358 000	358 000			168 700	182 500	233 500	119 700
Profit remaining 31.12.19–3					13 800			13 800
	358 000	358 000			182 500	182 500	233 500	233 500

AT Trading Ltd
Trading and Profit and Loss Account for the year ended 31 December 19–3

Sales		130 000
Less: Cost of goods sold:		
Opening stock	23 000	
Purchases	51 000	
	74 000	
Less: Closing stock	24 500	49 500
Gross profit		80 500
Less: Expenses:		
Depreciation provided:		
Equipment	1 500	
Vehicles	6 000	
Vehicle expenses	9 000	
Rent and rates	14 000	
Debenture interest	4 000	
Administration expenses	18 000	
Directors' remuneration	26 000	
General expenses	4 000	82 500
Loss for the year before taxation		(2 000)
Less: Corporation tax		2 000
Loss for the year after taxation		(4 000)
Add: Retained profits from last year		28 000
		24 000
Less: Appropriations:		
Transfer to general reserve	3 000	
Preference share dividend	2 400	
Ordinary share dividends:		
Interim	2 000	
Proposed final	2 800	10 200
Retained profits carried forward to next year		13 800

AT Trading Ltd
Balance Sheet as at December 19–3

Fixed assets:	Cost	Depreciation	Net
Buildings	136 000	—	136 000
Equipment	15 000	6 500	8 500
Vehicles	18 000	12 000	6 000
	169 000	18 500	150 500

Current assets:			
Stock	24 500		
Debtors	16 000		
Bank	24 000	64 500	

Less: Current liabilities:			
Creditors	13 000		
Debenture			
Interest accrued	2 000		
Corporation tax	2 000		
Proposed dividends:			
Ordinary shares	2 800		
Preference shares	2 400	22 200	

Net current assets		42 300
Total assets *Less*: Current liabilities		192 800
Less: Long term liabilities:		
10% Debentures		40 000
Financed by:		152 800

Capital and reserves:		
Authorized share capital:		
50 000 Preference shares of £1	50 000	
100 000 Ordinary shares of £1	100 000	150 000

Issued share capital:		
8% Preference shares	30 000	
Ordinary shares	80 000	110 000
Share Premium Account		18 000
General reserve		11 000
Profit and Loss Account		13 800
		152 800

Exercises

1. The following is the Trial Balance of Pecan Ltd as at 30 June 19–3:

	£	£
Authorized and allotted share capital:		
120 000 ordinary shares of £1 each		120 000
50 000 7% preference shares of 50p each		25 000
Freehold premises at cost	160 000	
Loose tools (cost £14 000)	9 100	
Plant and machinery (cost £90 000)	66 900	
Stock	9 400	
Debtors/creditors	11 200	8 300
Bank		7 800
Purchases/sales	49 700	135 250
Directors' salaries	20 000	
Rates	4 650	
Electricity	3 830	
Plant hire	6 600	
Interest on debentures	1 200	
General expenses	1 270	
10% Debentures		24 000
Provision for bad debts		1 200
Share Premium Account		25 000
Profit and Loss Account		3 750
Revenue reserve		8 200
Interim dividend on ordinary shares	3 250	
Audit fees	1 750	
Listed investments	11 000	
Investment income		1 350
	359 850	359 850

The following additional information is available:
(a) Stock at 30 June 19–3 is valued at £12 900.
(b) Rates include a payment of £2300 for the six months from 01 April 19–3.
(c) Depreciation on plant is 15 per cent per annum of cost and the loose tools were valued at £7400 on 30 June 19–3.
(d) The provision for bad debts is to be 10 per cent of the debtors.
(e) The preference share dividends are outstanding at the end of the year and the second half year's interest on the debentures has not been paid.
(f) The corporation tax on this year's profits is £5880.
(g) The directors propose to declare a final dividend on the ordinary shares of 08 pence per share and transfer £2000 to the revenue reserve.

You are required to prepare a Profit and Loss Account for the year ended 30 June 19–3 and a Balance Sheet at that date.

2. The following is the Trial Balance of Kneale Ltd as at 31 December 19–3:

	£	£
Bank	6 720	
Debtors	18 910	
Creditors		12 304
Stock at 01 January 19–3	40 360	
Buildings at cost	100 000	
Equipment at cost	45 000	
Profit and Loss Account as at 31 December 19–2		15 283
General reserve		8 000
Equipment replacement reserve		4 200
Authorized and issued share capital (£1 ordinary shares)		100 000
Purchases	72 360	
Sales		135 480
Carriage inwards	1 570	
Carriage outwards	1 390	
Salaries	18 310	
Rates	4 235	
Administration expenses	3 022	
Miscellaneous expenses	1 890	
Provisions for depreciation at 31.12.19–2:		
Buildings		32 000
Equipment		16 000
Directors' remuneration	9 500	
	323 267	323 267

You are required to produce a Trading and Profit and Loss Account and Balance Sheet as at 31 December 19–3 after adjusting for the following:
(a) Stock at 31 December 19–3 £52 460.
(b) Rates owing £280; administration expenses owing £190.
(c) Proposed dividend at 10p per share.
(d) Transfers to reserves: General £1000; Equipment replacement £800.
(e) Depreciation on cost: Buildings 5 per cent; Equipment 20 per cent.

3. From the Trial Balance of Quantum Ltd as at 31 December 19–6, you are to produce a Profit and Loss and Appropriation Account and a Balance Sheet as that date:

	Dr £	Cr £
Issued share capital (£1 ordinary shares)		30 000
Premises at cost	40 000	
Vehicles:		
At cost	10 000	
Depreciation to 31 December 19–5		4 000
Expenses	11 000	
Stock at 01 January 19–6	12 000	
Purchases	70 000	
Sales		100 000
10% Debentures		15 000
Debenture interest	750	
Bank		1 000
Bank interest	250	
Debtors and creditors	25 000	15 000
Dividends paid	1 500	
Profit and Loss Balance as at 31 December 19–5		5 500
	170 500	170 500

Adjustments required:
(a) Closing stock is £10 000.
(b) The debentures were issued on 01 April 19–6.
(c) The bank reconciliation at 31 December 19–2 reveals the following:
  (i) cheque in cash book not on bank statement £600
  (ii) standing order included on bank statement but not in cash book £300 (expenses)
  (iii) credit transfer from a debtor on bank statement but not in cash book £600.
(d) The vehicles were purchased in 19–4. Depreciation is provided at the rate of 25 per cent per year on cost. On 31 December 19–6, one vehicle, purchased on 01 January 19–4 for £4500, was traded in for £2750 against a new vehicle costing £7000. No entries have been made in the books with regard to these transactions, and no money has been paid or received.
(e) Corporation tax for the year to 31 December 19–6 is estimated at £5000.
(f) A final dividend of 5p per share is proposed.
(g) Authorized share capital is 50 000 £1 ordinary shares.

4. Burgess plc has an authorized capital of 500 000 ordinary shares of £0.50 each.
   (a) At the end of its financial year, 31 May 19–6, the following balances have been extracted:

	£
Issued share capital: 400 000 ordinary shares fully paid	200 000
Land and buildings at cost	320 000
Stock	17 800
10% Debentures	30 000
Trade debtors	6 840
Trade creditors	8 500
Prepaid expenses	760
Share premium account	25 000
General reserve	20 000
Accrued expenses	430
Profit and Loss Account balance (01 June 19–5)	36 200
Bank	3 700
Equipment	
At cost	54 000
Provision for depreciation	17 500

The company's Trading and Profit and Loss Accounts had been prepared and revealed a net profit of £58 070. However, this figure and certain balances shown above, need adjustment for the following:

(i) A trade debtor who owes £300 is not able to pay. It was decided to write the account off as a bad debt.

(ii) An examination of the company's stock on 31 May 19–6 revealed that some items shown in the accounts at a cost of £1800 had deteriorated and had a resale value of only £1100.

(iii) At the end of the financial year, some equipment which had cost £3600 and which had a net book value of £800 had been sold for £1300. A cheque for this amount had been received on 31 May 19–6.

You are required to produce:
A statement showing the changes which should be made to the net profit of £58 070.

(b) The directors proposed to pay a final dividend of 10 per cent and to transfer £50 000 to general reserve on 31 May 19–6.

You are required to produce:
The profit and loss appropriation account for the year ended 31 May 19–6.
Extracts from the company's balance sheet as at 31 May 19–6, showing in detail:
(i) The current assets, current liabilities and working capital.
(ii) The items which make up the shareholders' funds.

(c) The directors are concerned about the company's liquidity.

You are required to state:
THREE transactions which will increase the company's working capital. State which Balance Sheet items will change as a result of each transaction.

Unit 23

Cash flow statements

___

Introduction and outline

We have seen that limited companies, by law, have to produce a Profit and Loss Account and Balance Sheet. Having examined these two vital, final reports, we now need to turn our attention to another statement which must, also by law, be produced with the final accounts of all limited companies except the very smallest. This 'new' statement is the *cash flow statement*. Do not confuse this with the *cash flow forecasts* we covered in Units 14 and 15. While much of the logic is the same, they are two completely separate statements and serve different purposes.

The cash flow statement (as its title suggests) analyses the flow of *actual money* into and out of the business, and shows the reason for changes in the cash and bank balances from the start of a year to the end. We know from our previous studies that not every transaction involves the movement of actual money. Provisions for depreciation or doubtful debts are prime examples of these non-monetary transactions. We are only interested in those accounts which do represent a flow of actual money and the following illustrations will help us grasp this concept.

Concept of Cash Flow Analysis

	In	Out
1. Fixed assets		
Sale of fixed assets	XX	
Purchase of fixed assets		XX
2. Current assets		
Decrease in debtors	XX	
Increase in debtors		XX
3. Stocks		
Decrease in stocks	XX	
Increase in stocks		XX
4. Current liabilities		
Increase in creditors	XX	
Decrease in creditors		XX
5. Long-term liabilities		
Loans received	XX	
Loans repaid		XX
6. Capital account(s)		
Capital introduced	XX	
Shares sold	XX	
Drawings		XX
Dividends paid		XX
7. Profit and Loss Account		
Profit	XX	
Loss		XX
(after adjustment for non-monetary entries)		

Sources of cash flow

We will now look, in a little more detail, at the reasoning behind the categories shown in the previous illustration.

1. *Fixed assets.* Cash received from selling fixed assets is a cash flow into a business whereas cash paid in purchasing fixed assets is a flow out.
2. *Current assets.* If debtors have reduced over the year, it means that the difference between opening and closing debtors represents an inflow of cash. Conversely, if the value of debtors has increased then the difference represents an outflow of cash (the business is financing an increased level of debtors).
3. *Stocks.* A decrease in stockholding means the reduction has been turned into cash. Increasing stock takes cash out of a business.

4. *Current liabilities.* An increase in creditors over the year represents an inflow of cash. The business has increased the amount of financing from its creditors. (If the business had paid the creditors represented by the increase then it would have less cash.)

5. *Long-term liabilities.* If loans have been received (this could include selling debentures) then they have brought in cash. If loans have been repaid then, obviously, cash has flowed out.

6. *Capital accounts.* Capital introduced or shares sold bring cash into the business, while drawings taken by a proprietor or share dividends paid result in an outflow of cash.

7. *Profit and Loss Account.* As we know, the balance on the Profit and Loss Account (net profit or net loss) is the net figure obtained by deducting all expenses from income. The majority of the income and expenses represents actual cash movement *less* receipts for income and payments for expenses. However, some items found in the Profit and Loss Account are not represented by actual cash movement, they are just 'book' transactions. Prime examples of these non-monetary transactions are:

(a) Provisions for depreciation

(b) Provisions for doubtful debts

(c) Profit or loss on sale of fixed assets.

This last item, profit or loss on sale of fixed assets, warrants further explanation. Let us assume an asset with a net book value of £1000 has been sold for £1400. The cash inflow is £1400 and has been added to the bank balance. The £400 profit shown in the Profit and Loss Account is a 'book' entry only to show the profit on sale, i.e. the difference between the book value of £1000 and the actual receipt of £1400.

When we use the profit figure drawn from the Profit and Loss Account in a cash flow statement we must deduct all 'non-monetary' income or expenses from the net profit, i.e. 'Book entries only'.

Illustrating cash flow

We will now move directly to a worked example of a cash flow statement and then examine the layout in some detail.

A Able
Balance Sheet as at: 31.12.19–2

				31.12.19–3
Fixed assets				
Plant and equipment at cost		70 000		78 000
Less: Depreciation provided		14 000		21 800
		56 000		56 200
Current assets				
Stock		18 000		16 500
Debtors	14 000		16 000	
Less: Provision for doubtful debts	1 000	13 000	1 500	14 500
Bank		7 000		5 700
		94 000		92 000
Less: Current liabilities:				
Creditors		9 000		11 900
		85 000		81 000
Financed by:				
Capital		70 000		75 000
Add: Net profit		25 000		24 000
		95 000		99 000
Less: Drawings		20 000		26 000
		75 000		73 000
Long-term loan		10 000		8 000
		85 000		81 000

A Able
Cash Flow Statement for the year ended 31 December 19–3

Source of funds:		
Net profit		24 000
Depreciation provided	7 800	
Increase in doubtful debts provision	500	
Decrease in stock	1 500	
Increase in debtors	(2 000)	
Increase in creditors	2 900	10 700
Funds generated from operations:		34 700
Plant and equipment purchased	(8 000)	
Drawings	(26 000)	
Loan repaid	(2 000)	
Funds applied other than in operations		36 000
Decrease in cash funds		(1 300)
Bank balance 31.12.19–2	7 000	
Bank balance 31.12.19–3	5 700	(1 300)

Let us look briefly at each item in turn:

1. *Net profit*. Picked up directly from the 31.12.19–3 Balance Sheet.
2. *Depreciation provided*. Increase in depreciation provided from 31.12.19–2 to 31.12.19–3.
3. *Increase in doubtful debts provision*. Again, the increase between 31.12.19–2 and 31.12.19–3.
4. *Decrease in stock*. The reduction in stocks from £18 000 to £16 500.
5. *Increase in debtors*. Debtors have increased from £14 000 to £16 000. The £2000 increase represents funds of A Able tied up in financing this increase in the level of debtors. Note how this negative cash flow is shown in brackets.
6. *Increase in creditors*. The £2900 increase represents an increase in the amount of financing obtained from suppliers. If creditors had been held at the same level as 19–2 then there would be £2900 less in the bank.
7. Having started with the profit for the year and adjusted that figure by the items in 2–6 above, we now arrive at the 'adjusted profit figure' representing cash inflow from normal trading activities. This is described as 'Funds generated from operations'.
8. *Plant and equipment purchased*. It is clear from the fact that the value of plant and equipment (at cost) has grown from £70 000 to £78 000 that additional assets have been bought costing £8000.
9. *Drawings*. The proprietor has taken £26 000 out of the business.
10. *Loan repaid*. The loan balance has dropped from £10 000 to £8000. Clearly, £2000 has been expended in paying off part of the loan.
11. *Funds applied other than in operations*. This is the total of the non-trading aspects of the business to which cash has been applied.
12. *Decrease in cash funds*. In our example, the funds applied to the non-trading aspects of the business have exceeded the funds generated from trading. Overall, there has therefore been a net decrease in cash of £1300.
13. We then take the difference between the closing bank balance at 31.12.19–2 and 31.12.19–3 and see that this reduction of £1300 reconciles with the figure in 12 above.

Hints

1. Producing Profit and Loss Accounts and Balance Sheets is in many ways much easier than constructing cash flow statements. With the former we have structured double entry accounting producing a Trial Balance to make life relatively easy. With cash flow statements, we have no such precise mechanism. We must examine every item and make informed judgements as to whether, and in what way, they affect cash flow.
2. The safest way to proceed is to work carefully down the Balance Sheet, line by line. The layout of the cash flow statement does not necessarily follow the same sequence but if we have an outline statement drawn up, it is only a matter of inserting each item in the appropriate place. This is far safer than going looking for cash movements in the Balance Sheet in a haphazard, disorganized way. To do so will certainly result in missing items.

Cash flow statements and meaning

We must understand that profitability and cash flow are two different things. Comparison of a Profit and Loss Account and a cash flow statement vividly illustrates this most important point. For this reason, it seems sensible that companies have to produce a cash flow statement as part of their published final accounts. We should also accept that, while there is no statutory requirement for the accounts of a sole trader to include a cash flow statement, the additional information it provides can be just as useful as it is to the owners of a company.

Most people, not well versed in the intricacies of accounting, can identify more readily with actual cash than profit. Cash flowing in and out are more observable events than, what to many people, are the abstract and subjective non-cash adjustments used in formatting Profit and Loss Accounts and Balance Sheets.

Ultimately, the success of any business depends in large measure upon the ability to use cash efficiently and the cash flow statement is designed to be a measure of this. Profit is one measure of efficiency and performance, cash flow is another.

Most importantly, creditors and shareholders depend, for their payments and dividends, on the availability of cash. Cash flow statements allow these groups to make a more accurate assessment of the ability of a business to meet these commitments.

Exercises

1. From the following summarized Balance Sheets of Akron Limited you are to produce a cash flow statement as at 30 September 19–5.

Balance Sheets as at 30 September

	19–4 £000	19–5 £000
Fixed assets at cost	500	650
Depreciation provided	200	300
	300	350
Investments at cost	200	50
Current assets		
Stock	400	700
Debtors	1350	1550
Bank	100	–
	1850	2250
Less: Current liabilities		
Bank overdraft		(60)
Creditors	(650)	(790)
Taxation	(230)	(190)
Proposed dividend	(150)	(130)
	(1030)	(1170)
	1320	1480
Capital and reserves		
Share capital (£1 ordinary shares)	500	750
Share premium account	150	200
Profit and Loss Account	670	530
	1320	1480

Notes

(i) During the year to 30 September 19–5, some fixed assets, originally costing £25 000, had been sold for £20 000 in cash. The accumulated depreciation on these fixed assets at 30 September 19–4 amounted to £10 000.

(ii) The taxation balances, disclosed in the above balance sheets, represent the actual amounts agreed with the Inland Revenue. All taxes were paid on their due dates. Advance corporation tax may be ignored.

(iii) Some of the investments, originally costing £150 000, had been sold for cash at their book value.

2. The following Balance Sheets and cash flow statement relate to David Johnson:

David Johnson
Balance Sheet as at 31 December

	19–7 £	19–7 £	19–6 £	19–6 £
Fixed assets		40 000		25 000
Stock		24 000		15 000
Debtors		24 000		10 000
Bank		—		4 000
		88 000		54 000
Capital	17 000		12 000	
Add: Net profit	40 000		10 000	
	57 000		22 000	
Less: Drawings	8 000	49 000	5 000	17 000
11% Loan		11 000		20 000
Creditors		22 000		17 000
Bank overdraft		6 000		—
		88 000		54 000

Cash Flow Statement for year ended 31 December 19–9

	£
Sources of cash	
Trading profit	40 000
Increase in creditors	5 000
	45 000
Applications of cash	
Purchases of fixed assets	15 000
Increase in stock	9 000
Increase in debtors	14 000
Repayment of loan	9 000
Drawings	8 000
	55 000
Decrease in cash	10 000

Answer the following questions using the above information to illustrate your answers:
(a) What is the meaning of the term cash flow?
(b) What is the main purpose of a cash flow statement?
(c) How can the cash flow of a business be measured?
(d) Will the following improve or worsen the cash flow of a business? Explain your answers.
 (i) An increase in debtors.
 (ii) A decrease in creditors.
(e) Give *two* reasons why David Johnson had an overdraft as at 31 December 19–7.
(f) Explain why a business selling goods on credit can make a profit on sales while not receiving any cash.

3. The following information relates to Reach Limited as at 31 December 19–9:

Profit and Loss Account year ended 31 December

	19–3 £000	19–4 £000
Profit before taxation	9 500	20 400
Taxation	(3 200)	(5 200)
Profit after taxation	6 300	15 200
Dividends:		
Preference (paid)	(100)	(100)
Ordinary: interim (paid)	(1 000)	(2 000)
final (proposed)	(3 000)	(6 000)
	2 200	7 100

Balance Sheets as at 31 December

	19–3 £000	19–4 £000
Fixed assets		
Plant, machinery and equipment, at cost	17 600	23 900
Less: Accumulated depreciation provided	9 500	10 750
	8 100	13 150
Current assets		
Stock	5 000	15 000
Debtors	8 600	26 700
Prepaid expenses	300	400
Bank	600	—
	14 500	42 100
Less: Current liabilities		
Bank	—	16 200
Creditors	6 000	10 000
Accrued expenses	800	1 000
Dividends	3 000	6 000
Taxation	3 200	5 200
	13 000	38 400
	9 600	16 850
Share capital		
Ordinary shares of £1 each	5 000	5 000
10% preference shares of £1 each	1 000	1 000
Profit and Loss Account	3 000	10 100
Loans	9 000	16 100
10% debenture	600	750
	9 600	16 850

Additional information
During the year to 31 December 19–4, fixed assets originally costing £5 500 000 were sold for £1 000 000. The accumulated depreciation on these assets at 31 December 19–3 was £3 800 000.

You are to prepare a cash flow statement for the year ended 31 December 19–4.

Unit 24

Interpretation of company accounts by ratio analysis

Ratios for companies outlined

In Unit 7, we examined the way in which performance-related ratios analysis could help interpret the accounts of a sole trader. In particular, we looked at ratios measuring:

- Profitability
- Return on investment
- Liquidity
- Controls on working capital.

All these ratios are just as relevant to companies but there are other, additional ratios which can also be applied to company accounts. In particular, the ratios we are about to explore are primarily concerned with providing information to shareholders and indeed some of these ratios are published in the financial press as a guide to those making investment decisions.

The ratios we shall be looking at are:

1. Earnings per share
2. Dividend yield
3. Dividend cover
4. Price/earnings ratio
5. Return on equity shareholders' interest
6. Gearing ratio.

In our worked examples of the various ratios we will use the following Profit and Loss Account and Balance Sheet as the basis for our analysis.

Ratio Limited
Summary Profit and Loss Account for year ended 19–3

	£	£
Sales		120 000
Cost of sales		132 200
		168 000
Gross profit		
Expenses:		
Administration expenses	12 000	
General expenses	6 800	
Rent and rates	11 200	
Depreciation provided	40 000	70 000
		98 000
Less: Interest		
Bank	3 200	
Mortgage	10 000	
Debenture	4 800	18 000
		80 000
Less: Corporation tax		36 000
		44 000
Less: Dividend		40 000
Transfer to general reserve		4 000

Balance Sheet as at 31 December 19–3

	£	£	£
Fixed assets			720 000
Depreciation provided			200 000
Current assets			520 000
Stock		120 000	
Trade debtors		100 000	
Cash		60 000	
		280 000	
Less: Current liabilities:			
Trade creditors	28 000		
Taxation	52 000	80 000	
Net current assets			200 000
Total assets Less: Current liabilities			720 000
6% Debenture		80 000	
5% Mortgage		200 000	
Bank loan		40 000	320 000
			400 000
Financed by:			
Capital and reserves:			
Share capital: Ordinary £1 shares authorized			250 000
Ordinary shares issued			240 000
General reserve			160 000
			400 000

Investment ratios explored

Earnings per share

This is an important ratio evidenced by the fact that all companies quoted on the Stock Exchange must disclose this ratio in their published accounts. The ratio is calculated as:

$$\frac{\text{Profit after corporation tax} - \text{Preference share dividends}}{\text{Number of ordinary shares issued}}$$

Quite simply, by taking the net profit after taxation and deducting preference share dividends we arrive at the profit remaining which can be distributed to ordinary shareholders. When the resulting figure is divided by the number of ordinary shares issued, we have an earnings for each share.

As shareholders obviously have a great interest in the level of profit available to be distributed to them we can see the importance of the ratio.

Ratio Limited
Earnings per share

$$\frac{\text{Profit after tax } £44\,000 - \text{Preference share dividends } £\text{nil}}{\text{Number of ordinary shares issued } 240\,000}$$
$$= 18.3\text{p per share}$$

This means that the ordinary shareholders could have received a dividend of 18.3 per cent (18.3p per £1 share). We can see from the Profit and Loss Accounts appropriation that £4000 has been transferred to general reserve and that £40 000 has actually been distributed. The actual dividend paid is therefore

$$\frac{£40\,000}{240\,000} = 16.6\text{p per share}$$

Dividend yield

The dividend yield is broadly a means whereby an ordinary shareholder can compare the rate of return on investment with that which could be obtained elsewhere. The ratio is calculated as:

$$\frac{\text{Dividend on ordinary shares} \times 100}{\text{Current market value of ordinary shares}}$$

For the purpose of this exercise, we will assume that the current market value of Ratio Limited shares is £1.80.

Ratio Limited
Dividend yield

$$\frac{\text{Ordinary shares dividend}}{\substack{\text{Current market value of ordinary shares} \\ (240\,000 \times £1.80)}} \qquad \frac{40\,000 \times 100}{432\,000}$$

$$= 9.26 \text{ per cent}$$

We can now see the important difference between the earnings per share, which is the return on the nominal (face) value of a share, and the dividend yield, which shows the actual dividend distributed as a percentage of the current market value of an investment in a share.

Dividend cover

This ratio is designed to indicate the extent to which a company can maintain dividends on ordinary shares even if future profit levels were to fall.

The calculation is:

$$\frac{\text{Profit after corporation tax} - \text{Preference dividends}}{\text{Ordinary dividends}}$$

Ratio Limited
Dividend cover

$$\frac{\text{Profit after tax } £44\,000 - \text{Preference dividends } £\text{nil}}{\text{Ordinary dividends } £40\,000}$$

$$= 1.1$$

The extent to which the ratio exceeds 1 is the 'margin of safety'. In our example, this is relatively slender and something nearer 2 would be more acceptable, this being nearer the average we could expect to find.

Price/earnings ratio

The price/earnings ratio attempts to assess the number of years it will take for the current value of shares to be recouped (paid back) at the current level of earnings per share. If we think about this rather convoluted statement clearly, we can see that essentially it is a means of assessing risk. If the shares are in a company engaged in a type of business where, traditionally, the risk factor has been high then we would be looking for a short price/earnings ratio (short pay-back period). Conversely, if the type of business is traditionally low risk, then we will likely settle for a longer pay-back period.

The calculation is:

$$\frac{\text{Current market value of an ordinary share}}{\text{Current earnings per share}}$$

Ratio Limited
Price/earnings ratio

$$\frac{\text{Current market value of ordinary share} \quad £1.80}{\text{Current earnings per share} \quad £0.183}$$

$$= 9.84$$

This means that, assuming the market value of the shares and the earnings per share remain stable, the current value of the share would be recouped in just under 10 years. Great caution must be exercised before drawing any firm conclusions from this ratio. Earnings per share are not necessarily actually paid out by way of dividends (earnings per share covers dividends and retained profits). In any event, we would almost certainly need to compare the ratio with that of other companies engaged in a similar type of business.

Return on equity and gearing

Return on equity shareholders' interests

The return on equity shows earnings as a percentage of the nominal value of ordinary shares. It is in common use as a means of evaluating the degree to which profit is available for distribution to ordinary shareholders. The calculation is:

$$\frac{\text{Profit and corporation tax} - \text{Preference dividends}}{\text{Ordinary shareholders' interests}} \times 100$$

Ratio Limited

$$\frac{\text{Profit after tax } £44\,000 - \text{Preference shares } £\text{nil} = £44\,000}{\text{Ordinary shareholders' interests* } £400\,000} \times 100$$

$$= 11 \text{ per cent}$$

*Ordinary shareholders' interests warrants some explanation. The 'net worth' of the business belongs to the ordinary shareholders who represent the equity capital of a company. The easiest way of getting this figure is to take the total of the capital and reserves section of the Balance Sheet, deduct preference share capital and we have ordinary shareholders' interests.

Gearing

Gearing essentially measures the relationship or proportion of capital on which fixed interest is paid (loans, debentures and preference shares) to ordinary (equity) share capital. It is a measure of the risk taken by ordinary shareholders who rank behind the fixed interest capital in having a claim on the income and assets of a company. It is calculated as:

$$\frac{\text{Nominal value of fixed interest capital}}{\text{Nominal value of fixed interest capital} + \text{nominal value of ordinary shares}} \times 100$$

Ratio Limited

Gearing

$$\frac{\text{Fixed interest capital}^*}{\text{Fixed interest capital £320 000} + \text{Ordinary share capital £240 000}} \quad \frac{£320\,000 \times 100}{}$$

$$= 57 \text{ per cent}$$

*	6% Debentures	80 000
	5% Mortgage	200 000
	Bank loan	40 000
		320 000

In general, we can say that if the fixed interest capital (sometimes referred to as debt capital) of a company is less than the equity capital (ordinary share capital) then the company has low gearing. Conversely, when the fixed interest capital exceeds the value of equity capital, the company has high gearing. In our example, where fixed interest capital is 57 per cent of the total capital structure of the company, then the company can be said to have relatively high gearing.

Exercises

1. Summary accounts of two trading companies are as follows:

Balance sheets as at 31 July 19–3

	A Ltd £000	£000	B Ltd £000	£000
Fixed assets				
Premises		5 000		8 000
Equipment		500		1 000
		5 500		9 000
Current assets				
Stock	800		900	
Debtors	50		60	
Bank	330		720	
	1 180		1 680	
Current liabilities	850		980	
		330		700
		5 830		9 700
Long-term loans		800		5 000
		5 030		4 700
Share capital				
Ordinary shares of £1		3 000		2 000
Retained profits		2 030		2 700
		5 030		4 700

Profit and Loss Accounts for the year ended 31 July 19–3

	£000	£000	£000	£000
Sales		13 360		16 020
Cost of sales		8 685		10 090
		4 675		5 930
Distribution costs	2 300		2 870	
Administration costs	1 375		1 670	
		3 675		4 540
Trading profit		1 000		1 390
Interest paid		65		400
Net profit		935		990
Dividend		300		400
Retained profit		635		590

You are required to:
(a) Compute for each of the two companies:
   (i) one liquidity ratio
   (ii) one gearing ratio
   (iii) three ratios assessing profitability and performance.

2. Study the following Balance Sheet and answer the questions below:

Balance Sheet

	Cost	Depn	Net
Equipment	10 000	4 000	6 000
Vehicles	50 000	10 000	40 000
			46 000

Investments at cost	50 000
Land	43 000
Stock	55 000
Debtors	40 000
Bank	3 000
	237 000

Ordinary shares £1 each	40 000
Share premium	12 000
Revaluation reserve	—
Profit and Loss Account	25 000
10% debentures	100 000
Creditors	40 000
Proposed dividend	20 000
Bank	—
	237 000

Profit and Loss Account

	£
Sales	200 000
Cost of sales	100 000
	100 000
Expenses	60 000
	40 000
Dividends	20 000
	20 000
B/Fwd	5 000
C/Fwd	25 000

Calculate the following ratios:
  Return on capital employed
  Return on shareholders' funds
  Debtors turnover
  Creditors turnover
  Working capital ratio
  Acid test
  Gross profit percentage
  Net profit percentage
  Gearing ratio

3. The following balances remained in the Ledger of Burrows Limited after the Trading and Profit and Loss Accounts had been prepared for the year ended 30 April 19–3.

	Debit £	Credit £
Premises at cost	86 000	
General reserve		4 000
Ordinary shares: fully paid		100 000
8% Preference shares: fully paid		50 000
Electricity		100
Cash at bank	13 100	
Profit and Loss Account balance 01 May 19–2		14 500
Debtors and creditors	20 000	12 900
Profit and Loss Account	16 500	
Machinery at cost	60 000	
Provision for depreciation on machinery		40 000
Stock	60 000	
Provision for bad debts		4 000
Insurance	900	
Preference share dividend paid	2 000	
	242 000	242 000

Burrows Limited had an authorized capital of £200 000 divided into 100 000 ordinary shares of £1 each and 200 000 8 per cent preference shares of 50p each.

The Directors have recommended a transfer of £5000 to general reserve; an ordinary dividend of 15p per share; and a provision for the unpaid preference share dividend.

You are required to :
(a) Prepare the profit and loss appropriation account for year ended 30 April 19–3.
(b) Prepare the balance sheet as at 30 April 19–3, showing clearly the *working capital* and the *shareholders' funds*.
(c) Prepare:
    (i) one ratio indicating the firm's profitability
    (ii) two ratios indicating the firm's liquidity.

Unit 25

Clubs

Objectives outlined

Unlike the businesses we have been studying, many clubs and associations do not exist to make profit. They are run primarily for the benefit of their members in pursuit of leisure or sporting activities. Because they are non-profit making they do not require a Trading and Profit and Loss Account. What they do need is a meaningful financial statement which relates to their particular activities.

We need to clear up a common misunderstanding. To say that a club is non-profit making is not to say that it will never engage in a particular activity which is designed to make a profit. Many clubs do just this. We can all think of clubs we know which organize events such as bring and buy sales, dances, fêtes, etc., with a view to making a profit. However, the 'profit' generated by a particular event is a contribution to the resources of the club and does not detract from the fact that, as an entity, the purpose of the club is not to make profit for the personal benefit of individual members. Instead of a Trading and Profit and Loss Account, clubs produce one of two possible financial statements:

- A Receipts and Payments Account.
- An Income and Expenditure Account.

Receipts and Payments Account

This really is the simplest of accounts to produce. It is merely a summarized analysis of the Cash Book. In fact, a Cash Book with analysis columns is a sensible arrangement for this type of organization. Let us look at an example for a club.

Payments Side of Analysed Cash Book

Date	Detail	Cash	Bank	Rent	Stationery	Telephone	Bar Purchases	Transport	Barman's Wages	Fête Expenses
31.01.19–3	TOTALS			100.00	20.00	40.00	340.00	50.00	280.00	60.00

Receipts Side of Analysed Cash Book

Date	Detail	Cash	Bank	Subs	Bar Takings	Donations	Fête Receipts			
01.01.19–3	Balance B/FWD		180.00							
31.01.19–3	TOTALS			220.00	630.00	50.00	240.00			

Note For clarity, the detailed figures have been omitted.

In columnar form, the Receipts and Payments Account would be:

Receipts and Payments Account for the month ended 31.01.19–3

Receipts
Opening bank balance 01.01.19–3 .... 180.00
Subscriptions 220.00
Bar takings 630.00
Donations 50.00
Fête receipts .... 240 00 .... 1140.00
1320.00

Less: Payments

Rent	100.00	
Stationery	20.00	
Telephone	40.00	
Bar supplies	340.00	
Transport	50.00	
Bar staff	280.00	
Fête expenses	60.00	890.00
Bank balance 31.01.19–3		430.00

While this form of accounts may suffice for some small clubs, it would not be sufficient for the majority because it takes no account of any assets owned or outstanding liabilities. In the next section we will examine the account which is more commonly used.

Income and Expenditure Account

An Income and Expenditure Account gets round the deficiencies of a simple Receipts and Payments Account in that it includes provision for prepaid and unpaid expenses, and adjusts income to relevant accounting periods. Indeed, an Income and Expenditure Account follows the same general format and rules as a Trading and Profit and Loss Account except that some items are described differently.

The most noticeable difference is that instead of a 'Net profit', there is a 'Surplus of income over expenditure'. If the club makes the equivalent of a net loss, this is described as 'Excess of expenditure over income'.

We have already discussed the fact that clubs often engage in activities which in themselves are designed to create a profit contribution to their general finances. For this type of activity a separate Trading and Profit and Loss Account is drawn up and any profit or loss is then transferred into the Income and Expenditure Account. Based on the example in the previous section and using the following information, we will now explore this method:

	31.12.19–2	31.01.19–3
Bar stock	190.00	210.00
Subscription owing	45.00	40.00
Subscriptions in advance	10.00	15.00
Bar purchases owing	105.00	80.00

The club owns equipment valued at £1800 at 31.12.19–2.

The equipment is depreciated at 24 per cent per annum.

Before we can complete the Bar Trading Account, we need to establish the cost of purchases:

Bar Purchases

		Balance B/D (owing 01.01.19–3)	105.00
Bank	340.00		
Balance C/D (owing 31.01.19–3)	80.00	Bar Trading Account	315.00*
	420.00		420.00
		Balance B/D	80.00

* Balancing figure.

Now we can complete a Bar Trading Account:

Sales			630.00
Less: Cost of goods sold:			
Stock	01.01.19–3	190.00	
Purchases		315.00	
		505.00	
Less: Stock	31.01.19–3	210.00	295.00
Gross profit			335.00
Less:			
Barman's wages			280.00
Net profit transferred to Income and Expense Account			55.00

Before we construct the Income and Expenditure Account, there is another area requiring attention: the matter of subscriptions. You can be almost certain that these will figure in any exercise or examination involving club accounts. The most reliable way of dealing with this area is to construct a Subscription Account. By doing so, there is less likelihood of error.

All we need do is slot in the information we have and then the balance on the account will represent the amount to be credited to the Income and Expenditure Account.

Subscriptions

Subs owing B/D 01.01.19–3	45.00	Subs in Advance B/D 01.01.19–3	10.00
Income and Expenditure A/c	210.00	Bank	220.00
Subs in advance C/D 31.01.19–3	15.00	Subs owing C/D 31.01.19–3	40.00
	270.00		270.00
Subs owing B/D	40.00	Subs in advance B/D	15.00

In practice, it is highly likely that if subscriptions are owed for any extended period, they never get collected so most clubs would not usually provide for unpaid subscriptions. However, for our purposes, we must include them as this is the approach demanded in most assignments or examinations, unless we are told differently.

Another common area of difficulty with membership subscriptions is life membership where members can pay one specified subscription which ensures membership for life. Quite simply, we must follow the rules laid down in a particular exercise. However, the approach will invariably involve the following:

1. Crediting all life membership subscriptions to a Life Membership Account. This account is a liability as it holds payments in advance.
2. Transferring from the Life Membership Account an annual sum as income into the Income and Expenditure Account.
3. Showing the end-of-year balance on the Life Membership Account as a liability in the Balance Sheet.

Preparing final accounts

Most clubs will not keep a set of double entry books so we will not have as our start point the luxury of a balanced set of books, represented by a Trial Balance. At best, we will probably have an analysed Cash Book and records of income and expenditure from particular organized events.

We can be pretty sure that in a given exercise or examination, the Income and Expenditure Account or Balance Sheet for the previous year will not be supplied. Rather, we will be given random information, sufficient to make our task possible. The say way to proceed is to approach the problem in a structured manner, as follows:

From the information given, prepare a 'Statement of Affairs' at the end of the last period of account.

A statement of affairs simply involves listing known information in a meaningful way and then using our accounting knowledge to work out missing figures. We will do this by slotting into what is essentially a balance sheet structure all the information we have relating to the end of the last period of account at 31 December 19–2.

Statement of Affairs at 31.12.19–2

Fixed assets			
Equipment			1800.00
Current assets			
Bar stock	190.00		
Subscriptions owing	45.00		
Bank	180.00	415	
Less: Current liabilities:			
Creditors (bar purchases)	105.00		
Subscriptions in advance	10.00	115	
Working capital			300.00
			2100.00
Financed by:			
Accumulated fund*			2100.00

* This is the information we were not given. In order to make the statement balance, we simply slot in the balancing figure which is described as 'Accumulated fund'. This is the club equivalent of the Capital Account with which we are familiar.

We could now, if we wished, open up a balanced set of accounts and track all current transactions through by double entries. However, our accounting knowledge is now sufficiently developed to enable us to prepare final accounts without going through this procedure, perhaps with the exception of some of the more complex accounts such as bar trading and subscriptions which we have already covered.

Income and Expenditure Account for the month ended 31 December 19–3

Income:		
Subscriptions		210
Profit from bar		55
Profit from fête (1)		180
Donations		50
		495
Less: Expenditure		
Rent	100	
Stationery	20	
Telephone	40	
Transport	50	
Depreciation on equipment (2)	36	246
Surplus of income over expenditure		249

Notes
(1) Receipts £240 *Less*: Expenses £60 = £180
(2) £1800 × 2%   = £36

Balance Sheet as at 31 December 19–3

Fixed assets:		
Equipment	1800	
Less: Depreciation	36	1764
Current assets:		
Bar stock	210	
Subscriptions owing	40	
Bank (1)	430	680
Less: Current liabilities:		
Creditors (bar purchases)	80	
Subscriptions in advance	15	95
Working capital		585
		2349
Financed by:		
Accumulated fund 01.01.19–3		2100
Surplus of income over expenditure		249
		2349
Note (1) Opening balance	180	
Receipts	1140	
	1320	
Payments	890	
	430	

Exercises

1. The following is a Receipts and Payments Account for the Advance Social Club as at 30 November 19–6.

Receipts and Payments Account for the year ended 30 November 19–6

	£		£
Bank balance b/f	810	Office expenses	685
Members' subscriptions	4250	Rent	2500
Donations	1480	Visiting speakers' expenses	1466
Sales of social tickets	1126	Donations	380
		Prizes for social	550
		Purchase of equipment	1220
		Printing	469
		Balance c/f	396
	7666		7666

On 01 December 19–5, the club owned equipment which had cost £3650 and which was valued at £2190. The club's equipment as at 30 November 19–6 (inclusive of purchases during the year) was valued at £1947.

The following additional information is available:

	01 December 19–5 £	30 November 19–6 £
Stocks of prizes	86	108
Owing to suppliers of prizes	314	507
Subscriptions in arrears	240	580
Subscriptions in advance	65	105

You are required to:
(a) Prepare a statement of the accumulated fund of the club as at 01 December 19–5.
(b) Prepare a Subscriptions Account for the year ended 30 November 19–6.
(c) Prepare an Income and Expenditure Account and Balance Sheet as at 30 November 19–6.

2. The secretary of the Cliveden Sports Club gives you the following summary of his Cash Book for the year ended 31 December 19–4.

	£		£
Opening balances:			
Bank	63	Rent	234
Cash	10	Office expenses	18
Income		Secretary's expenses	37
Members 19–4	170	Refreshments	61
Members 19–5	20	Annual social	102
Fees for games	150	Equipment purchased	26
Annual social	134	Donations	12
		Balance at close of year	
		Bank	49
		Cash	8
	547		547

The secretary also gives you the following information:

	December 19–3 £	December 19–4 £
Amounts due		
Members' subscriptions	14	12
Letting charges	78	53
Re annual social	6	—
Amounts owing		
Rent	72	54
Office expenses	—	3
Secretary's expenses	4	8
Refreshments	13	12

On 31 December 19–3, the club's equipment stood at £204 — 10 per cent is to be written off the equipment cost as at 31 December 19–4.

You are required to:
(a) Prepare a statement of the club's accumulated fund as on 31 December 19–3.
(b) Prepare the Income and Expenditure Account for the year ended 31 May 19–4, and the Balance Sheet as at that date.

3. From the following information, for the Greenland Social Club as at 31 December 19–7, you are to prepare:
   (a) A statement showing the general fund of the club as on 31 October 19–6.
   (b) An Income and Expenditure Account for the year ended 31 October 19–7 (showing gross profit on bar sales and catering); and a Balance Sheet as at 31 October 19–7.

	£		£
Cash 01 November 19–6	10	Bar purchases	1885
Bank 01 November 19–6:		Secretary's honorarium	306
Current account	263	Rent	184
Deposit account	585	Electricity	143
Spectators' entrance fees	54	New projector	
Subscriptions to 31.10.–6	30	(less allowance for old one £40)	120
31.10.–7	574	General expenses	132
31.10.–8	44	Catering purchases	80
Bar takings	2285	Furniture	460
Deposit account interest	26	Cash at 31 October 19–7	8
Catering receipts	120	Bank 31 October 19–7:	
		Current account	176
		Deposit account	497
	3991		3991

(i) The book value of the furniture, on 31 October 19–6, was £396 (cost £440) and projector £20 (cost £120).

(ii) The current assets and liabilities were as follows:

	31 October 19–6	31 October 19–7
	£	£
Bar stock	209	178
Bar purchases	186	248
Due for rent	12	26
Due for electricity	9	11
Subscriptions in arrear	30	50

(iii) The Club Secretary is to receive 50 per cent of the gross profit from catering in addition to her honorarium.

(iv) Furniture is to be depreciated at a rate of 10 per cent on cost. No depreciation is to be provided on the new projector, but a full year on the new furniture.

4. From the following Receipts and Payments Account for the year ended 31 March 19–3 of the Low Reaches Fishing Club and the additional information given, prepare the Income and Expenditure Account and Balance Sheet.

	£	£
Bank balance brought forward 01 April 19–2		1 347
Receipts:		
Membership subscriptions:		
For the year ended 31 March 19–2	252	
For the year ended 31 March 19–3	6 810	
For the year ended 31 March 19–4	330	
	7 392	
Sale of photographic equipment	28 100	
Sale of small transit coach	2 560	38 052
		39 399
Payments:		
Purchase of fishing equipment	22 734	
Lecturer for rural hobbies course	460	
Purchase of fishing rights	10 000	
Bank investment deposit account	3 000	
Office expenses	600	
Printing costs	810	
Advertising	230	
National affiliation fee	180	
Meeting room hire	340	
Secretary's expenses	300	38 654
31 March 19–3 Bank balance carried forward		745

Notes
(i)   Subscriptions are not accounted for until received.
(ii) The Society's assets and liabilities, as at 01 April 19–2, were as follows:

	£
Stock of fishing equipment for resale, at cost	3420
Subscriptions for the year ended 31 March 19–3 received prior to 31 March 19–2	420

(iii) *Further information:*
   –   All receipts and payments are passed through the Club's bank account.
   –   The Club buys fishing equipment for sale to members at favourable prices; the fishing equipment in stock at 31 March 19–3 has been valued, at cost, at £1800.
       Members have requested that the Club's annual accounts show the profit from the sale of fishing equipment.
   –   The Club's bank investment deposit account was credited with interest of £82 on 31 March 19–3.

5. From the following Receipts and Payments Account of the Rockerbie Sports Club, and the additional information given, prepare:
   (a) An Income and Expenditure Account and Balance Sheet as at 31 October 19–5.
   (b) An account to show the profit or loss on the bar.

19–4		£	19–5		£
01 Nov	Balance B/f	1 700	31 Oct		
19–5				Rent and insurance	380
31 Oct	Subscriptions	8 600		Repairs	910
	Bar takings	13 800		Annual dance — catering	650
	Donations	1 168		Bar purchases	9 200
	Annual dance			Printing	248
	(sale of tickets)	470		New equipment	2 463
				Hire of coach	89
				Steward's salary	4 700
				Petty cash	94
				Balance c/f	7 004
		25 738			25 738

The following additional information has been given:

	19–4 £	19–5 £
Premises, at cost	15 000	15 000
Bar stocks	1 840	2 360
Petty cash	30	10
Bank deposit account	600	730
Subscriptions received in advance	210	360
Creditors for bar supplies	2 400	1 900

Depreciation is to be provided on the premises at the rate of 10 per cent of cost and on the new equipment at the rate of $33\frac{1}{3}$ per cent of cost.
The petty cash float is used for office expenses.
The only entry in the bank deposit account, during the year ended 31 October 19–5 was for interest.
One-quarter of the steward's salary and one-half of the premises costs, including depreciation, are to be apportioned to the bar.

Unit 26

Partnerships

Partnerships — agreements and law

If two or more people join together to carry on a business then they are said to be in partnership. Indeed, the Partnership Act of 1890 says that a partnership is: 'The relation which subsists between persons carrying on business in common with a view to profit.'

Normally, there is a minimum of two partners and a maximum of twenty partners. However, the maximum number restriction does not apply to certain professions such as solicitors, accountants, Stock Exchange members, etc., who can have an unlimited number of partners.

The relationship of partners is subject to legal constraint in two ways. Partners are free to make their own arrangements as to the terms of their partnership and the arrangements should be set down in a legal agreement, commonly referred to as a *Deed of Partnership*. Should there then be any dispute over matters relating to the partnership, the Deed of Partnership can be relied on as a legal agreement determining how the matter(s) should be resolved. However, in the absence of a Deed of Partnership or if the Deed does not cover the particular matter which is disputed, then the relevant provisions of the Partnership Act 1890, are applied.

Broadly, the Partnership Act 1890 has the following main provisions:

1. The liability of every partner to meet the debts of the business is unlimited. Creditors can sue the partnership, or any individual partner, because the partners are 'jointly and severally liable for the debts of the partnership'. This means, for example, that if a partnership collapsed and, say, one partner was forced into bankruptcy while the other had private wealth, then creditors could sue the solvent partner for the whole of any debt.
2. Every partner is entitled to take part in the management of the business.
3. Each partner has one vote:
    (a) Decisions requiring a vote will normally be determined by a majority vote.
    (b) Decisions affecting the structure of the partnership, such as admitting a new partner, or the type of business the partnership carries out require the consent of all partners.
4. Each partner can sign contracts on behalf of the partnership as an agent of the partnership.
5. All partners have access to the financial records and other papers of the partnership.

6. A partnership is dissolved by:
   (a) The death of any partner.
   (b) A partner who gives notice to the other partner(s) of his or her intention to leave the partnership.
7. (a) Profits or losses are to be shared equally.
   (b) No interest is chargeable on capital.
   (c) No interest is chargeable on drawings.
   (d) Salaries are not allowed.
   (e) If a partner contributes more capital than an agreed amount, then that partner is entitled to interest on the excess at 5 per cent per annum.

We can see therefore that partners are well advised to draw up their own agreement in the form of a Deed of Partnership. At the minimum, such an agreement should cover:

1. The capital to be contributed by each partner.
2. The basis on which profits or losses are to be shared.
3. The rate of interest to be paid on capital.
4. Arrangements for partners' drawings.
5. The rate of interest, if any, to be charged on drawings.
6. The salaries to be paid to partners.
7. Arrangements for the preparing of accounts and their audit.
8. The circumstances under which the partnership will be dissolved.
9. How disputes between partners are to be resolved.
10. How the voting rights of the partnerships are to be distributed.

Note   These points are not exhaustive but cover the majority of circumstances which are relevant to the accounting requirements of a partnership.

There is no average or norm for partnership agreements because, as we have seen, partners are free to make their own arrangements. However, from our point of view, there are a number of key points on a critical path which we will look for in any exercise involving partnerships:

- Agreed salaries. These usually recognize the degree of responsibility taken and time devoted to the business by each partner.
- Interest, if any, to be allowed on capital contributed by each partner.
- Interest, if any, to be charged on drawings.
- The ratio in which profits, or losses, are to be distributed. If this is not specified, then the equal shares provision of the Partnership Act 1890 applies.

Partnerships — Capital and Current Accounts

We know from our previous studies that the relationship of the proprietor to the business is expressed in two accounts — the Capital Account and a Drawings Account. The relationship of partners to their business is expressed somewhat differently.

1. Each partner will have his or her own Capital Account but this only shows the capital actually put into the business. It does not receive any other entries for transactions such as profit share or drawings.
2. Each partner will have a Current Account (these are sometimes referred to as Drawings Accounts although we will not be using this description). Into this Current Account goes all transactions relating to the partner's position with the business, except capital introduced which is put to the Capital Account. Typically, the Current Account will contain entries for:

   (a)   Drawings
   (b)   Interest chargeable on drawings
   (c)   Interest payable on loans made to the business
   (d)   Interest payable on capital introduced
   (e)   Salary
   (f)   Share of profit or loss.

Accounting for any of the above transactions follows the normal double entry rules and, to make life easy, we need only remember that the double entry for most of these transactions within the Current Account is to an account called an Appropriation Account. This account is similar to a company's Appropriation Account in that it is the vehicle for accounting for distribution of profit. We will see later how the Appropriation Account fits into the final accounts of a partnership. For now, we will just accept the existence of the account and use it as we now explore the accounting entries that may confront us in a partnership.

   To illustrate the entries, we will use the information below:

The A and B partnership

A and B are partners sharing profits in the ratio 3 : 2. Capital Accounts at the start of 19–3 show:

	A	B
	80 000	60 000

During the year 19–3 the following transactions occurred:

		A	B
Drawings	01.07.19–3	15 000	8 000
	01.10.19–3	—	4 000
Salaries		22 000	18 000
Capital introduced		20 000	

Notes

1. Interest is charged on drawings at 10 per cent per annum.
2. Interest is credited to capital at 5 per cent per annum.
3. Net profit for the year is £76 250.

We will now track the accounting entries for these transactions.

Capital Accounts:

A Capital		
	Bal B/D 01.07.19–3	80 000
	Bank	20 000

B Capital		
	Balance B/D	60 000

Current Accounts:

A Current Account

01.07.19–3 Bank (drawings)	15 000	Salary	22 000	(1)
Interest on drawings	750	Interest on capital	4 500	(2)
Balance C/D	28 750	Share of profit	18 000	(4)
	44 500		44 500	
		Balance B/D	28 750	

B Current Account

01.07.19–3 Bank (drawings)	8 000	Salary	18 000	(1)
01.10.19–3 Bank (drawings)	4 000	Interest on capital	3 000	
Interest on drawings (3)	500	Share of profit	12 000	(4)
Balance C/D	20 500			
	33 000		33 000	
		Balance B/D	20 500	

Appropriation Account

Salaries A	22 000	Net profit B/D	76 250
B	18 000	Interest on drawings	
Interest on capital		A	750
A	4 500	B	500
B	3 000		
Share of profit			
A	18 000		
B	12 000		
	77 500		77 500

Notes

(1) Partners' salaries are *not* charged on the Profit and Loss Account. Salaries in the sense that they apply to partners are really a predetermined share of profit. For this reason, they are credited to partners' Current Accounts and debited to the Appropriation Account.

(2)
Capital 01.01.19–3	£80 000 × 5%	=	4 000
Capital introduced 01.07.19–3	£20 000 × 0.5 (yr) × 5%	=	500
			4 500

(3)
Drawings 01.07.19–3	£8 000 × 0.5 (yr) × 10%	=	400
Drawings 01.10.19–3	£4 000 × 0.25 (yr) × 10%	=	100
			500

(4)
Net profit remaining before profit share		30 000
A	£30 000 ÷ 5 × 3	18 000
B	£30 000 ÷ 5 × 2	12 000

(5) If there is a net loss, all the agreed adjustments to the partners' Current Accounts, including salaries, are still entered in the accounts. The resulting net loss in the Appropriation Account is then shared out in the agreed ratio. The reason for this is simple. Only by doing the full, agreed adjustments can the ultimate burden of the loss reflect the intentions of the partnership agreement.

Partnerships — final accounts

These really are good news!

Profit and Loss Account

The Profit and Loss Account of a partnership is identical to that of a sole trader except for the Appropriation Account, which is effectively tacked on to the end of what would otherwise be a sole trader's Profit and Loss Account.

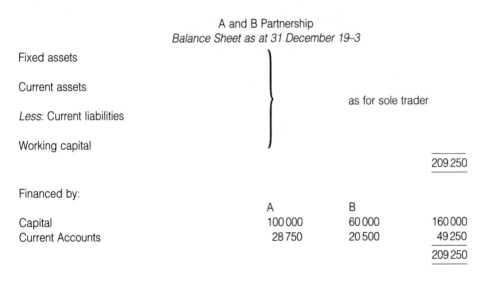

A and B Partnership
Profit and Loss Account for the year ended 31 December 19–3

Sales			
Less: Cost of sales			
Gross profit			as for sole trader
Less: Expenses			
....			
....			
....			
Net profit			76 250
Appropriations:	A	B	1 250
Interest on drawings	750	500	77 500
Less:			
Salaries	22 000	18 000	40 000
Interest on capital	4 500	3 000	7 500
			30 000
Balance of profit shared			
	18 000	12 000	30 000

Balance Sheet

Again, the Balance Sheet is identical to that prepared for a sole trader, except for the layout of the Capital Account section.

A and B Partnership
Balance Sheet as at 31 December 19–3

Fixed assets			
Current assets			
			as for sole trader
Less: Current liabilities			
Working capital			
			209 250
Financed by:			
	A	B	
Capital	100 000	60 000	160 000
Current Accounts	28 750	20 500	49 250
			209 250

Note

If a Current Account is a debit balance, i.e. overdrawn, then it would be bracketed and deducted to produce a net figure in the total column. For example, say B's Current Account had been a debit balance of £20 500 instead of a credit (as above), the Balance Sheet entry would be:

	A	**B**	
Current Accounts	28 750	(20 500)	8 250

Exercises

1. Thomas and Pollard are in partnership sharing profits and losses in the ratio 7:3. The following information has been taken from the partnership records for the financial year ended 31 May 19–7.

Partners' Current Accounts, balances as at 01 June 19–6:

    Thomas £15 000 Cr
    Pollard £13 000 Cr

Partners' Capital Accounts, balances as at 01 June 19–6:

    Thomas £200 000
    Pollard £140 000

During the year ended 31 May 19–7 the partners had the following drawings:

Thomas	£10 000 on 31 August 19–6
	£10 000 on 30 November 19–6
	£10 000 on 28 February 19–7
	£10 000 on 31 May 19–7
Pollard	£7 000 on 31 August 19–6
	£7 000 on 30 November 19–6
	£7 000 on 28 February 19–7
	£7 000 on 31 May 19–7

Interest is charged on drawings at the rate of 12 per cent per annum. Interest is allowed on capital accounts and credit balances on current accounts at the rate of 12 per cent per annum. Pollard is to be allowed a salary of £15 000 per annum.

The net profit of the partnership for the year ended 31 May 19–7 is £102 940.

You are to produce:
(a) A statement of the amount of interest chargeable on partners' drawings for the year ended 31 May 19–7.
(b) The partnership Appropriation Account for the year ended 31 May 19–7.
(c) A statement of the balance on each partner's Current Account as at 31 May 19–7.

2. The following list of balances, as at 30 September 19–6, has been extracted from the books of Lyme & Regis, a partnership, sharing profits and losses in the proportions 3:2.

	£
Printing	3 500
Sales	322 100
Stock at 01 October 19–5	23 000
Purchases	208 200
Rent	10 300
Electricity	8 700
Staff salaries	36 100
Telephone	2 900
Vehicles running costs	5 620
Discounts allowed	950
Discounts received	370
Returns inwards	2 100
Returns outwards	6 100
Carriage inwards	1 700
Carriage outwards	2 400
Plant & equipment: at cost	26 000
provision for depreciation	11 200
Vehicles: at cost	46 000
provision for depreciation	25 000
Provision for doubtful debts	300
Current account balances at 01 October 19–5:	
Lyme	3 600 Cr
Regis	2 400 Cr
Capital account balances at 01 October 19–5:	
Lyme	33 000
Regis	17 000
Drawings: Lyme	24 000
Regis	11 000
Debtors	9 300
Creditors	8 400
Bank	7 700

Notes
(i) Lyme transferred £10 000 from his Capital Account to a newly opened Lyme Loan Account on 01 July 19–6.
Interest at 10 per cent per annum on the loan is to be credited to Lyme.
(ii) Regis is to be credited with a salary at the rate of £12 000 per annum from 01 April 19–6.
(iii) Stock at 30 September 19–6 has been valued at cost at £32 000.
(iv) Telephone charges accrued due at 30 September 19–6 amounted to £400 and rent of £600 prepaid at that date.
(v) During the year, Regis has taken goods costing £1000 for his own use.
(vi) Depreciation is to be provided as follows:

Plant and equipment	10 per cent
Vehicles	20 per cent

Required:
(a) Prepare a Trading and Profit and Loss Account for the year ended 30 September 19–6.
(b) Prepare a Balance Sheet as at 30 September to include summaries of the partners' Capital and Current Accounts for the year ended on that date.

3. The partnership of Seaward, Groves and Johannes has just completed its first year. Profits are to be apportioned in the ratio of Seaward 3, Groves 2 and Johannes 1 after allowing interest on capital at 12 per cent per annum and crediting Seaward with a salary of £12 000.

The following information relates to their first financial year which ended on 31 October 19–7.
(a) The partners introduced the following amounts as capital on 01 November 19–6:

	£
Seaward	50 000
Groves	40 000
Johannes	20 000

(b) Drawings during the year were:

	£
Seaward	3 900
Groves	4 500
Johannes	2 400

(c) The draft Profit and Loss Account for the year showed a net trading profit of £61 720.
(d) Included in the vehicle running costs for the year was a bill for £300 which related to Groves' private motoring expenses.
(e) No entries had been made in the accounts to record the following:
   – Groves invested a further £10 000 as capital with effect from 01 May 19–7, and on the same date Johannes brought into the business items of equipment at an agreed valuation of £6000. In order to settle a debt, Johannes had privately undertaken some work for Fraser, a creditor of the partnership. Fraser accepted the work as full settlement of the £2000 the partnership owed him.
   – Seaward had accepted a car from Milnes, a debtor of the partnership. The car, which was valued at £1000, was accepted in full settlement of a debt of £2500 that Milnes owed to the partnership.
   – Each partner had taken goods for private use during the year as follows:

	£
Seaward	1 400
Groves	2 100
Johannes	2 100

You are to produce:
(i) Profit and Loss Appropriation Account for the year ended 31 October 19–7 showing the corrected net profit of the first year's trading.
(ii) The Capital and Current Accounts of Seaward, Groves and Johannes for the year ended 31 October 19–7.

Unit 27

Incomplete records

The problem

Many small traders and businesses do not maintain a set of books using a double-entry system. At best they will maintain a detailed Cash Book and subsidiary records on a single entry basis. At worst, financial records may be very sparse indeed, to the extent that it is impossible to prepare a full detailed set of final accounts.

This is, however, a very interesting area because it draws deeply on our basic understanding and accounting knowledge. Apart from our own initiative, the only other tool we need is access to keys which will open the door to many of the problems inherent in an exercise of this type. As we progress through this unit we will identify many of these 'keys'.

We will use the following exercise and work through it, step by step. When we have finished we will have covered most of the problem areas which are likely to confront us in this area.

Introduction to the basics

In Unit 25 covering club accounts, we used the concept of a statement of affairs which is essentially a Balance Sheet format into which all known figures are slotted. In most questions concerning incomplete records there is a requirement to find the opening capital figure. An opening statement of affairs is the ideal vehicle for doing this because, having inserted the known figures, capital can then be found by using a 'key'.

$$\text{Capital} = \text{Assets} - \text{Liabilities}$$

A Peters is a retailer. He does not keep complete records but can supply the following information:

Position 01 January 19–3

Stock	3 000
Debtors	2 600
Creditors	1 600
Vehicle	5 100
Shop fittings	4 000
Electricity owing	300

Summary Cash Book 31.12.19–3

Balance 01.01.19–3	2 400	Payments to creditors	22 000
Receipts from debtors	44 000	Telephone	400
Cash sales	4 200	Shop fittings	2 500
		Insurances	900
		Vehicle expenses	2 000
		Electricity	1 300
		Drawings	15 500
		Balance 31.12.19–3	6 000
	50 600		50 600

All cash and cheques had been banked.

1. At 31.12.19–3 £150 was owing for electricity and insurances were paid in advance £100.
2. Fittings are depreciated at 10 per cent and vehicle at 20 per cent. A full year's depreciation is charged on additions.
3. Balances at 31.12.19–3

Debtors	4 000
Creditors	2 500
Stock	4 000

We are to prepare a Trading and Profit and Loss Account and Balance Sheet as at 31 December 19–3.

Statement of affairs 01.01.19–3

Assets:	Vehicle	5 100	
	Shop fittings	4 000	
	Stock	3 000	
	Debtors	2 600	
	Bank	2 400	17 100
Less: Liabilities:			
	Creditors	1 600	
	Electricity owing	300	1 900
			15 200
Capital			15 200

Trading and Profit and Loss Account

Trading Account

If we examine the available information and think about what we require for a Trading Account we will see that, somehow, we have to get at figures for sales and purchases.

Sales

Open a Debtors' Account and insert known information

Debtors

Balance 01.01.19–3	2 600	Bank	44 000
		Balance 31.12.19–3	4 000

Sales must be the missing figure to balance the account

Debtors

Balance 01.01.19–3	2 600	Bank	44 000
Sales	45 400	Balance 31.12.19–3	4 000
	48 000		48 000

Therefore total sales:

Credit sales	45 000
Cash sales	4 200
Total sales	49 600

Purchases

Open a Creditors' Account and find the missing purchases figure*

Creditors

Bank	22 000	Balance 01.01.19–3	1 600
Balance 31.12.19–3	2 500	Purchases	22 900*
	24 500		24 500

Profit and Loss Account

Clearly, most of the expense items can be 'picked up' direct from the Summary Cash Book. Electricity and insurances, however, need some adjustment.

This time (for demonstration purposes) we will use an alternative technique to drawing up a T account which we may find quicker to use.

Electricity	DR	CR
Balance 01.01.19–3		300
Bank	1 300	
Balance 31.12.19–3 (owing)	150	
* Profit and loss		1 150
	1 450	1 450

Insurances:		
Bank	900	
Prepaid		100
* Profit and loss		800
	900	900

* Missing figure inserted to balance account

Trial Balance

We can now prepare a Trial Balance from which final accounts can be produced after adjusting for depreciation.

Trial Balance at 31.12.19–3

	DR	CR
Stock 01.01.19–3	3 000	
Capital		15 200
Shop fittings	6 500	
Vehicle	5 100	
Debtors	4 000	
Creditors		2 500
Sales		49 600
Purchases	22 900	
Telephone	400	
Insurances	800	
Insurances prepaid	100	
Vehicle expenses	2 000	
Electricity	1 150	
Electricity accrued		150
Drawings	15 500	
Bank	6 000	
	67 450	67 450

In the time constraint of an examination we could dispense with the Trial Balance and go straight to final accounts. In this study, we are primarily concerned with finding 'missing' figures. We will stop at the Trial Balance as working through what is now a simple set of final accounts would serve little purpose.

Worked exercise

We will now work through a rather more complex problem based on the following information.

R Rogers wants us to produce accounts for the year ended 31 December 19–3 but can only produce the following:

Assets and liabilities at:	01.01.19–3	31.12.19–3
Bank balance	2 300	1 650
Cash	360	330
Debtors produce by sales	4 000	4 500
Creditors (purchases)	7 200	9 000
Stock	8 500	13 700
Electricity owing	230	190
Rent in advance	200	320

All takings from sales have been banked after taking out:

Staff wages	1 200
Stock purchases	1 800
Drawings	*

* R Rogers cannot say how much these have been. However, in addition, £600 (cost) of goods have been taken for personal use. Net takings have been marked up $33\frac{1}{3}$ per cent on cost.

Analysis of bank payments:

Rent	5 040	
Wages	6 620	
Electricity	1 390	
Carriage costs (to customers)	3 000	
Purchases	101 500	

Statement of affairs 31.12.19–2

Assets		
Stock	8 500	
Debtors	4 000	
Pre-paid rent	200	
Bank	2 300	
Cash	360	15 360
Less: Liabilities:		
Creditors	7 200	
Accrual — electricity	230	7 430
		7 930
Capital		7 930

Purchases: Cash payments	1 800	
Bank payments	101 500	
Increase in creditors	1 800	
Total purchases	105 100	
Less: Drawings (goods own use)	600	
	104 500	

Sales (marked up $33\frac{1}{3}$ per cent on cost):

Cost of sales		
Opening stock	8 500	
Purchases	104 500	
	113 000	
Less: Closing stock	13 700	
	99 300	
99 300 + $33\frac{1}{3}$ per cent =	132 400	
Total sales	132 400	
Less: Increase in debtors	500	
Takings from sales	131 900	

Summary Cash Book

	Cash	Bank			Cash	Bank
Balances 01.01.19–3	360	2 300	(3) Drawings		12 030	
Sales takings	131 900		Wages		1 200	6 620
			Purchases		1 800	101 500
			Rent			5 040
			Electricity			1 390
			Carriage			3 000
			Balances 31.12.19–3		330	1 650
		116 900 (1)	(2) Cash to bank		116 900	
	132 260	119 200			132 260	119 200

Notes
(1) Balancing figure.
(2) Figure at (1) from Cash.
(3) Balancing figure.

Electricity		DR	CR
	Balance 01.01.19–3		230
	Bank	1 390	
	Balance 31.12.19–3 accrual	190	
	Profit and loss*		1 350
		1 580	1 580

*Balancing figure.

Rent		DR	CR
	Balance 01.01.19–3	200	
	Bank	5 040	
	Balance 31.12.19–3 Prepaid		320
	Profit and loss*		4 920
		5 240	5 240

*Balancing figure.

Although not strictly necessary we will now prepare a Trial Balance:

Trial Balance 31.12.19–3

	DR	CR
Capital		7 930
Cash	330	
Bank	1 650	
Electricity	1 350	
Electricity accrual		190
Rent	4 920	
Rent prepaid	320	
Stock 01.01.19–3	8 500	
Purchases	104 500	
Sales		132 400
Debtors	4 500	
Creditors		9 000
Drawings*	12 630	
Wages	7 820	
Carriage	3 000	
	149 520	149 520

*Drawings	Cash taken	12 030
	Goods taken	600
		12 630

R Rogers
Trading and Profit and Loss Account for the year ended 31 December 19–3

Sales		132 400
Less: Cost of Sales:		
Stock 01.01.19–3	8 500	
Purchases	104 500	
	113 000	
Less: Closing stock	13 700	99 300
Gross profit		33 100
Less: Expenses:		
Electricity	1 350	
Rent	4 920	
Wages	7 820	
Carriage	3 000	17 090
Net profit		16 010

Balance Sheet as at 31 December 19–3

Current assets:		
Stock	13 700	
Debtors	4 500	
Prepaid rent	320	
Bank	1 650	
Cash	330	20 500
Less: Current liabilities:		
Creditors	9 000	
Accrual — electricity	190	9 190
		11 310
Financed by:		
Capital 01.01.19–3	7 930	
Profit for year	16 010	
	23 940	
Less: Drawings	12 630	11 310

Exercises

1. Geraldine Jackson is a retailer who does not maintain full accounting records. The Trading and Profit and Loss Account and Balance Sheets are prepared annually, from records consisting of a bank statement and a list of unpaid suppliers and outstanding debtors.
   The following balances were shown on her Balance Sheet at 01 January 19–6:

	£
Creditors	245
Shop fittings (cost £2500) at written-down value	2 000
Stock	4 750
Debtors	500
Bank	1 100
Cash in till	100

   The following is a summary of her bank statement for the year ended 31 December 19–8:

	£
Takings banked	69 830
Payments to suppliers	62 900
Rent of premises to 31 December 19–6	400
G Samson — shopfitter	85
Advertising in local newspaper	500
General expenses	38

   Additional information
   (a) Takings are banked daily and all suppliers are paid by cheque. Geraldine keeps £150 per week for herself and pays her assistants £110 per week out of the takings.
   (b) The work done by G Samson was for providing display stands.
   (c) The cash float in the till was considered insufficient and raised to £150.
   (d) Geraldine Jackson took £750 worth of goods for her own use without payment.
   (e) Charges for preparing the accounts will be £250.

(f)   £2300 is outstanding to suppliers; £100 in respect of general expenses; £850 outstanding debtors.

(g)   Depreciation is provided on shop fittings at 10 per cent on cost, a full year's charge is made in the year of purchase.

(h)   Stock in hand at 31 December 19–6 was £7100.

You are to prepare:

(i) A Trading and Profit and Loss Account for the year ended 31 December 19–6.

(ii) A Balance Sheet as at 31 December 19–6.

2. Joan Carter started a boutique on 01 April 19–4 but has not kept proper records. She had put £15 000 of her own money into the business bank account. The transactions in the bank account, during the year ended 31 March 19–5, have been summarized from the bank account as follows:

	£
Receipts:	
Loan from Frank Shuker 01 April 19–5	10 000
Sales takings	42 000
Payments:	
Purchase of stock for resale	26 400
Electricity to 31 December 19–4	760
Rent of premises — 15 months to 30 June 19–5	3 500
Rates of premises for the year ended 31 March 19–5	1 200
Staff wages	14 700
Purchase of van — 01 October 19–4	7 600
Purchase of car for Joan Carter's private use	8 500
Van running costs	250

The bank statement shows the balance on 31 March 19–5 was £4090 in Joan Carter's favour. In addition to cash drawings, the following payments were made out of takings before being banked:

Van running costs	890
Sundry expenses	355

On 31 March 19–5, takings waiting to be banked amounted to £640. It has been discovered that an amount of £340, paid into the bank on 29 March 19–5, was not credited to Joan's account until 02 April 19–5 and a cheque, to the value of £120, drawn on 28 March 19–5 for purchases, was not cleared until 10 April 19–5. The rate of gross profit on goods sold is 50 per cent on sales. However, during the year stock costing £600 was not moving so Joan sold it off at cost price.

Interest, at the rate of 5 per cent per annum is payable on the loan from Frank Shuker but had not been paid at 31 March 19–5.

Depreciation on the van is to be provided on the straight line basis. It is estimated that the vehicle will be disposed of, for £100, after 5 years' use.

The stock for resale at 31 March 19–5 has been valued at cost at £1900.

Creditors for purchases, at 31 March 19–5, amounted to £880. Electricity charges due on that date were £180.

Trade debtors at 31 March 19–5 totalled £2300.

You are to:

Prepare Joan Carter's Trading and Profit and Loss Account for the year ended 31 March 19–5, together with a Balance Sheet.

3. A retailer, Jayne Hollingworth, does not keep detailed accounts. However, she is able to provide information as follows:

Business bank account for the year ended 31 August 19–6 (Summary):

	£		£
01 September 19–5 balance b/f	1 970	Payments to creditors	72 000
Receipts from debtors	96 000	Purchase of motor van (L97 PPD)	13 000
Sale of private flat	20 000	Rent	2 600
Sale of motor van (E65 LBJ)	2 100	Wages	15 100
		Postages and stationery	1 360
		Vehicle running costs	3 350
		Drawings	9 200
		Repairs to premises	650
		Insurances	800
		31 August 19–6 balance c/f	2 010
	120 070		120 070

Other assets and liabilities:

As at:	01 Sept 19–5	31 Aug 19–6
	£	£
Creditors	4 700	2 590
Debtors	7 320	9 500
Rent unpaid	200	260
Motor vans E65 LBJ — At cost	10 000	—
Provision for depn	8 000	—
L97 PPD — At cost	—	13 000
Provision for depn	—	?
Stock	4 900	5 900
Insurances prepaid	160	200

All receipts are banked and all payments are made from the business bank account.

A trade debt of £300 owing by Jack Sharpe, included in debtors at 31 August 19–6, is to be written off as a bad debt.

Jayne wishes to provide depreciation at 20 per cent on the cost of motor vans held at the end of each financial year; no depreciation is provided for in the year of sale or disposal of a motor van.

Discounts received during the year ended 31 August 19–6 from creditors amounted to £1100.

You are to:
Prepare a Trading and Profit and Loss Account for Jayne Hollingworth for the year 31 August 19–6 together with a Balance Sheet at that date.

Index

To accompany this book

PC BASED ACCOUNTING TRAINING SYSTEMS

David Farrow and Alec Danyshchuk

ACCOUNTING I   INTERACTIVE TRAINING SYSTEM   ACCOUNTING I   LECTURE THEATRE
ACCOUNTING II   INTERACTIVE TRAINING SYSTEM   ACCOUNTING II   LECTURE THEATRE

▶ Knowledge is tested at every stage of transaction entries, account adjustments and account allocations

▶ Easy access to detailed explanations in the tutorial and quick reference – a special feature of the operating system

▶ Allows for continual and extensive practice

▶ Comprehensive lectures on each topic and technique

▶ All lectures include rolling demonstrations of accounting techniques

▶ Includes workbook of exercises for each topic covered

▶ Includes playback of A to Z model answers for each exercise

▶ Affordable, innovative and unique, state-of-the-art software packages specifically designed for learning accountancy from basic to intermediate level

▶ No computer training, experience, or manual is required

▶ Systems run on any IBM compatible, or network

▶ Each level follows the chronology of this book

▶ Demonstration disks sent on a 30-day inspection period.

TO   University and College Marketing Department
McGraw-Hill Book Company Europe
Maidenhead
Berkshire
ENGLAND SL6 2QL

Please send me the following demonstration disks:

Accounting I: Interactive Training System ☐   Lecture Theatre ☐
Accounting II: Interactive Training System ☐   Lecture Theatre ☐

Name: ....
Organization: (if applicable) ....
Department: (if applicable) ....

Address: ....
....
Post Code ....

Telephone No: ....
Course: (if applicable) ....